SWEET BASIL BLOSSOMS
IN REFUTATION OF
TAHQIQ AL-BAYAN

*A Critical Response to What Qasim ibn Nu'aym al-Ta'i Wrote
Concerning Ibn Abi Sufyan*

By

Shaykh Hasan al-Saqqaf

Appended to this work:
The Sayings of the Greatest Messenger
concerning
Mu'awiya ibn Abi Sufyan

Translated by
Walid Abdurrahim

Sweet Basil Blossoms in Refutation of Tahqiq al-Bayan

By Shaykh Hasan al-Saqqaf

ISBN: 979-8-90514-205-5

First published in English, 2026

Translated by Walid Abdurrahim

Independently published

ABOUT THIS WORK

This volume presents the English translation of *Zahr al-Rayhan fi al-Radd 'ala Tahqiq al-Bayan* by Shaykh Hasan al-Saqqaf, a direct rebuttal of Qasim ibn Nu'aym al-Ta'i's defence of Mu'awiya ibn Abi Sufyan. In this work, Shaykh Hasan responds to arguments built upon alleged consensus, claims of absolute uprightness for every Companion, fabricated virtues, and attempts to excuse grave wrongdoing under the language of ijtihad.

The importance of the work lies in its correction of a widespread misconception in later Sunni discourse: the claim that Ahl al-Sunna unanimously regarded Mu'awiya as a righteous Companion beyond serious criticism. This claim has been repeated so often that many have come to assume it is an agreed Sunni doctrine. Yet repetition is not proof, and inherited caution is not consensus.

Shaykh Hasan shows that the Sunni scholarly record is far broader than this later apologetic convention. Major Sunni authorities criticized Mu'awiya, rejected reports invented in his praise, denied the soundness of alleged virtues attributed to him, and condemned the Umayyad practice of cursing Sayyiduna 'Ali, may Allah be pleased with him. The work also demonstrates that Mu'awiya's status as a Companion was not treated as beyond dispute by all scholars, and that the evidence concerning his conduct places even the reality and sincerity of his Islam under grave question. The work therefore distinguishes between honoring the Companions and sanctifying political power, and between reverence for the righteous and the falsification of history.

The appended material at the end of this volume continues the same purpose. It gathers Prophetic reports and scholarly statements concerning Mu'awiya, including reports of censure and statements from leading Sunni authorities who criticized him or rejected the alleged virtues attributed to him. It should therefore be read as an evidentiary continuation of the main refutation.

This book is not a call to sectarian hatred. It is a call to moral clarity, to love of the Prophetic Household, and to a more honest engagement with the Qur'an, the Sunnah, and the full range of the Sunni scholarly inheritance.

Walid Abdurrahim

Translator

TRANSLATOR'S PREFACE

This work enters a subject that many Muslims have been taught to avoid, not because the evidence is weak, but because the subject has been surrounded by fear, inherited formulas, and accusations. The name of Mu'awiya ibn Abi Sufyan has often been placed behind a wall of slogans: "do not speak about the Companions," "they all exercised ijtihad," "Ahl al-Sunna agreed upon their uprightness," and "criticizing Mu'awiya is an attack on the Companions." Yet when one returns to the books of hadith, tafsir, history, legal theory, and Sunni scholarship itself, the matter is far more complex.

The purpose of this translation is not to promote sectarian hostility, nor to import a foreign framework into Sunni Islam. Rather, it is to make available in English a work that speaks from within a Sunni scholarly inheritance many readers have not encountered. That inheritance gives the Household of the Prophet, may Allah bless him and his household and grant them peace, their proper rank, refuses to sanitize injustice, and does not confuse political success with spiritual virtue.

One of the assumptions challenged by this book is the claim that Ahl al-Sunna unanimously placed Mu'awiya beyond serious moral and scholarly criticism, or that exposing his actions necessarily amounts to attacking the Companions. This claim is repeated so often that many assume it to be a settled Sunni doctrine. Yet repetition is not proof, and inherited caution is not consensus. When one returns to the books of hadith, history, tafsir, legal theory, and Sunni scholarly commentary, one finds a much wider record. Major Sunni authorities criticized Mu'awiya, rejected reports invented in his praise, denied the authenticity of alleged virtues attributed to him, and condemned the Umayyad practice of cursing 'Ali and the Prophetic Household. The reader should therefore not mistake a later defensive convention for an actual binding consensus.

A reader must also understand that 'Ali ibn Abi Talib, may Allah be pleased with him, is not treated in this work as merely one

Companion among others. He is from the Household of the Prophet, may Allah bless him and his household and grant them peace. He is the husband of Fatima, the father of al-Hasan and al-Husayn, the one whom the Prophet loved, raised, made his brother, and described in reports whose meanings cannot be reduced to ordinary companionship. The Prophet said to him, as narrated in Sahih Muslim: "None loves you except a believer, and none hates you except a hypocrite."[1] He also said, in a report authenticated by a number of hadith scholars: "Whoever curses 'Ali has cursed me."[2] For this reason, the question of Mu'awiya's cursing of 'Ali is not a minor historical dispute between two political figures. It touches love of the Prophet himself, reverence for his Household, and the moral integrity of the Ummah's memory.

Some Sunni authorities went further and held that the Household of the Prophet occupy a distinct rank that cannot be measured by ordinary Companion-ranking. Imam Ahmad is reported to have said of 'Ali: "My son, 'Ali ibn Abi Talib is from a Household to whom no one can be compared."[3] Ahmad ibn al-Siddiq al-Ghumari expressed this even more explicitly, stating that the best of people after the Messenger of Allah, may Allah

----

[1] Muslim, *Sahih*, Book of Faith, no. 78; al-Tirmidhi, *Sunan*, no. 3736. The wording in Muslim is from 'Ali, may Allah be pleased with him: "By the One who split the seed and created the soul, it is a promise from the unlettered Prophet, may Allah bless him and his household and grant them peace, to me that none loves me except a believer, and none hates me except a hypocrite." Al-Tirmidhi narrated it with similar wording and graded it *hasan sahih*.

[2] Ahmad, *Musnad*, no. 26748, from Umm Salama, may Allah be pleased with her, with the wording: "Whoever curses 'Ali has cursed me." It was also cited by al-Haythami in *Majma' al-Zawa'id*, 9:130, who said that its narrators are the narrators of the Sahih, except Abu 'Abd Allah al-Jadali, who is trustworthy. It was also narrated by al-Nasa'i in *al-Sunan al-Kubra*, Ibn Abi Shayba, Abu Ya'la, and al-Tabarani.

[3] Reported by Ibn al-Jawzi in *Manaqib al-Imam Ahmad*, p. 219, from 'Abd Allah ibn Ahmad ibn Hanbal, who said: "I asked my father: Who are the best people after the Messenger of Allah, may Allah bless him and grant him peace? He said: Abu Bakr. I said: Then who? He said: 'Umar. I said: Then who? He said: 'Uthman. I said: Then 'Ali? He said: My son, 'Ali ibn Abi Talib is from a Household to whom no one can be compared." It is also cited in *al-Jami' li-'Ulum al-Imam Ahmad: al-'Aqida*, in the section on the virtues of 'Ali ibn Abi Talib, citing *Tabaqat al-Hanabila*, 3:216.

bless him and his household and grant them peace, are Fatima, then 'Ali, then al-Hasan and al-Husayn, then the wives of the Prophet, and then the Companions.[4] Whether or not every reader adopts that precise ranking, it is enough to show that reverence for Ahl al-Bayt is not a sectarian excess. It is a rooted Sunni inheritance.

The same must be said regarding Mu'awiya. Many contemporary Muslims have inherited the idea that any criticism of him is necessarily Rafidism or sectarian excess. This too is historically false. Major Sunni authorities spoke about him with severe criticism. Some denied that any sound report exists concerning his virtues. Others condemned Mu'awiya's political project and its hostility toward 'Ali and the Prophetic Household. The reader will see in this book that these positions were not invented by modern polemicists. They are preserved in the works of recognized Sunni scholars, hadith masters, and exegetes.

One reason this misconception became so deeply rooted is that it was not repeated only by extremists or political partisans. It also entered the writings of respected scholars who, in this matter, were affected by inherited narratives concerning Mu'awiya. Among the most important examples is Ibn Hajar al-Haytami,[5] whose work defending Mu'awiya was relied upon heavily by al-Ta'i. Al-Haytami was a great and respected Shafi'i scholar, especially in law, theology, and devotional counsel. However, hadith criticism was not his strongest area, and his

---

[4] Ahmad ibn al-Siddiq al-Ghumari, *al-Jawab al-Mufid li-l-Sa'il al-Mustafid.* He states: "In my belief, the best of people after the Messenger of God, may Allah bless him and his household and grant them peace, is his daughter Fatima, then 'Ali, then al-Hasan and al-Husayn, then the wives of the Prophet, may Allah bless him and his household and grant them peace, then the Companions."

[5] The reader should distinguish between Ibn Hajar al-Haytami and al-Hafiz al-Haythami. Ibn Hajar al-Haytami was the Shafi'i jurist Ahmad ibn Muhammad ibn Hajar al-Haytami, associated in this book with the defence of Mu'awiya. Al-Hafiz al-Haythami was the hadith scholar 'Ali ibn Abi Bakr al-Haythami, author of *Majma' al-Zawa'id.* They are two different scholars, and both names appear in this work.

grading or defence of reports concerning Mu'awiya cannot be treated as decisive when it conflicts with hadith masters who denied the authenticity of Mu'awiya's alleged virtues. The stature of a scholar does not make every argument in every book correct, and in this subject the inherited apologetic framework surrounding Mu'awiya led even scholars of great rank into serious error.

Nor is the interpretation of the "accursed tree" in Qur'an 17:60 as referring to Banu Umayya a modern invention. It appears in the classical tafsir tradition. Al-Tabari records, among the transmitted explanations of the verse, reports connecting the vision to people ascending the Prophet's pulpit.[6] Al-Qurtubi also records the interpretation that the accursed tree refers to Banu Umayya, attributing it to Ibn 'Abbas and others.[7] Al-Suyuti likewise gathers reports on this meaning in al-Durr al-Manthur.[8] One may debate the strength, scope, or application of this interpretation, but one cannot honestly describe it as a late sectarian fabrication. It is part of the transmitted interpretive record.

At the same time, fairness requires precision. Condemning the Umayyad political project does not mean condemning every individual of Umayyad lineage. Accountability in Islam is based on faith, action, repentance, justice, and moral choice, not bloodline. Figures such as Mu'awiya ibn Yazid, who renounced Umayyad rule, and 'Umar ibn 'Abd al-'Aziz, who ended the public cursing of 'Ali from the pulpits and restored many

---

[6] Al-Tabari, Jami' al-Bayan 'an Ta'wil Ay al-Qur'an, commentary on al-Isra' 17:60. Al-Tabari records reports concerning the Prophet's vision of people ascending his pulpit, while preferring the interpretation that the vision refers to the Isra'.

[7] Al-Qurtubi, al-Jami' li Ahkam al-Qur'an, commentary on al-Isra' 17:60, under the words "wa'l-shajarata al-mal'unata fi'l-Qur'an." Al-Qurtubi records the view that the accursed tree refers to Banu Umayya, attributing it to Ibn 'Abbas and others.

[8] Al-Suyuti, al-Durr al-Manthur fi'l-Tafsir bi'l-Ma'thur, commentary on al-Isra' 17:60. Al-Suyuti gathers reports on the connection between the verse, Banu Umayya, and the Prophet's pulpit, including reports transmitted through Ibn Abi Hatim, Ibn Mardawayh, al-Bayhaqi, and Ibn 'Asakir.

injustices, cannot be treated as identical to those who institutionalized oppression. The issue is not ancestry. The issue is the corrupt political model, built on power, injustice, and hostility toward Ahl al-Bayt, that Mu'awiya initiated and institutionalized.

A further reason this subject requires care is that Nasb, meaning hostility toward or denigration of the Prophet's Household, did not disappear with the Umayyads. It became a culture. At times, it entered scholarly circles, political institutions, and even hadith criticism. Praising 'Ali too openly could lead to accusations of Shi'ism. Narrating the virtues of Ahl al-Bayt could bring suspicion. Some reports were fabricated to diminish their rank, while other reports in their favor were treated with undue severity. Imam al-Hakim al-Naysaburi's testimony regarding those who belittled 'Ali and Fatima to please authority is a painful example of how political power distorted religious judgment.[9]

The reader should therefore approach this book with two principles in mind.

First, loving Ahl al-Bayt, defending their rank, and condemning those who wronged them is not Rafidism. It is part of the religion of Muhammad, may Allah bless him and his household and grant them peace. The Prophet's Household are not an ornamental appendix to Islam. They are central to its moral memory and spiritual inheritance. The Prophet said: "I have left among you that which, if you hold fast to it, you will never go astray after me: the Book of Allah and my 'itra, my Ahl al-Bayt."[10]

Second, refusing to sanctify Mu'awiya is not a rejection of the Companions. The Qur'an itself praises some who accompanied the Prophet and censures others. The Sunnah itself contains

---

9 Al-Hakim al-Naysaburi, *Fada'il Fatima al-Zahra'*, introduction.

10 Narrated by al-Tirmidhi, *Sunan*, no. 3788; Muslim, *Sahih*, no. 2408, with the wording of the two weighty things and the exhortation regarding Ahl al-Bayt; and Ahmad, *Musnad*, from Abu Sa'id al-Khudri, with the wording: "the Book of Allah... and my 'itra, my Ahl al-Bayt."

reports about hypocrites among those outwardly counted with the Muslim community. The books of Ahl al-Sunna themselves contain criticism of individuals who lived in the Prophetic age. To recognize this is not to attack the Companions. It is to distinguish between reverence and historical falsification.

This does not diminish the rank of the true and upright Companions, such as Abu Bakr, 'Umar, 'Uthman, 'Ali, and the righteous men and women who believed, sacrificed, remained faithful, and carried the religion with sincerity. Their honor is preserved, and their service to Islam is not denied. The issue is whether the noble rank of companionship should be turned into a blanket slogan used to shield anyone who is merely claimed to have been a Companion, even when the evidence of his conduct reveals corruption, injustice, hostility toward the Prophet's Household, or hypocrisy. The Qur'an and Sunnah themselves show that there were people outwardly present among the Muslims in the Prophet's time whose inward reality was hypocrisy. Therefore, when a person's actions disclose what he truly was, the evidence should not be silenced by a slogan. Respect for the upright Companions is not a license to sanctify someone like Mu'awiya, nor to turn the name of companionship into a refuge from evidence.

This book by Shaykh Hasan al-Saqqaf belongs to that corrective effort. It asks the reader to return to evidence rather than inherited fear, to the Qur'an and sound Sunnah rather than political theology, and to the actual range of Sunni scholarship rather than a simplified narrative produced by later repetition. The author's language is sometimes sharp because the issue is not merely historical. It concerns the honor of the Messenger of Allah, the dignity of his Household, and the integrity of the religion's moral witness.

The English-speaking reader may find some of the arguments unfamiliar, and unfamiliarity can sometimes feel unsettling. That is especially true of the interpretation of the "accursed tree" in the Qur'an as referring to Banu Umayya. For many Sunnis today, this interpretation may at first sound severe or even unthinkable. Yet unfamiliarity is not evidence of unsoundness. This interpretation is not foreign to the Sunni tafsir tradition. It is a transmitted interpretation preserved in classical sources, reported from early authorities, and discussed by major exegetes.

More importantly, the reader who proceeds through the evidence presented in this work may find his understanding transformed. What initially appears severe may, after careful reading, appear not only plausible, but strong, coherent, and deeply consistent with the Qur'anic language of trial, corruption, and historical consequence. The verse speaks of a vision shown to the Prophet, may Allah bless him and his household and grant them peace, and of a trial for the people. When read in light of what later occurred to the Prophet's Household, the public cursing of 'Ali, the transformation of the caliphate into kingship, the killing of the righteous, and the tragedies inflicted upon the Ummah, this interpretation becomes far more compelling than many readers may have expected.

This is part of what makes the present work eye-opening. It does not merely ask the reader to revisit Mu'awiya as an isolated historical figure. It asks the reader to reconsider an inherited framework: how political power shaped later religious memory, how reverence for Ahl al-Bayt was sometimes recast as sectarianism, and how criticism of injustice was often treated as an attack on the Companions themselves. The result is not a departure from Sunni Islam, but a return to a neglected Sunni moral clarity.

The purpose of this translation is to reopen the archive, restore the discussion to its sources, and show that love for 'Ali, Fatima, al-Hasan, al-Husayn, and the Prophetic Household is not a sectarian intrusion into Sunni Islam.

Walid Abdurrahim

Translator

Contents

**In the Name of Allah, the Most Gracious, the
Most Merciful**

AUTHOR'S INTRODUCTION

All praise is due to Allah, Lord of all worlds, and may blessings and peace be upon our master Muhammad, and upon his pure and noble household, and may Allah be pleased with his pious Companions.

To proceed:

I came across a treatise by Shaykh Qasim ibn Nu'aym al-Ta'i which he titled *Tahqiq al-Bayan fi Radd Shubhat 'an Mu'awiya ibn Abi Sufyan* (The Verified Clarification in Refuting Doubts Concerning Mu'awiya ibn Abi Sufyan). In it he took issue with this humble servant regarding what I had written about Mu'awiya ibn Abi Sufyan as a commentary on *Daf' Shubah al-Tashbih* by Ibn al-Jawzi. I was astonished by his audacity in speaking without knowledge, and by his strange eagerness to defend Mu'awiya — even if that required relying on feeble foundations of weak and worthless hadiths and narrations that contradict fact and reality, and twisting the texts of the Quran and the sound Sunnah, forcing them to serve as alleged virtues of Mu'awiya — despite the explicit statements of the leading hadith masters of the era of the righteous early generations, such as al-Nasa'i, Ishaq ibn Rahawayh, and Judge Isma'il, among others, and Hafiz Ibn Hajar's agreement with them, that nothing sound has been transmitted regarding the merits of Mu'awiya, as will be demonstrated shortly.

Some scholars and many students of knowledge in our country and in many other lands had repeatedly asked me, from time to time and period to period, to clarify this subject and to uncover its obscured and concealed issues, questions, and evidence. Many of our brothers from Ahl al-Sunna across the world also wrote to me seeking to resolve certain difficulties and doubts raised by those who fanatically defend falsehoods and the Umayyad ideology that is hostile to the Hashimite household of the Prophet, may Allah's peace be upon them. I therefore saw this as an opportunity to bring forth some of what I have to offer in clarifying certain matters, in following the Noble Quran and the sound and purified Prophetic Sunnah, and in fulfilling our duty to our masters the Hashimite household of the Prophet — may Allah raise their standing and firmly establish their honor and status.

Whoever sincerely seeks the face of Allah must pursue the truth and grasp it, and must not turn away from it out of fear or cowardice before the common people and those who merely adorn themselves with the appearance of knowledge — fearing that such people will accuse him of Rafidism, [T.N. Rafidism is a polemical label applied to those accused of rejecting the first three caliphs and holding excessive devotion to 'Ali and the Prophet's household. The term is often used broadly as a term of condemnation against anyone who criticizes certain Companions.] Mu'tazilism, or Shi'ism. We live in an age in which people are not compelled in matters of belief and opinion. People are free in their thinking and their convictions, and every person has the right to choose what he adopts for himself. The opinions of men are not among the legal proofs of the Shari'a. As it is said: know the truth and you will know its people. May Allah have mercy on Imam al-Shafi'i when he said:

If loving the family of Muhammad is Rafd, then let both the Thaqalayn bear witness that I am a Rafidi.

And so I say, and with Allah alone is all success, guidance, and assistance:

CHAPTER 1: THE ESTABLISHED RECORD

Mu'Awiya's Cursing And Reviling Of Imam 'Ali

Attacks on Imam 'Ali

Mu'awiya and his followers' attacked Imam 'Ali, the master of the Prophet's household and the father of the two masters of the youth of Paradise.

The author of Tahqiq al-Bayan has turned a blind eye to the faults of Mu'awiya and to what has been reported from the greatest Messenger, may Allah's blessings and peace be upon him and his household, and from the Companions and scholars, in censure of him.

When I saw what this writer had done, I resolved to expose the falsehood of what he put forward in his book by critically examining the foundations upon which he built his arguments on this subject. I ask Allah and beseech His beloved Prophet to make this work of mine purely for His noble face — in defense of the Noble Quran, the honored and sound Sunnah, and the noble and pure household of the Prophet — making clear the condition of those who bore enmity toward them, who reviled and abused them, and who committed acts that cause children's hair to turn white: fighting the people of truth, rebelling against the rightly-guided Imam, killing the best and most righteous of the Companions and others, and more besides — until he became the leader of the faction that calls to the Fire, as stated in the hadith of al-Bukhari (447) and Ahmad: "Ammar will be killed by the transgressing faction — he calls them to Paradise and they call him to the Fire." And as stated in the hadith of Muslim in *al-Sahih* (1844), on the authority of 'Abd al-Rahman ibn 'Abd Rabb al-Ka'ba, who said to 'Abd Allah ibn 'Amr ibn al-'As:

"This cousin of yours, Mu'awiya, commands us to consume one another's wealth unjustly and to kill one another, while Allah, Exalted be He, says: {'O you who believe, do not consume one another's wealth unjustly, unless it be through trade conducted with your mutual consent, and do not kill yourselves. Indeed Allah is ever Merciful to you.'}" [al-Nisa': 29]

Mu'awiya commanded the people — including senior Companions — to curse and revile our master 'Ali, may Allah's peace and pleasure be upon him, of whom the Messenger of Allah, may Allah's blessings and peace be upon him and his household, said, as reported in *Sahih Muslim* (78) and elsewhere: "None loves you except a believer, and none hates you except a hypocrite."[11] And of whom he said, may Allah's blessings and peace be upon him and his household, as in the authenticated hadith in *Musnad Ahmad* (6/323) and elsewhere: "Whoever curses 'Ali has cursed me."

It has been established that Mu'awiya used to curse and revile our master 'Ali, may Allah's peace and pleasure be upon him, and would order others to do so. In *Sahih Muslim* (2404), on the authority of 'Amir ibn Sa'd ibn Abi Waqqas, from his father, it is reported:

Mu'awiya ibn Abi Sufyan commanded Sa'd and said: "What prevents you from cursing Abu Turab?" Sa'd replied: "As for the three things I recall that the Messenger of Allah, may Allah's blessings and peace be upon him and his household, said to him — I will never curse him; for any one of those three things would be dearer to me than red camels..."

Ibn Maja narrated (121) with an authenticated chain[12] on the authority of Sa'd ibn Abi Waqqas: Mu'awiya came on one of his

---

[11] The wording in *Sahih Muslim* (78) is on the authority of Sayyiduna 'Ali, may Allah be pleased with him: "By the One who split the grain and created the soul — it is the covenant of the unlettered Prophet, may Allah's blessings and peace be upon him and his household, to me: none loves me except a believer, and none hates me except a hypocrite." Al-Tirmidhi (3736), al-Nasa'i (5018), and others narrated it with the wording mentioned above.

[12] This was authenticated by the self-contradicting scholar of our era, al-Albani, in *Sahih Ibn Maja* (1/26).

pilgrimage visits. Sa'd visited him, and they mentioned 'Ali. Mu'awiya cursed and abused him. Sa'd became angry and said: "You say this about a man of whom I heard the Messenger of Allah, may Allah's blessings and peace be upon him and his household, say: 'Whoever I am his master, 'Ali is his master'; and I heard him say: 'You are to me as Harun was to Musa, except that there is no prophet after me'; and I heard him say: 'I will give the banner today to a man who loves Allah and His Messenger.'"

This narration is explicit in establishing that Mu'awiya cursed and abused our master 'Ali.

Mu'awiya also commanded his governors to curse and revile our master 'Ali and order the people to do so. Among the evidence for this is what Muslim narrated in *al-Sahih* (2409) from the noble Companion Sahl ibn Sa'd: "A man from the family of Marwan was appointed over Madinah. He summoned Sahl ibn Sa'd and ordered him to curse 'Ali. Sahl refused. The man said: 'If you refuse, then at least say: May Allah curse Abu Turab.' Sahl said: 'No name was dearer to 'Ali than Abu Turab, and he used to rejoice when called by it.'"

By this, what Qasim al-Ta'i denies in his treatise — that Mu'awiya used to curse our master 'Ali, may Allah be pleased with him, and order the people to curse him — is conclusively established. And it has been confirmed, as stated above, that the Prophet, may Allah's blessings and peace be upon him and his household, said: "Whoever curses 'Ali has cursed me."

Ahmad narrated in *al-Musnad* (6/323) from Abu 'Abd Allah al-Jadali who said: I entered upon Umm Salama and she said to me: "Is the Messenger of Allah, may Allah's blessings and peace be upon him and his household, being cursed among you?" I said: "Allah forbid!" or "Glory be to Allah!" or words to that effect. She said: "I heard the Messenger of Allah, may Allah's blessings and peace be upon him and his household, say: 'Whoever curses 'Ali has cursed me.'"[13]

Since the matter of Mu'awiya is as described — a documented truth established in the books of the leading hadith scholars and the scholars of Ahl al-Sunna wa'l-Jama'a — and since Qasim al-Ta'i stubbornly rejects and attempts to deny and refute what is established in the authenticated collections, going so far as to devote a special chapter in his book titled "The Ninth Pearl: Exonerating Mu'awiya from Cursing and Reviling Sayyiduna 'Ali" — I have considered it obligatory to expose the falsehood of what he wrote in that book, argument by argument, and to restore the truth to its proper place.

The Claim That Later Generations Disparaged the Earlier Generations

Al-Ta'i begins by claiming that later generations of the Ummah disparaged its earliest generation. The author turns this claim back upon Mu'awiya himself.

Al-Ta'i says [*Tahqiq al-Bayan*, p. 3]:

"When I saw that the age had become corrupt and reversed, and that most of its people had fallen back and grown sluggish in pursuing knowledge, and that the later generations of this community were reviling the first generation due to the doubts and falsehoods spread by certain spiteful individuals upon reading the books of the historians — I decided to move my pen and write some pages on the moral uprightness of the Companions, may Allah be pleased with them, and the ruling on reviling them, mentioning thereafter the noble Companion Mu'awiya ibn Abi Sufyan, who is the true and original subject of this brief treatise, clarifying therein many realities that may be

---

[13] Narrated also by al-Nasa'i in *al-Sunan al-Kubra*, 5:133. It is transmitted through numerous routes, many of which were cited by al-Haythami in *Majma' al-Zawa'id*, 9:130. It is also transmitted with other wordings through numerous routes. See Ibn Abi Shayba, *al-Musannaf*, 12:76-77; al-Tabarani, *al-Mu'jam al-Kabir*, 23:322; and Abu Ya'la, *al-Musnad*, 12:444. Shu'ayb al-Arna'ut authenticated it in his commentary on the *Musnad*, 44:329, as did al-Albani in *al-Silsila al-Sahiha*, no. 3332.

obscure to many researchers, explaining what has been difficult for many Muslims to understand, and refuting the groundless doubts that history has falsely attributed to the Companion Mu'awiya."

I say: Al-Dhahabi spoke truthfully when he said in *Siyar A'lam al-Nubala'* (3/128): "Mu'awiya left behind a great number of people who loved him and held him in exaggerated esteem and elevated him above others — either because he had won them over through generosity, forbearance, and giving, or because they were born in Syria and grew up upon Nasb." [T.N. Nasb refers to hostility toward Imam 'Ali and the household of the Prophet, may Allah's blessings and peace be upon him and his household.] "We seek refuge in Allah from following one's desires."

As for al-Ta'i's phrase "the later generations of this community were reviling the first generation" — this very description applies to Mu'awiya himself, who was among the last to embrace Islam and then cursed and reviled our master 'Ali, may Allah's peace and pleasure be upon him, who was among the very first generation of the Companions, may Allah be pleased with them. The Messenger of Allah, may Allah's blessings and peace be upon him and his household, was informed that Khalid ibn al-Walid had abused 'Abd al-Rahman ibn 'Awf, and so the Prophet said: "Do not curse my Companions — for if one of you were to spend gold equal to the mountain of Uhud it would not reach the measure of one of them, nor even half of it."[14]

The Prophet, may Allah's blessings and peace be upon him and his household, thus forbade someone like Khalid ibn al-Walid — who was among the later Companions — from abusing a man from the foremost pioneers such as our master 'Abd al-Rahman ibn 'Awf, may Allah be pleased with him. Yet Mu'awiya did not

---

[14] Muslim narrated from Abu Sa'id al-Khudri that an incident occurred between Khalid ibn al-Walid and 'Abd al-Rahman ibn 'Awf, and Khalid insulted him. The Messenger of Allah, may Allah bless him and his household and grant them peace, then said: "Do not insult any of my Companions..." Muslim, *Sahih*, no. 2541.

comply with the Prophet's command, and he went on to curse and revile our master 'Ali, may Allah be pleased with him, as has been established from what we have already presented.

The Claim of Historical Fabrications

The author next addresses al-Ta'i's claim that the reports concerning Mu'awiya are merely historical fabrications.

As for al-Ta'i's phrase "due to the doubts and falsehoods spread by certain spiteful individuals upon reading the books of the historians":

The response is: what is recorded in the Sahihs, the Sunans, and the Musnad collections — and what is transmitted through sound chains of narration regarding the faults of Mu'awiya and his disgraceful acts — does not belong to the category of doubts and falsehoods spread by certain spiteful individuals. Rather, these are established factual realities. Furthermore, the faults of Mu'awiya are not confined to the books of historians. They were transmitted, spread, narrated, and documented by historians and hadith masters alike — including al-Bukhari and Muslim.

Qur'an and Sound Sunnah Concerning Some Companions

The texts of the Qur'an and the sound Sunnah show that not every person counted among the Companions can be treated identically in uprightness, conduct, or rank.

As for al-Ta'i's phrase "I decided to write some pages on the moral uprightness of the Companions" — uprightness characterizes the majority of the Companions. However, there exists a group among them who were not upright, in light of Allah's words: {"And among the people of Madinah there are those who are entrenched in hypocrisy — you do not know them, but We know them"} [al-Tawba: 101], and His words: {"But when they see merchandise or entertainment they break away toward it and leave you standing"} [al-Jumu'a: 11]. In *Sahih al-Bukhari* (936), on the authority of our master Jabir, may Allah be pleased with him: "While we were praying with the Prophet, may Allah's blessings and peace be upon him and his household, a caravan arrived carrying food. The people turned toward it until no one remained with the Prophet, may Allah's blessings and peace be upon him and his household, except twelve men, and the verse was revealed."

How could they abandon Friday prayer with the Prophet, may Allah's blessings and peace be upon him and his household, and turn toward entertainment and trade? Is this praise or censure?

Allah, Exalted be He, also said concerning the Companions who built the Mosque of Harm: {"And those who built a mosque to cause harm and disbelief and division among the believers, and as an outpost for those who had previously made war against Allah and His Messenger — they will surely swear: 'We intended nothing but good.' But Allah bears witness that they are liars."} [al-Tawba: 107]. This verse affirms that a group among the Companions were liars — and they are not protected from this, as some fanatics imagine.

After these Quranic proofs, O Qasim, do you still claim uprightness for all of them?

If you insist and say that those referred to are the hypocrites, and that there were no hypocrites among the Companions — as some of your colleagues claim — then we say: certainly not! For the greatest Messenger, may Allah's blessings and peace be upon him and his household, ruled otherwise.

In *Sahih Muslim* (2779), on the authority of our master Hudhayfa, may Allah be pleased with him: the Messenger of Allah, may Allah's blessings and peace be upon him and his household, said: "Among my Companions are twelve hypocrites, eight of whom will not enter Paradise until a camel passes through the eye of a needle."

Al-Bukhari narrated in *al-Sahih* (6582): "Men from among my Companions will certainly come to me at the Hawd. When I recognize them they will be snatched away from me. I will say: 'My Companions!' And it will be said: 'You do not know what they introduced after you.'"

Muslim narrated in *al-Sahih* (2304), on the authority of our master Anas ibn Malik, may Allah be pleased with him: the Messenger of Allah, may Allah's blessings and peace be upon him and his household, said: "Men from among those who accompanied me will come to me at the Hawd. When I see them and they are brought before me they will be snatched away from me. I will say: 'O Lord, my little Companions, my little Companions!' And it will be said to me: 'You do not know what they introduced after you.'"

Al-Tirmidhi narrated (2423) from our master Ibn 'Abbas, may Allah be pleased with them both, in a chain traced back to the Prophet, which includes: "Men from among my Companions will be seized from the right and from the left. I will say: 'O Lord, my Companions!' And it will be said: 'You do not know what they introduced after you — they did not cease to apostatize on their heels from the moment you parted from them.'"

Al-Bukhari narrated in *al-Sahih* (6585) from Abu Hurayra that the Messenger of Allah, may Allah's blessings and peace be upon him and his household, said: "On the Day of Resurrection a company from among my Companions will come to me and will be driven away from the Hawd. I will say: 'O Lord, my Companions!' He will say: 'You have no knowledge of what they introduced after you — they turned back on their heels and apostatized.'" The word *yuhalla'un* means: they will be driven away, expelled, and turned back.

When Qasim al-Ta'i and those like him reflect carefully on these verses and sound hadiths, they will recognize that they are mistaken in their claim of uprightness for all of the Companions, and that what they claim is invalidated by the texts of the Quran and the sound Sunnah. The alleged consensus of Ahl al-Sunna on the uprightness of all the Companions is not correct — indeed it is false, because among the leading authorities of scholarship and the foremost hadith masters from Ahl al-Sunna there were those who criticized Mu'awiya and did not love him. Even if we hypothetically conceded that Ahl al-Sunna had reached consensus on this — which is not the case — the consensus of

Ahl al-Sunna alone, without the other Islamic sects and schools of thought, carries no binding force and does not constitute a valid consensus, as the leading scholars of legal theory from Ahl al-Sunna and the Ash'aris have explicitly stated.

As for the absence of consensus among Ahl al-Sunna — here is the proof, so that we may silence the objections of Qasim al-Ta'i, may Allah guide him:

Sunni Scholarly Criticism of Mu'awiya

Examples of Scholars Who Criticized Mu'awiya

The statements of the imams of Ahl al-Sunna who used to censure Mu'awiya, did not love him, and did not take him as an ally are very numerous. We mention here some of the most well-known among them — such as Imam al-Nasa'i, author of the *Sunan*; al-Hakim, author of the *Mustadrak*; and 'Abd al-Razzaq, author of the famous *Musannaf*, which is the relied-upon reference for the hadith imams such as Ahmad ibn Hanbal, al-Bukhari, and others.

1. Imam al-Nasa'i, author of the *Sunan* (died 303 AH):

Al-Dhahabi said in *Siyar A'lam al-Nubala'* (14/133) in the biographical entry for Imam al-Nasa'i: "He had a slight inclination toward Shi'ism and an aversion toward the opponents of Imam 'Ali, such as Mu'awiya and 'Amr."

Al-Dhahabi also mentioned in *Siyar A'lam al-Nubala'* (14/132) that al-Nasa'i left Egypt at the end of his life and traveled to Damascus, where he was asked about Mu'awiya and what had been transmitted regarding his virtues. He said: "Is it not enough for him to come out equal, that he must be elevated above others?" Al-Dhahabi says: "They kept pushing him in his groin until he was carried out of the mosque." Al-Daraqutni said: "He left to perform the Hajj, was tested in Damascus, and attained martyrdom."

Hafiz Ibn Hajar said in *Fath al-Bari* (7/104): "Many hadiths have been transmitted concerning the virtues of Mu'awiya, but none of them are sound in terms of chain of transmission. This was definitively stated by Ishaq ibn Rahawayh, al-Nasa'i, and others."

2. Imam al-Hakim, author of *al-Mustadrak* (died 405 AH):

In *Siyar A'lam al-Nubala'* (17/175) and *Tabaqat al-Shafi'iyya al-Kubra* by Imam al-Subki (4/163): when al-Hakim was told "Narrate hadiths about the virtues of Mu'awiya and they will leave you in peace," he said: "It does not come from my heart — meaning: Mu'awiya."

3. Imam 'Abd al-Razzaq, author of *al-Musannaf* (died 211 AH):

In *Siyar A'lam al-Nubala'* (9/570): 'Abd al-Razzaq said to a man: "Do not defile our gathering by mentioning Ibn Abi Sufyan."[15]

'Abd al-Razzaq is a major imam of Ahl al-Sunna, one of the teachers of Ahmad ibn Hanbal, and his *Musannaf* is a principal reference for Ahl al-Sunna in deriving hadiths and narrations.

4. Other hadith masters

For example, Abu Ghassan al-Nahdi al-Kufi, and the hadith masters and Kufi scholars among the teachers of al-Bukhari, Abu Zur'a, Abu Hatim, and their generation:

Al-Dhahabi reported in *Siyar al-Nubala'* (10/432) in the biographical entry for Abu Ghassan al-Nahdi — who is among the narrators of the Six Collections: "Abu Ahmad al-Hakim told us: al-Husayn al-Ghazi told us: I asked al-Bukhari about Abu Ghassan. He said: 'What are you asking about?' I said: 'His Shi'ism.' He said: 'He follows the school of the people of his region. If you had seen 'Ubayd Allah ibn Musa, Abu Nu'aym, and a group of our Kufi teachers, you would not have asked.'"

Al-Dhahabi adds: "Abu Nu'aym and 'Ubayd Allah venerated Abu Bakr and 'Umar, and it was only Mu'awiya and his associates that they cursed and abused." End of al-Dhahabi's words.

---

[15] See al-Dhahabi, *Mizan al-I'tidal*, 2:610, in the biographical entry of Imam 'Abd al-Razzaq; and al-'Uqayli, *al-Du'afa'*, 3:109.

As for 'Ubayd Allah ibn Musa: he would not allow anyone named Mu'awiya to enter his house, and he would not narrate to a group of people if someone named Mu'awiya was among them — as recorded in his biographical entry in *Siyar al-Nubala'* (9/556-557).

5. Sa'd al-Din al-Taftazani al-Hanafi

The scholar Sa'd al-Din al-Taftazani al-Hanafi (died 793 AH) — whose biographical entry Ibn Hajar recorded in al-Durar al-Kamina (4/350):

Al-Taftazani said in *Sharh al-Maqasid* (5/310): "What took place among the Companions in terms of battles and disputes — as recorded in the books of history and transmitted on the tongues of reliable narrators — indicates on its face that some of them deviated from the path of truth and reached the level of injustice and depravity. The driving force behind it was grudges and obstinacy, envy and enmity, and the pursuit of kingship and authority, and the inclination toward pleasures and desires — for not every Companion is infallible, and not everyone who met the Prophet, may Allah's blessings and peace be upon him and his household, is marked with good.

As for what took place after them in terms of oppression against the household of the Prophet, may Allah's blessings and peace be upon him and his household — this is so evident that there is no room to conceal it, so outrageous that there is no ambiguity in any mind's view of it, so that even inanimate objects and dumb animals would bear witness to it, and those in the earth and the heavens would weep over it, and mountains would be shaken by it.

May Allah's curse be upon whoever committed it, approved of it, or worked toward it — and the punishment of the Hereafter is more severe and more lasting."

The False Claim of Consensus

The alleged consensus regarding Mu'awiya is false and cannot withstand scrutiny.

How then can a consensus be formed after this great disagreement among Ahl al-Sunna, especially given that the consensus of Ahl al-Sunna alone — without the remaining sects — is not a proof, as is established in the science of legal theory?

I add further to Qasim al-Ta'i: among the Companions are those about whom the Noble Quran descended explicitly declaring their depravity — such as al-Walid ibn 'Uqba, concerning whom came the words of Allah, Exalted be He: {"If a depraved person brings you news, verify it"} [al-Hujurat: 6], in a well-known account.

Hafiz Ibn 'Abd al-Barr said in *al-Isti'ab*[16]: "There is no disagreement among the scholars of Quranic interpretation, to my knowledge, that the words of Allah, Exalted be He: 'If a depraved person brings you news, verify it,' were revealed concerning al-Walid ibn 'Uqba."

Al-Dhahabi said in *Siyar A'lam al-Nubala'* (3/415) about al-Walid: "Despite his depravity — may Allah pardon him — he was brave..."

Al-Dhahabi then adds: "Ibn Abi Layla narrated, from al-Hakam, from Sa'id ibn Jubayr, from Ibn 'Abbas, who said: Al-Walid ibn 'Uqba said to 'Ali: 'My spear is sharper than yours, my tongue more eloquent, and I fill the battle line more than you.' 'Ali said: 'Be silent — you are nothing but a depraved man.' Then the verse was revealed: {'Is one who is a believer like one who is depraved?'} I say: the chain is strong." End of al-Dhahabi's words.

As for al-Walid ibn 'Uqba leading the people in the Fajr prayer in Kufa while drunk, and saying afterward: "If you wish I can add more" — this is established in *Sahih Muslim* (1707). Let al-Ta'i read it and reflect upon that uprightness.

---

[16] Ibn 'Abd al-Barr, *al-Isti'ab fi Ma'rifat al-Ashab,* printed in the margin of Ibn Hajar's *al-Isaba,* 3:632, Dar Ihya' al-Turath edition. Ibn 'Abd al-Barr is among the authorities cited and relied upon by Qasim al-Ta'i in his treatise; see Qasim ibn Nu'aym al-Ta'i, *Tahqiq al-Bayan,* p. 6.

None of this, O Qasim, is from what history has falsely attributed to Mu'awiya. It is the verses of the Quran, the sound and strong hadiths, and the statements of the leading imams and hadith scholars. With this, what Qasim al-Ta'i seeks to establish collapses and falls on its face. And this is not all that history attributed falsely to Mu'awiya — as you have seen, and you will see more of it, Allah willing.

CHAPTER 2: COMPANIONSHIP AND IJTIHAD

Companion Status and Uprightness

The Real Aim Behind Defending the Companions

The true purpose of those who fanatically pretend to defend the Companions is the defence of Mu'awiya, and they fail even in that.

Al-Ta'i's words — "mentioning thereafter the noble Companion Mu'awiya ibn Abi Sufyan, who is the true and original subject of this brief treatise" — I say: note that this man — may Allah guide him — who brings before us these collapsing rules and discredited texts, has no purpose other than to defend Mu'awiya and to act as his advocate, occupying himself with rejecting the established foundations and sound texts that pass judgment on Mu'awiya as blameworthy, and that he is the leader of the faction that calls to the Fire — as stated in the hadith of al-Bukhari (447): "Ammar will be killed by the transgressing faction — he calls them to Paradise and they call him to the Fire."

And in order for us to see clearly the reality of this feeble and collapsing defense that Qasim al-Ta'i has offered, we need only continue laying out his arguments, proofs, and objections against us, so that we may demonstrate their invalidity and their failure to stand.

Al-Ta'i says [p. 3]: "I have only transmitted from the books of history what was authenticated in its chain by the hadith scholars."

I say: hearing is not the same as seeing. Our companion has in fact transmitted hadiths and reports — relying at times on his own judgment and at other times on al-Haytami[17] — that are among the fabrications and invented narrations, as will become clear. But I will not leave this point without giving one example here:

The Claim That Mu'awiya Loved Sayyiduna 'Ali

This section exposes the claim that Mu'awiya loved Sayyiduna 'Ali, may Allah be pleased with him.

Al-Ta'i says [p. 28]:

"What indicates complete love between Sayyiduna 'Ali and Mu'awiya... is that Ibn al-Jawzi transmitted, from Abu Salih, who said: Mu'awiya said to Dirar: 'Describe 'Ali to me'... Mu'awiya's tears flowed... then he said: 'May Allah have mercy on Abu al-Hasan.'"

I say: beyond this being among the laughable fabrications — for one who loves someone does not curse and revile his beloved, as has been established from Mu'awiya's conduct in the authenticated collections as presented above, making clear that this is pure lies — where is the chain of this story? Is it established or worthless?

If our companion does not know its chain, we will make it known to him. This is the chain, from Ibn al-Jawzi's *Safwat al-Safwa* (1/316):

"'Abd Allah ibn Muhammad ibn Yusuf told us, who said: Yahya ibn Malik ibn 'Abid told us, who said: Abu al-Hasan Muhammad ibn Muhammad ibn Salama al-Baghdadi told us in Egypt, who said: Abu Bakr Muhammad ibn al-Hasan ibn Durayd told us, who said: al-'Ukali informed us, from al-Harmazi, from a man from Hamdan, who said: Mu'awiya said to Dirar..."

Abu Bakr ibn Durayd: al-Daraqutni said: "People criticized him." Al-Azhari said: "I entered and found him drunk and never

---

returned to him." This is recorded in *Siyar A'lam al-Nubala'* (15/97). He died in 321 AH.

His teacher al-'Ukali: if this is Zayd ibn al-Hubab, then the Hafiz said in *al-Taqrib*: "Truthful but prone to many errors." He died in 203 AH, as stated in *Tahdhib al-Kamal* (10/46). The gap between their deaths is 117 years — making the chain broken. And if this is a different al-'Ukali then let Qasim al-Ta'i identify him for us.

As for al-Harmazi — it is not known who he is. He is certainly not the Companion mentioned by Hafiz Ibn Hajar in *Nuzhat al-Albab* (2/116), whom he described as "the lying al-Harmazi."

The teacher of al-Harmazi is unknown — "a man from Hamdan."

On the basis of such chains and such fabrications do the virtues of Mu'awiya and his love for Sayyiduna 'Ali, may Allah be pleased with him, rest in the view of Qasim al-Ta'i — who says: "I have only transmitted from the books of history what was authenticated in its chain by the hadith scholars." Which hadith scholar authenticated this? It becomes clear from this that our companion makes very large claims.

Companionship and Uprightness

Our companion mentioned on page 5 of his book a chapter he titled "The First Pearl: On the Definition of Companionship and the Uprightness of the Companions." This is a naive arrangement. In any case, it has already been dismantled by what we have quoted from the statements of the hadith scholars following the established texts of the Quran and the sound Sunnah, and the statements of the leading hadith masters of Ahl al-Sunna who used to curse and revile Mu'awiya and did not love him — such as Hafiz 'Abd al-Razzaq, author of the well-known *Musannaf*; al-Nasa'i, author of the *Sunan*; al-Hakim, author of the *Mustadrak*; and many, many others.

His only purpose in raising the uprightness of the Companions is to defend Mu'awiya.

This is why we find that the predecessors of Qasim al-Ta'i — from among those Nasibis within Ahl al-Sunna — when they mention someone who cursed Sayyiduna 'Ali and belittled him, they declare him reliable and praise him. But when someone criticizes the Umayyads or Mu'awiya, they impugn his character and accuse him of Rafidism, malice, lying, and so on.

If our companion doubts this, he should compare the biographical entry of Hariz ibn 'Uthman al-Himsi with that of Abu al-Salt 'Abd al-Salam ibn Salih in *Tahdhib al-Tahdhib*, and then read the book *al-'Atb al-Jamil 'ala Ahl al-Jarh wa'l-Ta'dil* by the learned Sayyid Muhammad ibn 'Aqil, may Allah have mercy on him, and our own commentary on that book. Perhaps he will return to his senses, recognize what is correct, awaken from his heedlessness, and abandon his fanatical attachment to falsehood.

On another note, I wish to draw our companion's attention to the fact that there are noble and distinguished Companions whom some hadith masters of Ahl al-Sunna criticized and whose narrations they rejected — the underlying assumption among such scholars being that whoever was close to Sayyiduna 'Ali, may Allah be pleased with him, is thereby under suspicion.

Companions Criticized by Sunni Scholars

Here are the examples:

1. The noble Companion Hind ibn Abi Hala, son of Sayyida Khadija and stepson of the Prophet, may Allah's blessings and peace be upon him and his household, who raised him in his home alongside Sayyiduna 'Ali, may Allah be pleased with them all.

Al-Bukhari placed him in his book *al-Du'afa' al-Saghir*. Abu Hatim al-Razi objected to this in *al-Jarh wa'l-Ta'dil* (9/116), saying: "Unknown narrators transmitted from him — but what is the fault of Hind ibn Abi Hala that al-Bukhari placed him in the book of weak narrators? I heard my father say: he should be transferred out of there."

2. The noble Companion 'Abd al-Rahman ibn 'Udayd al-Balawi.

Al-Dhahabi said in *Tarikh al-Islam*[18] (3/531):

"He had companionship, pledged allegiance under the Tree, and has narrations... He was among those who rose against 'Uthman and marched to fight him... Mu'awiya then captured him and imprisoned him in Palestine along with a group of others. He later escaped from prison. They caught up with him at Mount Lebanon and killed him. When they caught up with him he said to his killer: 'Fear Allah regarding my blood — I am one of the companions of the Tree.' The man said: 'Trees are plentiful in the mountains,' and killed him.

Muhammad ibn Yahya al-Dhuhali said: It is not permissible to narrate anything from him — he is the head of the fitna."

Reflect on how a man who pledged the pledge of al-Ridwan — of whom Allah said: {"Allah was pleased with the believers when they pledged allegiance to you under the Tree"} [al-Fath: 18] — was among the righteous, yet was not excused for fighting Sayyiduna 'Uthman, may Allah be pleased with him, in the way that Mu'awiya is excused for fighting Sayyiduna 'Ali, may Allah be pleased with him.

Reflect on a Companion whom the scholars of Ahl al-Sunna wa'l-Jama'a consider it impermissible to narrate from — so that you may understand the varieties and shades of fanaticism. And we do not know what new contrivances Qasim al-Ta'i and those like him will invent in response to situations such as this.

3. The noble Companion Abu al-Tufayl 'Amir ibn Wathila — the last of the Companions to die, may Allah be pleased with him.

Hafiz Ibn Hajar said in *Tahdhib al-Tahdhib* (5/72) in his biographical entry: "Abu al-Tufayl was reliable in hadith, and he inclined toward Shi'ism..."

Ibn al-Madini said: "I asked Jarir: did Mughira dislike narrating from Abu al-Tufayl? He said: Yes." — And here is one of the

---

[18] Section on the Era of the Rightly Guided Caliphs.

scholars of Ahl al-Sunna wa'l-Jama'a who disliked narrating from this noble Companion.

Where then is the consensus of Ahl al-Sunna on their uprightness that Qasim al-Ta'i claims? Is this how an upright and reliable Companion is treated? Is this how one narrates willingly from him?

4. The noble Companion Mudlaj ibn 'Amr al-Salami, may Allah be pleased with him.

Al-Dhahabi said in *al-Mizan* (4/86): "Mudlaj ibn 'Amr al-Salami: narrates from al-Rummani — or al-Zummari — it is not known who he is."

I say: Hafiz Ibn Hajar took issue with this in *Lisan al-Mizan* (6/15), saying: "This man is a Companion. Ibn Hibban and others mention him among the Companions. Ibn Hibban adds: an ally of Banu 'Abd Shams, who died in the year fifty. And Ibn Sa'd said: he was present at Badr, Uhud, and all the battles."

Note here that al-Dhahabi himself placed this Companion in his book of weak and criticized narrators, which Ibn Hajar then corrected. Yet none of this prevented al-Dhahabi from doing so in the first place.

5. The deviant Companion and one of the criminals: Busr ibn Arta'a — may he receive from Allah what he deserves.

Because he committed extremely shameful acts — killing people and taking the women of the believers as captives — some hadith scholars attempted to claim that his companionship was disputed, so that their principle of declaring all Companions upright would not collapse and fall on its face.

Al-Dhahabi said in *Siyar A'lam al-Nubala'* (3/409):

"Busr ibn Arta'a, the commander, Abu 'Abd al-Rahman, al-Qurashi al-'Amiri — the Companion, resident of Damascus... Ibn Yunus said: a Companion who witnessed the conquest of Egypt, and he had a house and bathhouse there. He governed the Hijaz and Yemen for Mu'awiya, committed abominations, and suffered mental deterioration at the end of his life."

Al-Daraqutni said: "He had companionship, but he had no uprightness after the Prophet, may Allah's blessings and peace be upon him and his household."[19]

I say: among his crimes and atrocities is what Hafiz Ibn 'Abd al-Barr mentioned in *al-Isti'ab*[20] in his biographical entry:

"He is the one who killed two young children of 'Ubayd Allah ibn 'Abbas ibn 'Abd al-Muttalib — 'Abd al-Rahman and Qutham... He came to the two sons of 'Ubayd Allah ibn al-'Abbas while they were small children and slaughtered them. Their mother witnessed something tremendous."

I say: he slaughtered them with a knife, as stated in some narrations.

Despite some scholars claiming he was not a Companion and had not heard from the Prophet, may Allah's blessings and peace be upon him and his household, some hadith scholars authenticated his direct narration from the Prophet — such as Ibn Hibban (2424 and 2425) and others.

Abu Dharr, may Allah be pleased with him, told Sayyida Umm Salama, Mother of the Believers, may Allah be pleased with her, that the pledge of allegiance taken on behalf of Mu'awiya through the hand of Busr ibn Arta'a was a pledge of misguidance — as recorded in *Tahdhib al-Kamal* (4/65), *al-Thiqat* by Ibn Hibban (2/300), *al-Isti'ab* by Ibn 'Abd al-Barr (1/162), and *al-Isaba* by Ibn Hajar (4/12), among others.

6. One of the Companions foretold to be in the Fire: Abu Ghaddiya — whose name was Yassar, and it was also said Muslim ibn Sab' — the one who directly killed Sayyiduna 'Ammar ibn Yasir, may Allah be pleased with him. The Prophet, may Allah's blessings and peace be upon him and his household, said: "The killer of 'Ammar and his despoiler are in the Fire."

---

[19] See al-Mizzi, *Tahdhib al-Kamal*, 4:62; and Ibn Hajar, *Tahdhib al-Tahdhib*, 1:381.

[20] Ibn 'Abd al-Barr, *al-Isti'ab fi Ma'rifat al-Ashab*, printed in the margin of Ibn Hajar's *al-Isaba*, 1:156.

Hafiz Ibn Hajar said in *Ta'jil al-Manfa'a* (p. 509): "He is the one who killed 'Ammar ibn Yasir. When he would seek permission to enter upon Mu'awiya and others he would say: 'The killer of 'Ammar is at the door' — boasting of it. And observe the strangeness of it: narrations from the Prophet forbidding killing are transmitted, and then he kills a man like 'Ammar."

Al-Albani said, responding to Hafiz Ibn Hajar in his *al-Silsila al-Sahiha* (5/19) regarding the Companion foretold to be in the Fire, Abu Ghaddiya al-Juhani: "The Hafiz — Ibn Hajar — said: the assumption regarding the Companions in those wars is that they were acting on their interpretation, and the mujtahid who errs receives one reward; and if this applies to ordinary people, it applies to the Companions all the more. I say: this is true, but applying it to every individual among them is problematic, because it forces a contradiction in the stated principle — for it is not possible to say that Abu Ghaddiya, who killed 'Ammar, is rewarded because he killed him by ijtihad, when the Messenger of Allah, may Allah's blessings and peace be upon him and his household, says: 'The killer of 'Ammar is in the Fire.'" End of al-Albani's words. And it is a sound and correct statement.

7. Midi'am — a servant who used to serve the Prophet, may Allah's blessings and peace be upon him and his household.

Al-Bukhari narrated in *al-Sahih* (6707) from Abu Hurayra, on the occasion of the Prophet's return from the battle of Khaybar:

"When they were at Wadi al-Qura, while Midi'am was unloading the saddle of the Messenger of Allah, may Allah's blessings and peace be upon him and his household, a stray arrow struck and killed him. The people said: 'Congratulations to him — Paradise!' The Messenger of Allah, may Allah's blessings and peace be upon him and his household, said: 'By no means — by the One in Whose hand is my soul, the garment he took on the day of Khaybar from the war spoils before they were distributed will burn upon him as fire.'"

Hafiz Ibn Hajar recorded in the introduction to *al-Isaba* the names of some Companions who apostatized and died in their apostasy — which establishes for us that they are not protected from disbelief, let alone from lesser matters.

All of these are Companions — despite any stubborn denier. The Prophet, may Allah's blessings and peace be upon him and his household, called them Companions and there is no counter-argument from any stubborn fanatical person — or any other — against the words of the Messenger of Allah, may Allah's blessings and peace be upon him and his household. And that settles the matter.

It has also been narrated from some of the Companions that they used to say: "We do not testify for any man that he is from the people of Paradise until we see him die upon faith — for people change, and the Companions are not infallible."

Al-Bazzar narrated in his *Musnad* (6/46) from the noble Companion al-Miqdad ibn al-Aswad, may Allah be pleased with him, who said: "By Allah, I will not testify for anyone that he is from the people of Paradise, after a hadith I heard from the Messenger of Allah, may Allah's blessings and peace be upon him and his household: 'The heart of the son of Adam fluctuates more violently than a boiling pot.'"

Al-Bazzar commented: "The correct attribution in our view is to al-Miqdad, and its chain is sound."[21] The Companions are from the sons of Adam and they are not infallible as the prophets are.

These are clear examples — and they are but a fraction of what is available. All of them establish what we have laid down and dismantle the sweeping claims made by Qasim al-Ta'i — may Allah guide him and forgive him.

Ibn Hajar's Claim on Uprightness

Al-Ta'i says [p. 5]: "As for uprightness, Hafiz Ibn Hajar said in *al-Isaba*: 'Ahl al-Sunna agreed that all of them are upright, and none disagreed with this except anomalous innovators.'"

---

[21] Al-Tabarani, *al-Mu'jam al-Kabir*, 20:252. Hamdi al-Salafi notes there, citing al-Albani's *Silsilat al-Ahadith al-Sahiha*, 2:703: "This chain is sound according to the conditions of Muslim."

This is an invalid statement that does not hold, given the clear and manifest proofs and evidences from the Quran and the Sunnah that we have presented. Ahl al-Sunna have not agreed on this at all. And even if they had, their agreement would not be binding and would not constitute proof — for proof consists in the agreement of the entire community across all its sects and schools, as al-Ghazali, al-Razi, 'Abd al-Qadir al-Baghdadi, and others have stated. This is in addition to the examples we have cited of hadith scholars themselves weakening some Companions, such as Hind ibn Abi Hala and others.

Furthermore, Hafiz Ibn Hajar himself undermined his own claim of consensus on the very same page by quoting:

"Al-Mazari said in *Sharh al-Burhan*: 'By our saying that the Companions are upright, we do not mean everyone who saw the Prophet, may Allah's blessings and peace be upon him and his household, for a day, or visited him, or met him for some purpose and then departed. We mean those who kept his company, revered him, supported him, and followed the light that was revealed with him — those are the successful ones.'"

Ibn Hajar then quoted from al-'Ala'i, who said that this is a strange view that would exclude many of those well-known for companionship and narration from the ruling of uprightness — such as Wa'il ibn Hujr.

Note that al-Mazari is not one of the anomalous innovators. He is among the leading scholars of Ahl al-Sunna wa'l-Jama‘a. Al-Dhahabi described him[22] saying: "The Shaykh, the Imam, the great scholar, the vast ocean of knowledge, Abu 'Abd Allah Muhammad ibn 'Ali ibn 'Umar ibn Muhammad al-Tamimi al-Mazari al-Maliki — author of *al-Mu'allim bi-Fawa'id Sharh Muslim*... He was one of the foremost minds and the deeply learned imams... and he was well-versed in the science of hadith."

---

[22] Al-Dhahabi, *Siyar A'lam al-Nubala'*, 20:104.

It is thus clear that the question of the uprightness of the Companions is not one of consensus among Ahl al-Sunna. Those who dissent from it are many. The rational person should follow what is correct — what is explicitly stated in the Quran and the Sunnah — and abandon fanatical attachment to Mu'awiya and those like him.

Applying Verses of Praise to All Companions

Citing verses that praise some companions and applying these verses to all is a form of deception.

Al-Ta'i says [p. 6], quoting al-Khattab al-Baghdadi as transmitted by Hafiz Ibn Hajar: "The uprightness of the Companions is established and known by Allah's endorsement of them, His report of their purity, and His choosing them..."

This is an invalid statement for the reasons already set forth from the texts of the Quran and the Sunnah and the statements of the scholars of Ahl al-Sunna and others. Beyond that there is nothing but fanaticism.

I say to Qasim al-Ta'i: al-Khattab erred in this, just as he erred in attacking Imam Abu Hanifa, may Allah have mercy on him, transmitting reprehensible statements criticizing him and quoting the words of leading hadith masters of Ahl al-Sunna who weakened Imam Abu Hanifa — including al-Bukhari and others. Al-Khattab and those he quoted from are mistaken in this, as the meticulous scholar al-Kawthari, may Allah's mercy and pleasure be upon him, demonstrated in his *Ta'nib al-Khatib 'ala ma Saqahu fi Tarjamat Abi Hanifa min al-Akadhib*. Take heed.

The correct position is to say: there are verses praising some of the Companions, and there are verses censuring some of the Companions. Likewise there are authentic hadiths praising some of the Companions and other hadiths censuring others. Nothing demonstrates this more clearly than what Muslim narrated in *al-Sahih* (2779): "Among my Companions are twelve hypocrites..." and what is in al-Bukhari (6582): "I will say: 'My Companions!' And it will be said: 'You do not know what they introduced after you.'"

The verses that Qasim al-Ta'i and the scholars he quoted cite contain no proof whatsoever for what he wants regarding Mu'awiya — such as the words of Allah: {"You are the best community brought forth for mankind"} — for this is not evidence of Mu'awiya's innocence and uprightness. This verse refers to the community as a whole and not to the Companions specifically. And praising the collective does not mean that no individual within it is without virtue, or that the verse applies to every single person.

And the words of Allah: {"The foremost — the first of the Muhajirun and the Ansar, and those who followed them in good conduct — Allah is pleased with them and they are pleased with Him"} — Mu'awiya is not included in this verse. Nor does it apply to every individual. Indeed a group from among the very foremost ones apostatized — such as 'Ubayd Allah ibn Jahsh and others. Hafiz Ibn Hajar said in the introduction to *al-Isaba* (1/8) about him: "He was the husband of Sayyida Umm Habiba. He accepted Islam with her and emigrated to Abyssinia, but then became a Christian and died a Christian. And such also was 'Abd Allah ibn Khatal, who was killed while clinging to the covering of the Ka'ba."

As for Mu'awiya — he did not follow the foremost Muhajirun and Ansar. On the contrary, he cursed them, abused them, reviled them, and commanded the people to abuse them — including, despite himself, his master Sayyiduna 'Ali ibn Abi Talib, may Allah be pleased with him. We have already presented the evidence for this — refer back to it.

I marvel at these people who cite noble verses praising some of the Companions while remaining silent about the verses that censure the other category of Companions — seeking to create a false impression in people's minds. Likewise they cite the praising hadiths while ignoring the authenticated censuring hadiths. This is what fanaticism does to its holder. {"Do you believe in part of the Book and disbelieve in part?"} [al-Baqara: 85]

Exaggeration and Excess

Al-Ta'i says [p. 6]: "Whoever diminishes one Companion or challenges his narration has rejected the Lord of all worlds and invalidated the laws of the Muslims."

Beyond being a pure error, this is a reprehensible excess. How did al-Bukhari diminish the Companion Hind ibn Abi Hala by placing him in his book of weak narrators? How did al-Dhuhali reject the narration of the Companion 'Abd al-Rahman ibn 'Udayd? How did Hariz ibn 'Uthman curse Sayyiduna 'Ali, may Allah be pleased with him, yet the majority of hadith scholars declared him reliable? How and how and how...

Qasim al-Ta'i has scattered in his book a number of statements of this excessive kind — to intimidate the general public and those who disagree with his refuted view that conflicts with the proofs, the evidences, and the statements of the scholars. He is in this respect like the rest of his Nasibi brothers.

Major Sins and Uprightness

Al-Ta'i says [p. 7]: "I say: the occurrence of some errors from them does not negate the uprightness established for them by Allah's and His Messenger's endorsement, for the errors that occurred were from pure ijtihad — not from desire or the pursuit of worldly power and leadership." He repeated this multiple times.

I say: this is not correct. Such conduct does indeed negate uprightness. For whoever kills a believer, or drinks an intoxicant, or oppresses people, or was from the transgressing faction that calls to the Fire — let alone being its leader — has forfeited uprightness and is a discredited narrator. Nothing demonstrates this more clearly than the evidences we have already presented.

What was previously cited from the statement of Imam and scholar Sa'd al-Din al-Taftazani al-Hanafi (died 793 AH) in

Sharh al-Maqasid (5/310) applies here: "What took place among the Companions in terms of battles and disputes... indicates on its face that some of them deviated from the path of truth and reached the level of injustice and depravity... for not every Companion is infallible, and not everyone who met the Prophet, may Allah's blessings and peace be upon him and his household, is marked with good."

And what was cited from al-Dhahabi in *Siyar A'lam al-Nubala'* (3/415) about al-Walid: "Despite his depravity — may Allah pardon him — he was brave..." A depraved person is not upright, as is known — unless Qasim al-Ta'i and those like him consider depravity a form of uprightness.

Imam al-Nawawi said in *Sharh Sahih Muslim* (16/139): "The Prophet did not kill the hypocrites because they outwardly professed Islam, and he was commanded to judge by outward appearance while Allah attends to what is inward. And because they were counted among his Companions, may Allah's blessings and peace be upon him and his household, and they waged jihad with him — either out of tribal pride, or in pursuit of worldly gain, or out of solidarity with their clansmen who were with him."

The Testimony and Narrations of All Companions

This section examines the claim that the testimony and narrations of all Companions are accepted, and demonstrates that no such consensus exists.

Al-Ta'i says [p. 7], quoting Imam al-Nawawi: "The people of truth and those who count in consensus agreed on accepting their testimonies, their narrations, their complete uprightness, and that they are excused for what issued from them."

This is refuted by what has already been presented. Al-Nawawi and Ibn Hajar and others have said things that reveal themselves to be errors which it is not permissible to follow — among them their claim that the early scholars practised tafwid and the later scholars practised ta'wil. Upon investigation we find that the early scholars did in fact practise ta'wil, as the books of Quranic interpretation are filled with the ta'wilat of Ibn 'Abbas regarding the divine attributes and other matters.

As for the claimed consensus on accepting their testimonies — this is refuted, among other things, by what al-Dhahabi recorded in *Siyar A'lam al-Nubala'* (3/7-8): "From Sa'id ibn al-Musayyab: 'Umar flogged Abu Bakra, Nafi' ibn al-Harith, and Shibl. Two of them repented and 'Umar accepted their testimony. But Abu Bakra refused to repent, and so 'Umar did not accept his testimony."

And as for the claimed consensus on accepting their narrations — this is likewise refuted by al-Dhuhali's statement about the noble Companion 'Abd al-Rahman ibn 'Udayd al-Balawi: "It is not permissible to narrate anything from him — he is the head of the fitna."[23]

Hafiz Ibn Hajar said in *Tahdhib al-Tahdhib* (5/72): "Ibn al-Madini said: I asked Jarir: did Mughira dislike narrating from Abu al-Tufayl? He said: Yes." And Abu al-Tufayl is a noble Companion — the last of the Companions to die.

The Imam and Hafiz Jarir al-Dabbi used to curse and abuse Mu'awiya openly. Hafiz Ibn Hajar said in *al-Tahdhib* (2/66): "Al-Khalili said in *al-Irshad*: 'He is reliable, agreed upon.' And Qutayba said: 'Jarir the foremost hafiz narrated to us — but I heard him cursing and abusing Mu'awiya openly.'"

With this, the alleged agreements and consensuses collapse entirely.

The Civil Wars and Ijtihad

The Wrongdoer Is Not a Mujtahid

A wrongdoer is not a mujtahid, especially one whom the Prophet identified as a transgressor calling to the Fire.

Al-Ta'i says [p. 7], claiming that Mu'awiya and his faction are rewarded: "The mujtahid who errs receives one reward, and the

---

[23] See al-Dhahabi, *Tarikh al-Islam*, 3:532.

mujtahid who is correct receives two. Sayyiduna 'Ali, may Allah be pleased with him, was correct, and some of those who fought him erred — but both are rewarded."

I say: the correct position is that Sayyiduna 'Ali, may Allah be pleased with him, is rewarded and Mu'awiya bears a burden of sin. For he is the one who calls to the Fire, as stated in *Sahih al-Bukhari* (447). The Prophet, may Allah's blessings and peace be upon him and his household, censured him in many hadiths. His acts are transgressions and violations of the commands of Allah, Exalted be He, and His Messenger. He cursed and reviled Sayyiduna 'Ali, and whoever curses 'Ali has cursed the Messenger of Allah, may Allah's blessings and peace be upon him and his household, as stated in the authenticated hadith: "Whoever curses 'Ali has cursed me."[24] He is the one who killed the noble Companion Hujr ibn 'Adi and others by execution because they objected to the cursing and reviling of Sayyiduna 'Ali, may Allah be pleased with him. He turned the caliphate into a biting kingship. And there is more, and more.

Ijtihad is not permissible where an explicit text exists — as is established. And clear violations of the Shari'a are not described as ijtihad. The acts of criminals — killing people, consuming their wealth unjustly, and so on — are not among the rewarded acts. The texts of the Quran and the Sunnah are clear that transgressions, whether committed by Companions or those after them, are transgressions, and their perpetrators deserve punishment. There is no evidence stating that transgressions go unpunished for their perpetrators.

What Qasim al-Ta'i and those like him must do is abandon their fanatical attachment to Mu'awiya and recognize that one who calls to the Fire, commits transgressions — including drinking wine — rebels against the rightly-guided and just caliph, and kills people, cannot be described as a mujtahid who is rewarded

---

[24] Ahmad ibn Hanbal, *al-Musnad*, 6:323; al-Nasa'i, *al-Sunan al-Kubra*, 5:133. The report was also authenticated by Shu'ayb al-Arna'ut in his commentary on the *Musnad*, 44:329, and by al-Albani in *al-Silsila al-Sahiha*, no. 3332.

and bears no sin. Only a fanatic — whoever he may be — would say such a thing.

{"Grave is the word that comes from their mouths — they say nothing but falsehood."} [al-Kahf: 5]

The Blood Shed Between the Companions

Al-Ta'i says [p. 7]: "Some distinguished scholars said: the blood spilled between the Companions, may Allah be pleased with them, is not included in the threat concerning two Muslims who fight each other."

I say: this is truly laughable. It is a refuted and invalid claim. What is the proof for this exemption? Does the Shari'a apply to those other than the Companions but not to the Companions themselves? By Allah, this is among the laughable things that demonstrate the naivety of its speaker and his bankruptcy of proofs and evidences.

Where then is the hadith — "Ammar will be killed by the transgressing faction — he calls them to Paradise and they call him to the Fire" — which is in the authenticated collections? And where is the mass-transmitted hadith: "Whoever I am his master, 'Ali is his master — O Allah, be an ally to whoever is his ally, and an enemy to whoever is his enemy"[25] — narrated by Ahmad in *al-Musnad* (4/372) and others? And where is the statement of the Prophet, may Allah's blessings and peace be upon him and his household: "The killer of 'Ammar and his despoiler are in the Fire"?[26] And where is the Prophet's statement in the two Sahihs about his Companions who are driven away from the Hawd: "I will say: 'O Lord, my Companions!' And He will say: 'You have no knowledge of what

---

[25] Al-Albani authenticated it in *al-Silsila al-Sahiha*, 4:330, no. 1750, and stated that it is transmitted through ten Companions. He added: "In summary, the hadith under discussion is sound in both of its parts; indeed, the first part of it is mass-transmitted from the Prophet, may Allah bless him and his household and grant them peace."

[26] Ahmad ibn Hanbal, *al-Musnad*, 4:198; Ibn Sa'd, *al-Tabaqat al-Kubra*, 3:260; and al-Hakim, *al-Mustadrak*. Al-Albani authenticated it in *al-Silsila al-Sahiha*, 5:18, no. 2008.

they introduced after you — they turned back on their heels and apostatized.'"[27] Wake up — may Allah grant you well-being — are these people upright?

The Killer of 'Ammar and His Despoiler

The Prophet, may Allah bless him and his household and grant them peace, explicitly stated that the killer of 'Ammar and his despoiler are in the Fire — in addition to the threat against the transgressing faction.

The Nasibi who contradicts himself in our time also agrees with us in what we maintain. He responds to Hafiz Ibn Hajar in his *al-Silsila al-Sahiha* (5/19) regarding the Companion foretold to be in the Fire, Abu Ghaddiya al-Juhani, saying: "The Hafiz — Ibn Hajar — said: the assumption regarding the Companions in those wars is that they were acting on their interpretation, and the mujtahid who errs receives one reward; and if this applies to ordinary people, it applies to the Companions all the more. I say: this is true, but applying it to every individual among them is problematic, because it forces a contradiction in the stated principle — for it is not possible to say that Abu Ghaddiya, who killed 'Ammar, is rewarded because he killed him by ijtihad, when the Messenger of Allah, may Allah's blessings and peace be upon him and his household, says: 'The killer of 'Ammar is in the Fire.'" End of al-Albani's words. And it is a sound and correct statement.

By the same logic: those who built the Mosque of Harm among the Companions exercised ijtihad! Those who abandoned Friday prayer and left the Prophet standing while they rushed off to entertainment and trade exercised ijtihad! Those who abandoned the Prophet's army, may Allah's blessings and peace be upon him and his household, on the march to Uhud and turned back under the leadership of Ibn Umm Salul — turning

---

[27] Al-Bukhari, *Sahih*, nos. 6585, 6586, and 6587. See also Ibn Hajar, *Fath al-Bari*, 11:385, in his commentary on hadith no. 6526, where he gathers the relevant wordings concerning those driven away from the Hawd and notes additional supporting reports from Ahmad and al-Tabarani.

away on the day of battle — and they numbered approximately three hundred Companions[28] — they exercised ijtihad!

Anyone who holds that such ijtihad earns its holder a reward, as these fabricators assert, is afflicted with a kind of madness.

The Transgressing Faction and Worldly Gain

Al-Ta'i says [p. 7], quoting an unnamed scholar, that those transgressing Companions "did not intend sin or purely worldly gain..."

What has already been presented dismantles and demolishes this entirely. Among the evidence: the statement of Imam al-Nawawi in *Sharh Sahih Muslim* (16/139): "The Prophet did not kill the hypocrites because they outwardly professed Islam, and he was commanded to judge by outward appearance while Allah attends to what is inward — and because they were counted among his Companions and waged jihad with him, either out of tribal pride, or in pursuit of worldly gain, or out of solidarity with their clansmen who were with him."

The Abstaining Companions and Their Regret

A small group of Companions who abstained from fighting were mistaken, and they later regretted it. Likewise, some of those who fought against Sayyiduna 'Ali repented. Mu'awiya, however, never repented of his crimes.

Al-Ta'i says [p. 8]: "Until a group of Companions became confused by the matter and abstained from both sides, refusing to fight."

I say: this statement is invalid for several reasons.

First: the actions of those Companions do not constitute a legal proof. The statement of a Companion is not among the legal proofs of the Shari'a, as is established in the science of legal theory. The proof is the Quran, the Sunnah, consensus, and rational evidence. Mentioning this or omitting it makes no

---

[28] See al-Bukhari; al-Bayhaqi, *al-Sunan al-Kubra*, 9:31; and others.

difference. And besides, they were not confused — rather they fell short in supporting the truth.

Second: their action contradicts what Allah, Exalted be He, commanded — namely, fighting the transgressing faction, in His words: {"Fight the one that transgresses"} [al-Hujurat: 9]. And Mu'awiya and his party are the transgressing faction, by the agreement of Ahl al-Sunna — let alone others. The words of the Prophet, may Allah's blessings and peace be upon him and his household, are explicit in the two Sahihs and others: "Ammar will be killed by the transgressing faction — he calls him to Paradise and they call him to the Fire." Al-Ta'i's argument here is an attempt to comb through thorns.

Third: he himself transmitted to us that some of those who abstained from fighting and did not support Sayyiduna 'Ali, may Allah's peace be upon him, deeply regretted their abstention.

Al-Hakim narrated in *al-Mustadrak* (3/115) that Ibn 'Umar said: "Nothing weighs upon me more in this matter than the fact that I did not fight this transgressing faction, as Allah, Exalted and Mighty, commanded me." Al-Hakim recorded this in the chapter on the virtues of Sayyiduna 'Ali, may Allah's peace be upon him.

Al-Hakim narrated in *al-Mustadrak* (3/116) the story of Sa'd ibn Abi Waqqas's abstention: a man said to Sa'd: "'Ali speaks against you, saying that you stayed behind from supporting him." Sa'd replied: "By Allah, it was a view I held, and my view was mistaken. 'Ali was given three things — had I been given even one of them, it would have been dearer to me than all the world and what it contains..."[29]

And Sayyida 'A'isha's regret for fighting Sayyiduna 'Ali, may Allah's peace be upon him, is also recorded in *al-Mustadrak* (3/119). Al-Dhahabi confirmed this in *Siyar A'lam al-Nubala'* (2/177), saying: "There is no doubt that 'A'isha deeply regretted her march to Basra and her presence at the Battle of the Camel."

---

[29] Al-Malla'i is reliable according to us.

With this, what Qasim al-Ta'i has said is rendered null and void.

The Hadith "O Allah, O Allah, Regarding My Companions"

Al-Ta'i says [p. 8]: "It is sufficient for every Muslim who recognizes the right of the Messenger of Allah, may Allah's blessings and peace be upon him and his household, to obedience, that he refrain from any offence or disparagement — whether explicit or implied — toward any Companion. For the Prophet, may Allah's blessings and peace be upon him and his household, said: 'O Allah, O Allah regarding my Companions — do not make them a target. Whoever loves them does so through love of me, and whoever hates them does so through hatred of me. Whoever harms them has harmed me, whoever harms me has harmed Allah, and whoever harms Allah — He will soon seize him.'"

I say: this hadith is not authenticated in the view of the hadith masters. It is among the weak and worthless narrations, and it furthermore contradicts those whom Allah, Exalted be He, censured in His Book, and those whom the Prophet, may Allah's blessings and peace be upon him and his household, censured — such as his statement in *Sahih Muslim*: "Among my Companions are twelve hypocrites..." and his statement in the Hawd hadith in the two Sahihs: "I will say: 'My Companions!' And it will be said: 'You do not know what they introduced after you...'"

In its chain is 'Abd al-Rahman ibn Ziyad — some call him 'Abd Allah ibn 'Abd al-Rahman — and he is unknown, declared reliable by none except Ibn Hibban alone.

Al-Dhahabi said in *al-Mizan* (4/135): "Al-Bukhari said: there is something problematic in him." See the hadith in *Du'afa' al-'Uqayli* (2/272) and *al-Kamil fi al-Du'afa'* by Ibn 'Adi (4/167). Al-Manawi said in *Fayd al-Qadir* (2/98): "Al-Sadr al-Manawi said: in it is 'Abd al-Rahman ibn Ziyad — al-Dhahabi said: he is unknown. And in *al-Mizan*: the hadith is unstable."

This hadith is among the fabrications and invented narrations that contradict what is established in the Quran and the Sunnah. With this the arguments of Qasim al-Ta'i collapse and are turned on their head by these weak and rejected evidences.

And even if this hadith were sound, it would hold no proof for the Nasibis — for the Shari'a forbids transgressing against and attacking the righteous, not the wicked. {"Shall We treat those who submit as We treat the criminals? What is the matter with you — how do you judge?"} [al-Qalam: 35-36] This is on one hand. On the other hand: Mu'awiya transgressed against the righteous — headed by Sayyiduna 'Ali, may Allah be pleased with him — so the warning applies to him. And the address in the hadith was primarily to the Companions.

The Hadith "When My Companions Are Mentioned, Hold Back"

Al-Ta'i then cited another hadith from among the fabrications to complete his construction built on a crumbling bank, saying: "And the Prophet, may Allah's blessings and peace be upon him and his household, said: 'When my Companions are mentioned, hold back.'"

I say: let our companion search for it in the books of fabricated, worthless, and weak narrations — he will find it there. We will direct him to some of them. Ibn 'Adi narrated it in *al-Kamil fi al-Du'afa'* (6/162 and 7/24), and Ibn Hibban in *al-Majruhin* (3/115). The Sayyid and Hafiz Ahmad ibn al-Siddiq al-Ghumari said in his book *al-Mudawi* (1/366), after mentioning its chains of transmission and clarifying their defects: "In sum, this hadith is false, invented, and fabricated."

Let al-Ta'i benefit from this and learn what he does not know.

CHAPTER 3: MU'AWIYA, THE CURSING OF 'ALI, AND FABRICATED VIRTUES

The Claim That All Companions Are Definitively in Paradise

Al-Ta'i then quoted from Hafiz Ibn Hajar in *al-Isaba* (1/10) a statement attributed to Ibn Hazm, saying: "Abu Muhammad ibn Hazm said: All the Companions are definitively from the people of Paradise."

I say: Ibn Hazm did not say that, as we will demonstrate. And even supposing it were established as his statement, it is refuted by the words of the Prophet, may Allah's blessings and peace be upon him and his household, in *Sahih Muslim*: "Among my Companions are twelve hypocrites, eight of whom will not enter Paradise until a camel passes through the eye of a needle."

So do you take, O Qasim, the statement of Ibn Hazm or the statement of the Messenger of Allah, may Allah's blessings and peace be upon him and his household?

This is alongside the words of Allah, Exalted be He: {"And among the people of Madinah there are those who are entrenched in hypocrisy — you do not know them, but We know them"}, and His words: {"And among them are those who made a covenant with Allah: 'If He gives us from His bounty, we will surely give charity and be among the righteous.' But when He gave them from His bounty, they withheld it and turned away — so He penalized them with hypocrisy in their hearts until the Day they meet Him, because they broke their covenant with Allah and because they used to lie."} [al-Tawba: 75-77]

Al-Tirmidhi narrated (2423), as mentioned previously, from our master Ibn 'Abbas, may Allah be pleased with them both, in a chain traced back to the Prophet, which includes: "Men from among my Companions will be seized from the right and from the left. I will say: 'O Lord, my Companions!' And it will be said: 'You do not know what they introduced after you — they did not cease to apostatize on their heels from the moment you parted from them.'"

Al-Bukhari narrated in *al-Sahih* (6585) from Abu Hurayra that the Messenger of Allah, may Allah's blessings and peace be upon him and his household, said: "On the Day of Resurrection a company from among my Companions will come to me and will be driven away from the Hawd. I will say: 'O Lord, my Companions!' He will say: 'You have no knowledge of what they introduced after you — they turned back on their heels and apostatized.'" The word *yuhalla'un* means: they will be driven away, expelled, and turned back.

And in a narration of al-Bukhari (6097 and 6528) and Muslim (367 and 4243), the Prophet, may Allah's blessings and peace be upon him and his household, says of them: "Away, away with those who changed after me."

Citing some of the verses praising the foremost Muhajirun and Ansar and those who spent and fought before the conquest therefore does not cover Mu'awiya and those like him who changed and altered and transgressed and rebelled — and of whom the Prophet, may Allah's blessings and peace be upon him and his household, informed us that they call to the Fire. Do these people not have minds to comprehend this?

The meaning of the words of Allah, Exalted be He — {"Those among you who spent and fought before the conquest are not equal — those are greater in degree than those who spent and fought afterward, though Allah has promised the best to both"} [al-Hadid: 10] — applies to those who remained in submission to Allah, Exalted be He, and His Messenger, showing gentleness and mercy toward the believers, not rebelling against the rightly-guided caliphs, not transgressing, not killing the believing pious Companions. As for those who committed such outrages — the pretense of Islam does not benefit them, nor does spending before the conquest, nor does fighting before or after it. And you know what does benefit them.

There are those who accepted Islam before the conquest and then apostatized or committed outrages — such as 'Abd Allah ibn Sa'd ibn Abi al-Sarh, the first scribe of revelation, who apostatized. And 'Ubayd Allah ibn Jahsh, who was the husband of Sayyida Umm Habiba — he accepted Islam with her and emigrated to Abyssinia, then became a Christian and died a Christian.[30] And 'Abd Allah ibn Khatal and others.

Do these and others like them fall under the generality of {"Allah has promised the best to both"}?

Hafiz Ibn Hajar said in *al-Isaba* (4/109): "'Abd Allah ibn Sa'd ibn Abi al-Sarh used to write for the Prophet, may Allah's blessings and peace be upon him and his household, but Satan caused him to slip, so he joined the disbelievers. The Prophet, may Allah's blessings and peace be upon him and his household, ordered that he be killed — meaning on the day of the conquest..." Narrated by Abu Dawud (4358) and al-Nasa'i (4069), with a sound chain.

This verse and others like it contain praise for the collective, not for every individual within it — individuals deviate from the norm through depravity and injustice, just as some deviated through apostasy.[31] It is like the praise for the collective of the Muslim community in the words of Allah, Exalted be He: {"You are the best community brought forth for mankind"} — this does not mean that there is no one within it who is of bad conduct and behavior, or who has committed depravity, or apostatized, or transgressed and wronged and thereby deserved to enter the Fire. Allah, Exalted be He, said: {"But yes — whoever earns evil and is encompassed by his sin — those are the companions of the Fire; they will abide therein."} [al-Baqara: 81]

For this reason it is stated in the Quran and the Sunnah that some of the Companions will be driven away from the Hawd

---

[30] See Ibn Hajar, introduction to *al-Isaba fi Tamyiz al-Sahaba*.

[31] See Hasan Farhan al-Maliki, *al-Suhba wa'l-Sahaba*, where he provides useful responses to such objections derived from this noble verse.

because they changed and altered after the Prophet, may Allah's blessings and peace be upon him and his household.

The rational and fair-minded person does not claim infallibility for them, as we claim infallibility for the prophets and messengers, may Allah's peace and blessings be upon them all.

Ibn Jarir al-Tabari said in his *Tafsir* (1/66): "Allah, Exalted be His praise, favored the community of our Prophet Muhammad, may Allah's blessings and peace be upon him and his household, above all previous communities and informed them of this in His words: {'You are the best community brought forth for mankind'}. It is therefore known from this that the Children of Israel in the era of our Prophet — despite their rejection of him — were not the best of all peoples. Rather, the best of all peoples in that era and after it until the Day of Resurrection are those who believed in him and followed his way — not those of other communities who rejected him and went astray from his path."

And this does not mean that every individual within this community is characterized by this excellence — for among them is the sinner, the depraved, the apostate who perishes, and others.

Al-Ta'i's Truncated Citation of Ibn Hazm

The statement of Ibn Hazm was quoted by al-Ta'i from the introduction of *al-Isaba* (1/10) by Hafiz Ibn Hajar al-'Asqalani, where Ibn Hajar said: "Abu Muhammad ibn Hazm said: All the Companions are definitively from the people of Paradise." This is a truncated extract from Ibn Hazm's actual words. What Ibn Hazm said in *al-Fasl fi al-Milal* (4/148-149), after mentioning the names of certain distinguished Companions, is:

"Every one of those previously mentioned from the Muhajirun and the Ansar, up to and including the completion of the pledge of al-Ridwan — we assert with certainty regarding the inward states of their hearts, that they are all believers, righteous, who died upon faith and guidance and piety — all of them from the people of Paradise...

Then we assert with certainty that every one who accompanied the Messenger of Allah with a sincere intention, even for an hour, is from the people of Paradise...

As for those who spent and fought after the conquest — among them were hypocrites whom the Messenger of Allah, may Allah's blessings and peace be upon him and his household, did not know... and for this reason we do not assert certainty regarding every individual among them specifically, but we say: every one of them who was not among the hypocrites is definitively from the people of Paradise."

This is what Ibn Hazm actually said. It is not among the legal proofs of the Shari'a, but it is not what Ibn Hajar attributed to him.

The Misuse of Qur'anic Praise as a Blanket Guarantee

Al-Ta'i then argued, after citing what he attributed to Ibn Hazm: "Allah, Exalted be He, said: {'Those for whom the best has preceded from Us — they will be kept far from it.'} [al-Anbiya': 101] — establishing that all of them are from the people of Paradise and that none of them will enter the Fire."

This is a sweeping and unfounded claim, and a corrupt use of this noble verse as proof.

The scholars of Quranic interpretation disagreed about the intended meaning of the verse. Some said: it refers to every person for whom Allah, Exalted be He, foreordained happiness among His creation — and this is not specific to the Companions. Others said: it refers to those who were worshipped instead of Allah while they themselves were obedient to Allah — such as Sayyiduna 'Isa and 'Uzayr and the angels, may Allah's peace be upon them.[32]

---

[32] See al-Tabari, *Jami' al-Bayan 'an Ta'wil Ay al-Qur'an*, 17:96.

The verse is in a different context entirely and does not speak about the Companions specifically, for it to be applied to them to the exclusion of the prophets, the angels, and the messengers.

Furthermore, al-Ta'i's claim that "all of them are from the people of Paradise and none of them will enter the Fire" is refuted by what Muslim narrated in *al-Sahih* (2779): the Prophet, may Allah's blessings and peace be upon him and his household, said: "Among my Companions are twelve hypocrites, eight of whom will not enter Paradise until a camel passes through the eye of a needle."

And it is refuted by what al-Bazzar narrated in his *Musnad* (6/46) from the noble Companion al-Miqdad ibn al-Aswad, who said: "By Allah, I will not testify for anyone that he is from the people of Paradise, after a hadith I heard from the Messenger of Allah, may Allah's blessings and peace be upon him and his household. I heard the Messenger of Allah say: 'The heart of the son of Adam fluctuates more violently than a boiling pot.'"

Al-Bazzar commented: "The correct attribution in our view is to al-Miqdad, and its chain is sound."[33]

With this, the arguments, statements, and deductions of Qasim al-Ta'i are scattered to the winds.

Al-Ta'i then philosophizes after this, as if he has silenced every orator, saying: "Some callers to Islam openly curse him out of ignorance and transgression, and have forgotten verses such as this one and the sound narrations — indeed they have deliberately ignored the plain truth in order to please the enemies of Islam..." and the rest of his ranting.

Here it is necessary to point out an extremely important matter: people like these slanderers claim that whoever exposes the faults of Mu'awiya, his crimes, the ruling of the Shari'a concerning him, and what was said about him by the Prophet, may Allah's blessings and peace be upon him and his household,

---

[33] Al-Tabarani, *al-Mu'jam al-Kabir*, 20:252. Hamdi al-Salafi notes there, citing al-Albani's *Silsilat al-Ahadith al-Sahiha*, 2:703: "This chain is sound according to the conditions of Muslim."

and the Companions — that such a person is cursing and abusing him, and cursing and abusing the Companions. This is the worst kind of fraud, the claim of those who are bankrupt of arguments, liars and deceivers.

You now know the extent of our companion's knowledge in these matters, and how utterly hollow his arguments are, and who it is that is truly ignorant, transgressing, and forgetting the verses and hadiths — and who it is that applies them outside their proper context and interprets them contrary to their actual meaning.

A Hollow Commotion About the Cursing of the Companions

Al-Ta'i then devoted a section on page 9 of his book which he titled "The Second Pearl: On the Ruling Concerning Cursing the Companions." This is empty noise, because there is not a single Muslim faction — not the Rawafid, not the Nawasib, not the Khawarij, not any other — that curses all the Companions collectively. Inflating the matter of the tyrant Mu'awiya, the leader of the transgressing faction that calls to the Fire, and those with him who call to the Fire, into a matter of "the Companions," and treating whoever curses or abuses him or criticizes him or exposes his true nature as someone who is cursing and abusing the Companions — and that the ruling on such a person is that he is a disbeliever — this is empty nonsense, cold and fallen speech, low and worthless words, evidencing only the fanatical attachment of its speaker to falsehood.

On this basis, Mu'awiya himself falls under what al-Ta'i wishes to brand upon those who criticize him — namely al-Nasa'i, al-Hakim, 'Abd al-Razzaq, Abu al-Yaman,[34] Jarir al-Dabbi, and the imams of Ahl al-Sunna who criticized Mu'awiya — since Mu'awiya used to curse and revile our master 'Ali, may Allah be pleased with him, and order that he be cursed, reviled, and

---

[34] See al-Dhahabi, *Siyar A'lam al-Nubala'*, 10:432.

abused. Until Hafiz Ibn Hajar said in *al-Fath* (7/71) that the Umayyads cursed Sayyiduna 'Ali "and made his cursing from the pulpits a regular practice."

Is an intelligent and just Islamic state one that makes the cursing of the rightly-guided caliphs and the best of the Companions from the pulpits a regular practice?

The Prophet, may Allah's blessings and peace be upon him and his household, said to our master 'Ali, may Allah be pleased with him, as narrated by Muslim (78) in his *Sahih* and others: "None loves you except a believer, and none hates you except a hypocrite."

Yet Mu'awiya cursed and reviled our master 'Ali and ordered the people to curse him.

Muslim narrated in *al-Sahih* (2404) from 'Amir ibn Sa'd ibn Abi Waqqas, from his father, who said: Mu'awiya ibn Abi Sufyan commanded Sa'd and said: "What prevents you from cursing Abu Turab?" Sa'd replied: "As for the three things I recall that the Messenger of Allah said to him — I will never curse him... And when the verse {'Let us call our sons and your sons'} [Al 'Imran: 61] was revealed, the Messenger of Allah called 'Ali, Fatima, al-Hasan, and al-Husayn and said: 'O Allah, these are my family.'"[35]

Reflect on how Mu'awiya commands the Companions to curse and revile our master 'Ali, may Allah be pleased with him.

Ibn Maja narrated (121) with a sound chain[36] on the authority of Sa'd ibn Abi Waqqas: Mu'awiya came on one of his pilgrimage visits. Sa'd visited him, and they mentioned 'Ali. Mu'awiya cursed and reviled him. Sa'd became angry...

This narration is explicit in establishing that Mu'awiya used to curse and revile our master 'Ali.

---

[35] As noted above, this hadith was narrated by Muslim, *Sahih*, no. 2404; al-Tirmidhi, *Sunan*, no. 3724; and others.

[36] Al-Albani authenticated it in *Sahih Ibn Maja*, 1:26.

Mu'awiya also commanded his governors to curse and revile our master 'Ali and order the people to do so. Among the evidence for this is what Muslim narrated in *al-Sahih* (2409) from the noble Companion Sahl ibn Sa'd: "A man from the family of Marwan was appointed over Madinah. He summoned Sahl ibn Sa'd and ordered him to curse 'Ali. Sahl refused. The man said: 'If you refuse, then at least say: May Allah curse Abu Turab.' Sahl said: 'No name was dearer to 'Ali than Abu Turab, and he used to rejoice when called by it.'"

By this it is established that Mu'awiya used to curse our master 'Ali, may Allah be pleased with him, and order the people to curse him. And it has been authenticated that the Prophet, may Allah's blessings and peace be upon him and his household, said: "Whoever curses 'Ali has cursed me."

Ahmad narrated in *al-Musnad* (6/323) from Abu 'Abd Allah al-Jadali who said: I entered upon Umm Salama who said: "Is the Messenger of Allah being cursed among you?" I said: "Allah forbid!" She said: "I heard the Messenger of Allah, may Allah's blessings and peace be upon him and his household, say: 'Whoever curses 'Ali has cursed me.'"[37] Al-Hakim adds in his narration (3/121): "And whoever curses me has cursed Allah."

The cursing and reviling of Sayyiduna 'Ali by Mu'awiya and his followers is well-known — indeed it is mass-transmitted — and collecting it would require a dedicated monograph on the subject.[38]

---

[37] Al-Nasa'i also narrated it in *al-Sunan al-Kubra*, 5:133. It has numerous routes of transmission, many of which were cited by al-Haythami in *Majma' al-Zawa'id*, 9:130. It is also transmitted with other wordings through numerous routes. See Ibn Abi Shayba, *al-Musannaf*, 12:76-77; al-Tabarani, *al-Mu'jam al-Kabir*, 23:322; and Abu Ya'la, *al-Musnad*, 12:444. Shu'ayb al-Arna'ut authenticated it in his commentary on the *Musnad*, 44:329, as did al-Albani in *al-Silsila al-Sahiha*, no. 3332.

[38] Ahmad ibn Hanbal, *al-Musnad*, 1:187; Abu Dawud, *Sunan*, nos. 4649 and 4650, with a sound chain, reporting the objection of the Companion Sa'id ibn Zayd to al-Mughira ibn Shu'ba when 'Ali ibn Abi Talib was being cursed in his presence. Al-Albani authenticated it in *Sahih Abi Dawud*, 3:880, no. 3887. See also Ibn Abi 'Asim, *al-Sunna*, no. 1350, from 'Abd al-Rahman ibn al-

The summary of the matter is that Mu'awiya cursed our master 'Ali and commanded that he be cursed, reviled, and abused — while the greatest Prophet, may Allah's blessings and peace be upon him and his household, says: "Whoever curses 'Ali has cursed me."

So are you with the Messenger of Allah, may Allah's blessings and peace be upon him and his household, or with Mu'awiya who curses our master 'Ali and thereby curses our master the Messenger of Allah, may Allah's blessings and peace be upon him and his household?

Is it permissible to love and defend one who curses our master 'Ali, may Allah be pleased with him, and thereby curses our master the Messenger of Allah, may Allah's blessings and peace be upon him and his household? Where is Allah-consciousness, where is faith, where is the fear of Allah, Exalted be He?

Qasim al-Ta'i turns a blind eye to all of this and to these explicit rulings — overlooking Mu'awiya the one who cursed and reviled the master of the believers 'Ali, may Allah be pleased with him, while inflating and prolonging and presenting Mu'awiya's case — though it is a losing case.

The words of al-Alusi that al-Ta'i brings are refuted, for if those words were accepted, the great hadith masters and imams of Ahl al-Sunna and the narrators of hadiths and reports — such as al-Nasa'i, 'Abd al-Razzaq, al-Hakim, the noble Companions who hated Mu'awiya and criticized him — would all be disbelievers, guilty of the gravest slander without doubt, as al-Alusi and Qasim al-Ta'i claim with their low and false words.

From all of this you will understand that fanaticism and intellectual and mental rigidity, and the deliberate ignoring of reality, have done to this man what they have done — leading him to reckless audacity and deviation from submission to the Shari'a, which has established that whoever deviates from the Book and the Sunnah is a deviant — and no exception is made

---

Bilmani, concerning Sa'id ibn Zayd's objection to Mu'awiya when 'Ali was cursed in his presence.

for this, not for the Companions, not for the Successors, not for those who came after them.

Leave off writing — you have no part in it, even if you blackened your face with ink.

The Claim That Muslim Historians Wronged Mu'awiya

Al-Ta'i then devoted a section on page 10 of his book which he titled "The Third Pearl: On the Islam of Mu'awiya." In the introduction to this section, which collapses under its own weight, he said: "In this Pearl and until the end of the treatise, we speak specifically about the noble Companion Mu'awiya ibn Abi Sufyan, whom some historical transmitters wronged by attributing to him what ears are ashamed to hear and hearts grieve over, and whose fabricated and lying reports were repeated by some people of knowledge..." and the rest of his ranting.

I say: the summary of the matter is that even if Mu'awiya had been the first person to accept Islam and from the foremost early Muslims — that would not benefit him in light of the well-known, mass-transmitted outrages and disasters attributed to him that contradict the command of Allah, Exalted be He, and His Messenger. For it has been established that people who accepted Islam before the conquest then apostatized, or were proven to be hypocrites.[39]

As for Mu'awiya — he is not noble. All Muslims counted the rightly-guided caliphs but did not count him among them, despite his being a Companion. Why is that? They counted someone like 'Umar ibn 'Abd al-'Aziz among the rightly-guided and did not count Mu'awiya — because he deviated from the straight path.

The exposure of Mu'awiya's condition was not limited to the historians whom al-Ta'i describes as ignorant, wrongdoers, and

---

[39] See the biographical entry of Harqus ibn Zuhayr in Ibn Hajar, *al-Isaba fi Tamyiz al-Sahaba*, 1:320, and elsewhere.

so forth — among them Ibn Hajar al-'Asqalani and al-Dhahabi. Rather, his condition was also exposed by the imams of Ahl al-Sunna — al-Nasa'i, Abu Ghassan al-Nahdi, 'Abd al-Razzaq, al-Hakim, and others from the imams, Companions, Successors, and those after them to our own day.

The reports, O al-Ta'i, are not fabricated — they are sound in chain and mass-transmitted, including the reports of Abu Mikhnaf Lut ibn Yahya — may Allah protect you.

As for the statement of al-'Awwam ibn Hawshab that you cited there — where is its chain? From which book did you quote it? It is rejected and refuted because it contradicts reality. Allah, Exalted be He, said: {"And among the people is one who worships Allah on the very edge — so if good befalls him he is reassured by it, but if a trial befalls him he turns on his face, losing both this world and the Hereafter — that is the manifest loss."} [al-Hajj: 11]

There were those among the early Muslims in Mecca — from the first to accept Islam — who apostatized on the very morning of the Night Journey. Sayyida 'A'isha, may Allah be pleased with her, said: "When the Prophet, may Allah's blessings and peace be upon him and his household, was taken by night to the Farthest Mosque, the people began talking about it the next morning — and some of those who had believed in him and affirmed him apostatized..." Narrated by al-Hakim (3/62) and al-Bayhaqi in *Dala'il al-Nubuwwa* (2/361).

Al-Bayhaqi narrated in *Dala'il al-Nubuwwa* (2/360) through another chain: "Then the Messenger of Allah, may Allah's blessings and peace be upon him and his household, returned to Mecca and informed them that he had been taken by night — and many people who had prayed with him were put to trial and apostatized."

Ahmad also narrated in *al-Musnad* (1/374) with a sound chain from Ibn 'Abbas: The Prophet, may Allah's blessings and peace be upon him and his household, was taken by night to Jerusalem, then came back that very night and told them of his journey and the sign of the Farthest Mosque and their caravan... Some people said: "We believe Muhammad in what he says" — while others apostatized and became disbelievers, and Allah struck their necks alongside Abu Jahl. Shu'ayb al-Arna'ut authenticated its chain in his commentary on the *Musnad*.

And I add: among those Companions who apostatized is what al-Bukhari narrated in *al-Sahih* (6802) from Anas, may Allah be pleased with him: "A group from 'Ukl came to the Prophet, may Allah's blessings and peace be upon him and his household, accepted Islam, but found the climate of Madinah disagreeable. He ordered them to go to the camels of the zakat charity and drink from their urine and milk. They did so and recovered — then they apostatized and killed the herdsmen and drove away the camels. He sent after them and they were brought back, and he cut off their hands and feet and gouged out their eyes and left them without cauterizing their wounds until they died."

False Virtues Invented for Mu'awiya

Al-Ta'i's words — "Mu'awiya has been a target of attack from many since the day he accepted Islam, and such is the lot of great men" — are empty inflation. Those who attacked him from the day he accepted Islam were the noble Companions themselves. The attack upon him came from the direction of the Messenger, may Allah's blessings and peace be upon him and his household, and the Companions. Among the evidence for this is the statement of the Messenger, may Allah's blessings and peace be upon him and his household, about him: "O Allah, do not fill his stomach," and his statement about Mu'awiya and his faction who killed our master 'Ammar: "They call to the Fire." And the statements of the noble Companions about him — headed by our master 'Ali, may Allah be pleased with him, and Ibn 'Abbas and those after them.

His words "such is the lot of great men" are refuted by the statement of the Prophet, may Allah's blessings and peace be upon him and his household, about him in *Sahih Muslim* (1480): "As for Mu'awiya, he is a pauper with no wealth." The

Prophet, may Allah's blessings and peace be upon him and his household, never blamed any person for having little wealth or for poverty — had he not seen evil in him, he would not have said about him what he said. Especially since Allah, Exalted be He, says in His Book: {"And marry off the unmarried among you and the righteous among your male slaves and female slaves. If they are poor, Allah will enrich them from His bounty."} [al-Nur: 32]

Al-Ta'i says: "I am astonished by a man we thought was among the people of knowledge — he used to refute some of the innovators and debate some of those who claim expertise in hadith criticism, and he benefited and excelled. But after these blessed efforts he edited a treatise on the divine names and attributes and wrote in its margins words in which he wronged Mu'awiya, filling it with lies, deception, distortion of scholarly facts, and fabricated and rejected chains... and I responded to him in the Eleventh Pearl..."

I say: the corruption of this statement is manifest, its hollowness apparent, and its worthlessness clear.

That same man is likewise astonished by Qasim — how he cites stories like bedtime tales and makes them a defense of some of the tyrants. And it will become clear who it is that owns the lies and deception, and who distorts scholarly facts and produces fabricated and rejected chains. It will be said to him: this is not your nest — crawl away from it.

Openly it is said to those who attempt to scale his heights: this is not your nest — crawl away from it.

The Mythical Titles "Uncle of the Believers" and "Scribe of Revelation"

Our companion repeats himself at length in what holds no benefit, saying on page 10 — repeating his previous words: "It is sufficient for Sayyiduna Mu'awiya that he accompanied the Messenger of Allah, and his sister Umm Habiba is with the Prophet making her a Mother of the Believers; and it is sufficient for him that he was among those who wrote the revelation on some occasions and the Prophet's correspondence to the tribes; and that he is among those who accepted Islam before the conquest of Mecca, and Allah has promised the best to the Muslims before and after the conquest."

I say: as for Mu'awiya accompanying the Prophet, may Allah's blessings and peace be upon him and his household — this did not benefit him. Among the Companions the Prophet, may Allah's blessings and peace be upon him and his household, said: "Among my Companions are twelve hypocrites, eight of whom will not enter Paradise..." as in *Sahih Muslim*. And in the two Sahihs, a group of Companions who changed and altered after him are driven away from the Hawd on the Day of Resurrection — and he says of them: "Away, away." We have already presented this with full documentation.

As for his sister Sayyida Umm Habiba being a Mother of the Believers — this will not benefit Mu'awiya in the least. There is no proof in either reason or transmitted sources stating that the brother of a Mother of the Believers is in Paradise, or is counted among the non-sinful, or is immune from being among the tyrants or criminals.

The father of Sayyida Safiyya, may Allah be pleased with her — a Mother of the Believers — was the Jew Huyayy ibn Akhtab, and we do not know who her brother is among the Jews. Should they then receive the same false and fabricated virtues attributed to Mu'awiya — virtues which the hadith masters and transmitters of Ahl al-Sunna explicitly stated are unsound?

And by this same logic, the Coptic Egyptians — the kinsmen of Sayyida Mariya al-Qibtiyya — would be uncles of the believers.

Ibn Kathir said, in his commentary on verse 6 of Surah al-Ahzab — {"The Prophet is more worthy of the believers than themselves, and his wives are their mothers"} — (3/477), published by Dar al-Ma'rifa, Beirut, second edition 1407 AH:

"Is it said of Mu'awiya and those like him: 'uncle of the believers'? There are two scholarly opinions on this. Al-Shafi'i, may Allah be pleased with him, explicitly stated: it is NOT to be said."[40]

The word "not" has been deleted from some modern editions in which sinful hands have tampered — reversing the meaning entirely. Be aware of this.

As for the claim that he wrote the revelation — this is not established. And even if we concede it hypothetically, how many men before him wrote the revelation and then apostatized — such as Ibn Abi al-Sarh, and that Christian mentioned in *Sahih al-Bukhari*.

Al-Bukhari narrated in *al-Sahih* (3617) and Muslim likewise (2781) — this is al-Bukhari's wording — from Anas ibn Malik, may Allah be pleased with him:

"There was a Christian man who accepted Islam, read al-Baqara and Al 'Imran, and used to write for the Prophet, may Allah's blessings and peace be upon him and his household. He then reverted to Christianity and used to say: 'Muhammad knows nothing except what I wrote for him.' Then Allah caused him to die — and when they buried him, the earth cast him out."

Ahmad narrated with a sound chain (3/120) and Ibn Hibban in his *Sahih* (3/19) from Anas: "There was a man who used to write for the Prophet, may Allah's blessings and peace be upon him and his household, and then he apostatized from Islam and joined the polytheists. When this reached the Prophet, may Allah's blessings and peace be upon him and his household, he said: 'The earth will surely not receive him.'"

---

[40] Some modern printed editions of Ibn Kathir's *Tafsir* have been tampered with by deleting the word "not" from the phrase "not to be called," thereby reversing the meaning. Ibn Kathir was transmitting from Imam al-Shafi'i that Mu'awiya and those like him are **not to be called** "uncles of the believers." The wording "not to be called" is preserved in reliable manuscripts and older printed editions, including the first al-Manar edition printed in Egypt in 1347 AH under the supervision of Muhammad Rashid Rida, the 'Isa al-Babi al-Halabi edition, the Dar Subh/Adisoft 2003 edition edited by Mahmud 'Abd al-Karim al-Dimashqi, and the Dar al-Ma'rifa Beirut edition introduced by Yusuf 'Abd al-Rahman al-Mar'ashli. The edition prepared by Hassan 'Abd al-Mannan unfortunately omits the word "not."

We therefore hope that Qasim al-Ta'i and those like him will not boast after this about the writing of the revelation. Let them invent another way to establish the virtues and merits of Mu'awiya through which to oppose reality and what the Prophet, may Allah's blessings and peace be upon him and his household, informed us of his blameworthy condition.

The Claim That Mu'awiya Accepted Islam Before the Conquest of Mecca

As for his words "he accepted Islam before the conquest and Allah has promised the best to those who accepted Islam before and after the conquest" — the refutation of this has already been presented. This is a familiar refrain we recognize. It has already been demonstrated that this does not benefit him whether before the conquest or after it, given his evil deeds and those outrages.

Mu'awiya is from the Tulaqa' — those released at the conquest. Al-Ta'i's claim that he is among those who accepted Islam before the conquest, and that the conquest refers to the conquest of Mecca, contains a chain of errors and distortions.

As for the claim that he accepted Islam before the conquest — Hafiz Ibn Hajar said in *al-Isaba*[41] in the introduction to Mu'awiya's biographical entry: "Al-Waqidi reported that he accepted Islam after al-Hudaybiyya and concealed his Islam until he declared it in the year of the conquest, and that during 'Umrat al-Qada' he was already Muslim. But this is contradicted by what is established in the authenticated hadith from Sa'd ibn Abi Waqqas, who said, regarding performing 'Umra during the months of Hajj: 'We did this while he was at that time a disbeliever...'"

What al-Waqidi reported is refuted by what is established in the authenticated hadith. Al-Waqidi in their view is weak and criticized. Hafiz Ibn Hajar said in *al-Taqrib*: "Abandoned."

---

[41] Ibn Hajar, *al-Isaba fi Tamyiz al-Sahaba*, 3:433.

In *Sahih al-Bukhari* (4150), al-Bara' ibn 'Azib said: "You count the conquest as the conquest of Mecca — and the conquest of Mecca was indeed a conquest. But we count the conquest as the pledge of al-Ridwan on the day of al-Hudaybiyya."

On the basis of such fabrications, fantasies, and wishful thinking does Qasim build his ideas, his objections, and his attacks on those who disagree with his mistaken views.

Applying the verse {"Those for whom the best has preceded from Us — they will be kept far from it"} [al-Anbiya': 101] to Mu'awiya is an injustice, a false claim — indeed it is misguidance.

Citing Mu'awiya's biographical entry from the book of Ibn Hajar al-Haytami, author of *Tathir al-Jinan*, is an injustice, an outrage, and an aggression against the truth — because al-Haytami is not among the masters of this discipline. He is a Shafi'i jurist and nothing more. He has no part in knowing these matters or venturing into the science of hadith and distinguishing its sound from its weak, its accepted from its false and rejected.

He wrote that book to please some of the former kings of India at their request — and so fell into error and mistakes, containing a great many blunders and delusions. No reliance whatsoever can be placed on his words in that book, and no attention should be paid to it.

The Report That He Trimmed the Prophet's Hair at al-Marwa

The most telling proof of what we say regarding al-Ta'i and al-Haytami is that Qasim al-Ta'i said on page 11 of his ill-omened book:

Al-Ta'i says:

"Let me begin with you, O noble reader, in clarifying his Islam. The Imam and hadith master, the seal of jurists, the scholar Ibn Hajar al-Haytami, said in *Tathir al-Jinan* — citing what al-Waqidi reported — that after al-Hudaybiyya he accepted Islam;

and others said: on the very day of al-Hudaybiyya. He concealed his Islam from his father before the conquest of Mecca by approximately one year — and what supports this is what Ahmad transmitted through the chain of Muhammad al-Baqir ibn Zayn al-'Abidin ibn al-Husayn, from Ibn 'Abbas, may Allah be pleased with them, that Mu'awiya said: 'I trimmed from the head of the Messenger of Allah at al-Marwa with a blade.' The root of this hadith is in al-Bukhari through the chain of Tawus from Ibn 'Abbas with the wording: 'He trimmed with a blade' — not mentioning al-Marwa in either of the two narrations. Thus contrary to those who restrict themselves to the first narration as proof that he was Muslim during 'Umrat al-Qada', the first is clear because it states that this was at al-Marwa — which specifies that the trimming was during the 'Umra, because during the Farewell Pilgrimage he shaved at Mina by consensus..." [p. 11]

I say: this is speech that al-Haytami took from Ibn Hajar al-'Asqalani's *al-Isaba* and dealt with as he pleased — going on and on about this al-Marwa matter and making it a proof in favor of Mu'awiya, when the Companions considered it to be proof against him.

Muslim narrated (1246) from Ibn 'Abbas: "Mu'awiya said to me: 'Did you know that I trimmed from the head of the Messenger of Allah, may Allah's blessings and peace be upon him and his household, at al-Marwa with a blade?' I said to him: 'I consider this to be proof against you, not in your favor.'"

Reflect on how the Companions considered this to be of no benefit to Mu'awiya — as they said in wisdom: "He was prevented from success even when standing at the very door of it."

Even if Mu'awiya the released one had accepted Islam before the Hijra in Mecca alongside the earliest Muslims — that would not benefit him given the ruinous and destructive things he did. And given the statement of the greatest Messenger, may Allah's blessings and peace be upon him and his household: "The killer of 'Ammar and his despoiler are in the Fire," and the hadith of al-Bukhari: "Ammar will be killed by the transgressing faction — they call him to Paradise and they call him to the Fire."

Mu'awiya also played games with that narration in which he says "I trimmed from the head of the Messenger of Allah..." — for Muslim narrated it immediately after with different wording: "I trimmed for the Messenger of Allah... or I saw him being trimmed for him with a blade." Reflect on the manipulation — did he trim or did he see the Prophet being trimmed?

Furthermore, Ahmad ibn Hanbal did not narrate the hadith through the chain of Muhammad al-Baqir ibn Zayn al-'Abidin ibn al-Husayn, from Ibn 'Abbas — and I do not know where al-Ta'i and al-Haytami came up with this. These names were inserted for decoration with falsehood, and to create the false impression that the household of the Prophet, may Allah's blessings and peace be upon him and his household, narrated this and counted it among Mu'awiya's virtues. None of that is true — it is pure lies and fabrication, for those pure ones did not narrate it. And Ibn 'Abbas, who is from the Prophet's household, considered it proof against Mu'awiya and not a virtue for him — and that is if Mu'awiya's claim was sound and truthful in the first place.

Let the fanatics who narrate nonsense and condemn established facts as lies of historians and spiteful people wake up.

All of this from Qasim al-Ta'i and those he quotes from is a waste of words on what holds no benefit — for what matters is not when a person accepted Islam, but what he did and what he put forward for himself, and whether he obeyed or transgressed and sinned.

The nonsense of Ibn Hajar al-Haytami in these matters is well-known, until one of the scholars said:

Do not deny the gathering of Tathir al-Jinan — for the clay of the two shaykhs is one: praising with lies one who transgressed and committed wickedness — that one is Ibn Sakhr, and this praiser is Ibn Hajar.

The Claim That He Concealed His Islam to Preserve His Allowance

Al-Ta'i says [p. 11], quoting al-Haytami: "If you say: his accepting Islam and concealing it and not emigrating to the Prophet, may Allah's blessings and peace be upon him and his household, is a deficiency — and what a deficiency. I say: the matter is not absolutely so, for this is what occurred with al-'Abbas, the uncle of the Messenger of Allah, according to the view preferred by some, that he accepted Islam at Badr and concealed his Islam until the conquest of Mecca. Indeed this is more serious because the period of his concealment was approximately six years, while Mu'awiya concealed his for approximately one year."

I say: how vast is the distance between the earth and the Pleiades. And all of his speech rests on possibilities, fabrications, hypotheses, and worthless claims.

For Mu'awiya and his father Abu Sufyan are the symbol of disbelief and war against the Prophet, may Allah's blessings and peace be upon him and his household, from the very beginning of his mission. Al-'Abbas, the uncle of the Prophet, may Allah's blessings and peace be upon him and his household, is nothing like that. And where are the outrages of al-'Abbas, may Allah be pleased with him, compared to the outrages of Mu'awiya?

Hafiz Ibn Hajar said in *al-Isaba* (2/271) in the biographical entry for al-'Abbas, may Allah be pleased with him:[42]

"He attended the pledge of al-'Aqaba with the Ansar before he accepted Islam, and he was present at Badr with the polytheists under compulsion and was taken captive. He ransomed himself and ransomed his nephew 'Aqil ibn Abi Talib. He returned to Mecca — and it is said that he accepted Islam and concealed it

---

[42] This wording indicates uncertainty or weakness. In any case, al-'Abbas, may Allah be pleased with him, who was not known for depravity, killing, recklessness, oppression, or transgression, cannot be compared to the leader of the transgressing faction that calls to the Fire. This alone demolishes al-Haytami's argument.

from his people, and began writing to the Prophet, may Allah's blessings and peace be upon him and his household, with news. He then emigrated shortly before the conquest and was present at the conquest, and stood firm on the day of Hunayn... and the Companions acknowledge the virtue of al-'Abbas and consult him and take his opinion..."

What al-Haytami put forward in comparing al-'Abbas, may Allah be pleased with him, to Mu'awiya the leader of the transgressing faction that calls to the Fire — who used to curse and revile and abuse the Prophet's household and their master after the Messenger of Allah, may Allah's blessings and peace be upon him and his household, 'Ali ibn Abi Talib, may Allah's peace and pleasure be upon him — while the Prophet, may Allah's blessings and peace be upon him and his household, says in *Sahih Muslim* to Sayyiduna 'Ali: "None loves you except a believer, and none hates you except a hypocrite" — is therefore false and invalid in comparing al-'Abbas, may Allah be pleased with him, to Mu'awiya.

Mentioning this comparison to establish the invented and fabricated virtues of Mu'awiya over Sayyiduna al-'Abbas, may Allah be pleased with him, is a departure from the subject into empty composition that advances nothing.

A Repeated Excuse Regarding His Allowance

The fanatics err when al-Haytami then says, as on page 12 of Qasim's book:

Al-Ta'i says:

"Emigration is only obligatory and binding where there is no excuse — including ignorance of its obligation in the case of one who is excused for such ignorance. And there has come a narration that his mother said to him: 'If you emigrate we will cut off your allowance.' And this is a clear excuse."

I say: rather this is a shameful and disgraceful excuse — indeed it is worse than a sin. It is colder than ice.

Al-Haytami wants to manufacture virtues for this tyrant from his very faults — by force.

Does a person not know the virtue of emigration — so that Mu'awiya does not know it, and al-Haytami excuses him for abandoning it, turning his abandonment of it into something praiseworthy when it is in fact among his faults — assuming he had accepted Islam at that time?

Does a rational person abandon emigration when people were leaving their wealth, their lands, and their families for the sake of Allah and out of desire for what is with Him, Exalted be He — while this tyrant abandons it — as al-Haytami claims — because his mother, the liver-eater, says to him: "We will cut off your allowance"?

By Allah, these are matters that would make even a bereaved mother laugh.

Al-Haythami says this is a clear excuse for Mu'awiya. But Allah, Exalted be He, says: {"Say: If your fathers, your sons, your brothers, your wives, your clan, wealth you have acquired, trade you fear will decline, and dwellings you are pleased with are more beloved to you than Allah and His Messenger and striving in His cause — then wait until Allah brings His command. And Allah does not guide the depraved people."} [al-Tawba: 24]

Let al-Ta'i and those like him who portray truth as falsehood and falsehood as truth take heed.

Ibn Hajar's Claim and Contradiction Regarding Mu'awiya's Islam

Al-Ta'i then cited on page 13 of his book the statement of Hafiz Ibn Hajar al-'Asqalani in *al-Fath* about Mu'awiya: "He accepted Islam before the conquest, his parents accepted Islam, he accompanied the Prophet and wrote."

I say: we leave Hafiz Ibn Hajar al-'Asqalani in *al-Isaba* (3/433) to contradict himself in *al-Fath*, where he says: "Al-Waqidi reported that he accepted Islam after al-Hudaybiyya and concealed his Islam until he declared it in the year of the conquest, and that during 'Umrat al-Qada' he was already Muslim. But this is contradicted by what is established in the authenticated hadith from Sa'd ibn Abi Waqqas, who said regarding performing 'Umra during the months of Hajj: 'We did this while he at that time was a disbeliever...'"

CHAPTER 4: FURTHER CLAIMS AND FALSE MERITS

Al-Ta'i's Criticism of Shaykh Yusuf al-Nabhani

Al-Ta'i then said [p. 13]: "It has thus become clear to you after these quotations that what Shaykh Yusuf al-Nabhani said — that Mu'awiya accepted Islam after the conquest — is not the preponderant view upon careful investigation."

I say: on the contrary — after careful investigation and examination it becomes clear that the statement of Shaykh al-Nabhani is the correct position that admits of no doubt. And that whoever relied on the saying of the abandoned al-Waqidi and abandoned the saying of the Companions as established in *Sahih al-Bukhari* — the one who contradicts al-Nabhani here has no investigation and no evidence, only the ill-omened fanaticism for tyrants and transgressors who call to the Fire.

The Claim of Jihad, Companionship, and Service to Religion

Al-Ta'i says [p. 13]: "The summary of what we have presented is that Sayyiduna Mu'awiya accepted Islam before the conquest, accompanied the Messenger of Allah, campaigned with him, waged jihad, and rendered the religion great services."

This is a false and rejected statement.

The summary of the response to it is: that his Islam before the conquest is the saying of the abandoned al-Waqidi — refuted by what is in al-Bukhari from Sayyiduna Sa'd ibn Abi Waqqas, may Allah be pleased with him, as the Hafiz stated in *al-Isaba*. And the conquest upon careful investigation is al-Hudaybiyya, as stated in *Sahih al-Bukhari* (4150): al-Bara' ibn 'Azib said: "You count the conquest as the conquest of Mecca — and the conquest of Mecca was indeed a conquest. But we count the conquest as the pledge of al-Ridwan on the day of al-Hudaybiyya."

The companionship of the Messenger of Allah, may Allah's blessings and peace be upon him and his household, does not benefit tyrants — for the Prophet, may Allah's blessings and peace be upon him and his household, said: "Among my Companions are twelve hypocrites, eight of whom will not enter Paradise until a camel passes through the eye of a needle" — narrated by Muslim (2779). And the hadith of the two Sahihs about those who are driven away from the Hawd for having changed and altered after the Prophet is among the strongest of the evidences supporting our position and demolishing the words of al-Ta'i and those who agree with him.

As for his words "he campaigned with him and waged jihad" — many a man fell between the two battle lines and Allah alone knows his true condition. He and his father had warred against the Messenger of Allah, may Allah's blessings and peace be upon him and his household, from the beginning of his mission until the conquest of Mecca — and then Mu'awiya warred against Sayyiduna 'Ali, may Allah be pleased with him, and those with him of the noble Companions and the best of the Muslims at the end of his life. What kind of jihad is that?

Ibn 'Umar said, during the caliphate of Mu'awiya, when Mu'awiya said: "Whoever wishes to speak about this matter, let him raise his head — for we are more entitled to it than he and his father": Ibn 'Umar said: "I was on the verge of saying: more entitled to this matter than you is one who fought you and your father for the sake of Islam." Narrated by al-Bukhari in his *Sahih* (4108).

Al-Bukhari narrated (7458) from Abu Musa: "A man came to the Prophet, may Allah's blessings and peace be upon him and his household, and said: 'A man fights out of tribal pride, a man fights out of bravery, a man fights for show — which of these is in the path of Allah?' He said: 'Whoever fights so that the word of Allah may be supreme — he is in the path of Allah.'"

Al-Bukhari narrated in his *Sahih* (6707) from Abu Hurayra: "While Midi'am — a servant — was unloading a saddle for the Messenger of Allah, may Allah's blessings and peace be upon him and his household — when they were returning from Khaybar — a stray arrow struck and killed him. The people said: 'Congratulations to him — Paradise!' The Messenger of Allah, may Allah's blessings and peace be upon him and his household, said: 'By no means — by the One in Whose hand is my soul, the garment he took on the day of Khaybar from the war spoils before they were distributed will burn upon him as fire.'"

As for his words "he rendered the religion great services" — this is among the fabrications and fantasies. What has already been presented from the words of the Prophet, may Allah's blessings and peace be upon him and his household, his Companions, and the fair-minded scholars of Ahl al-Sunna regarding the leader of the transgressing faction that calls to the Fire speaks for itself. Let al-Ta'i and those like him review it — perhaps they will be cured of what afflicts them.

All of his imagined virtues are fabrications, scattered to the winds.

Inflammatory Claims Without Scholarly Basis

Al-Ta'i then said after the above [p. 13]: "Whoever harms him, or considers it permissible to curse and revile him and his honor, and explicitly declares his diminishment and openly shows enmity toward him — has committed disbelief, as we have transmitted from the Imam and exegete al-Alusi."

I say: the matter has gone too far, O al-Ta'i. How can one who criticizes the leader of the transgressing faction that calls to the Fire — by the explicit statement of the master of all creation, may Allah's blessings and peace be upon him and his household — be declared a disbeliever? Enough of your fraudulence, deception, confusion, fabrication, lies, recklessness, and fanaticism.

How is it that you do not bristle and rage against those who curse Sayyiduna 'Ali, may Allah be pleased with him — of whom the Messenger said: "None loves you except a believer, and none hates you except a hypocrite," and of whom he said: "Whoever curses 'Ali has cursed me" — all of which has been established against Mu'awiya beyond any doubt as we have presented — yet you turn a blind eye to all of that and then take up this disgraceful fanaticism for Mu'awiya?

Why do you not direct these rulings of disbelief against Mu'awiya, who cursed Sayyiduna 'Ali, may Allah be pleased with him, and ordered the people to revile and abuse him?

Are you content to stand in the ranks of the hypocrites and those who cursed the Messenger of Allah, may Allah's blessings and peace be upon him and his household?

Al-Nasa'i, 'Abd al-Razzaq the author of *al-Musannaf*, al-Hakim the author of *al-Mustadrak*, and others who censured Mu'awiya and criticized him — they are all disbelievers according to your view and the sick view of al-Alusi.

Do you declare a disbeliever one who censures someone who drank wine, called to the Fire, killed the Companions and the righteous, abolished the rightly-guided caliphate and turned it into a biting tyrannical kingship, and more?

Or do you want us to love the son of Hind — you will not find a believer, as Allah's Messenger told us, who loves one who warred against the Almighty? The Prophet's hadith is the strongest bond of faith: hating the wicked is belief in Allah. He is a transgressor — and no honor for transgressors, for from the Fire fly sparks of rebellion and misguidance. He fought al-Murtada and poisoned the grandson of al-Mustafa — what a wretched decision he chose. He kills the righteous in cold blood — like Hujr — consuming the spoils, cursing the Ever-Returning. He persisted in spreading corruption among them, and in arrogance and pride over the land. Then he departed and appointed Yazid the drunkard — O what a disgrace and shame is this. He spent twenty years plunging into the depths of misguidance. And you say: a rewarded mujtahid — had no remorse after killing 'Ammar. If what you claimed were correct, what you did would be accepted and the excuses received. Does the Knower of hidden things approve of hadiths resembling bedtime tales? It is shameful that people argue narrated by those who worship the dinar. Their Nasb drove them to fabricate them — the imitator among them only increases in loss. And how many an imitator sought profit while deviating from the explicit text, as you do.

Al-Ta'i then began on page 14 to speak in a section claiming to establish that Mu'awiya was a scribe of the revelation — and we have already refuted that and shown that there is no benefit or virtue in it.

Mu'awiya accepted Islam near the end of the revelation, close to the descent of the words of Allah, Exalted be He: {"Today I have perfected your religion for you..."} [al-Ma'ida: 3] — and I do not know what Mu'awiya could have been writing after that. When the Companions gathered the Quran, the scribes and reciters among them came together — and Mu'awiya was not among them and had no connection to them.

Deception and Manipulation of the Hadith

We must point out here something in which Qasim engaged in deception. He said there: "And in the Musnad of Ahmad, with its root in Muslim, from Ibn 'Abbas who said: the Prophet, may Allah's blessings and peace be upon him and his household, said to me: 'Call Mu'awiya for me — and he was his scribe.'"

I say: Muslim narrated it — but he did not mention in it "and he was his scribe." The continuation of the hadith in *Sahih Muslim* (2604) is that the Prophet, may Allah's blessings and peace be upon him and his household, cursed Mu'awiya when he did not respond to his summons, saying: "O Allah, do not fill his stomach."

Al-Ta'i concealed this and did not disclose it — because it harms his purpose. And because it is a fault among the faults of

Mu'awiya, since he did not respond to the Messenger of Allah, may Allah's blessings and peace be upon him and his household — while Allah, Exalted be He, says in His noble Book: {"O you who believe, respond to Allah and the Messenger when He calls you to what gives you life."} [al-Anfal: 24]

As for al-Alusi's claim that he was among the senior Companions — this is a rejected claim. Rather he is among the paupers, by the statement of the Prophet, may Allah's blessings and peace be upon him and his household, about him: "A pauper with no wealth." His father was among the greatest merchants of Quraysh and was one of the leaders of disbelief and champions of war against the Prophet, may Allah's blessings and peace be upon him and his household. Claiming that this released man was among the senior Companions is a lie and an invalid claim.

Al-Ta'i's statement there that Mu'awiya used to write for the Prophet, may Allah's blessings and peace be upon him and his household — "as the scholars said: meaning the revelation and other matters" — where is the documentation for this claim? We have repeatedly stated that this going around in circles is of no benefit, and that writing the revelation does not protect its writer from the Fire, does not prevent him from transgression and sin and hypocrisy.

Further Fabricated Virtues

Al-Ta'i then devoted a section on page 15 which he titled "The Fifth Pearl: The Virtues and Merits of Mu'awiya," and said in it: "The verified position upon which all of Ahl al-Sunna wa'l-Jama'a stand is that Mu'awiya has the nobility of companionship established for him, and deep-rooted excellence in knowledge, and virtues and merits..." and the rest of his ranting.

I say: Qasim hurls words without care, stumbling blindly here and there, trying to patch up the case for the leader of the transgressing faction that calls to the Fire.

He turns a blind eye to the criticism of Imam al-Nasa'i against Mu'awiya — al-Nasa'i who is the Hafiz and hadith master, author of the *Sunan* relied upon by Ahl al-Sunna wa'l-Jama'a as one of their principal sources and references. And likewise 'Abd al-Razzaq, al-Hakim, and many, many others — among them quickly:

Jarir ibn 'Abd al-Hamid ibn Yazid, the Imam and Hafiz, Judge Abu 'Abd Allah al-Dabbi[43] — one of the narrators in al-Bukhari, Muslim, and the four Sunans. Hafiz Ibn Hajar said in *al-Tahdhib* (2/66): "Al-Khalili said in *al-Irshad*: 'Reliable, agreed upon.' And Qutayba said: 'Jarir the foremost Hafiz narrated to us — but I heard him cursing and abusing Mu'awiya openly.'"

This is alongside the statement of Ishaq ibn Rahawayh, al-Nasa'i, Judge Isma'il, and Hafiz Ibn Hajar — that nothing sound has been transmitted regarding Mu'awiya's virtues.

Hafiz Ibn Hajar said in *al-Fath* (7/104): "Ibn al-Jawzi also transmitted through 'Abd Allah ibn Ahmad ibn Hanbal: I asked my father — what do you say about 'Ali and Mu'awiya? He fell silent, then said: 'Know that 'Ali had many enemies. His enemies searched for a fault in him and found none. So they turned to a man who had fought him and heaped praise upon him as a stratagem against 'Ali.' By this he pointed to the virtues they fabricated for Mu'awiya — virtues that have no basis.

And in the virtues of Mu'awiya there have come many hadiths, but none of them are sound in terms of chain of transmission. This was definitively stated by Ishaq ibn Rahawayh, al-Nasa'i, and others."

Are these people from Ahl al-Sunna?

And where did his phrase "all of Ahl al-Sunna" go?

---

43 Al-Dhahabi described him in *Siyar A'lam al-Nubala'*, 9:9.

The Report That Ibn 'Abbas Praised Mu'awiya's Jurisprudence

Al-Ta'i says there: "because the apparent testimony of Ibn 'Abbas to his jurisprudence and companionship is indicative of great virtue."

The response: the narration of al-Bukhari in this regard is contradicted by your own Imam al-Tahawi the Hanafi, may Allah have mercy on him, in his *Sharh Ma'ani al-Athar*. What al-Bukhari mentioned (3765) from Ibn 'Abbas's statement about Mu'awiya — that he is "a jurist" — is a distortion by the narrators. Al-Tahawi contradicted this in *Sharh Ma'ani al-Athar* (1/289), narrating it with the wording: "Mu'awiya stood and prayed one rak'a as witr. Ibn 'Abbas said: 'From where do you think this donkey got that?'" — and its chain is sound.

It has also been transmitted that Mu'awiya was the first to deliver the Friday sermon while seated, and the deviant Umayyads followed this wicked practice — as stated in *al-Kamil* by Ibn al-Athir (4/555). Likewise Mu'awiya was the first to abandon the takbir in prayer[44] — as stated in *al-Fath* (2/270).

Al-Ta'i further deceives when he says: "How could it be otherwise, when many hadiths have come concerning Mu'awiya's virtues — among them some that are sound..." The man evidently hurls words without accountability, creating the impression among those without knowledge that he is producing evidence and proofs — when there is nothing behind it but trying to comb thorns.

The hadith masters themselves say nothing sound has been transmitted regarding his virtues — and he says "among them some that are sound." Let him bring us this sound report and we will examine it before him.

Perhaps among what has been "established" of his merits is that he calls to the Fire, curses Sayyiduna 'Ali, may Allah be pleased

---

44 Al-Nasa'i, *Sunan*, 8:249; al-Bayhaqi, *al-Sunan al-Kubra*, 2:49; al-Daraqutni, *Sunan*, 1:311; al-Hakim, *al-Mustadrak*; and others.

with him, drinks wine, kills the righteous, appoints the wicked over this community, and installs the depraved drunkard Yazid as Imam and caliph over the Muslims — and that he is rewarded and praised for all of this because the threats of the Quran do not apply to him.

Allah, Exalted be He, says in His mighty Book: {And if he had invented false sayings in Our name, We would have seized him by the right hand, and then cut his aorta, and none of you could have defended him. And indeed it is a reminder for the pious.} [al-Haqqa: 44-48]

Further Claims Concerning Fabricated Virtues

Al-Ta'i says [p. 15]: "And the weak hadith — as it is permissible to act upon it in matters of virtuous deeds, so too is it permissible to act upon it in matters of merits — as stated by the learned jurist and hadith master, the scholar Ibn Hajar, in *Tathir al-Jinan wa'l-Lisan.*"

This is truly laughable, by Allah.

It has grown so thin that its ribs show, and every bankrupt person covets it.

It is as if he is blind to the statement of Hafiz Ibn Hajar in *Fath al-Bari* (7/104), where he transmits from Ahmad ibn Hanbal: "Know that 'Ali had many enemies. His enemies searched for a fault in him and found none. So they turned to a man who had fought him and heaped praise upon him as a stratagem against 'Ali."

Then Hafiz Ibn Hajar al-'Asqalani said: "By this he pointed to the virtues they fabricated for Mu'awiya — virtues that have no basis."

The virtues of Mu'awiya are fabricated and invented — they have no basis. The issue is not merely that their chains are weak. But fanaticism blinds and deafens. There are no virtues for Mu'awiya — what has come from the Messenger of Allah, may Allah's blessings and peace be upon him and his household, and his noble Companions concerning him consists only of faults and censure.

Do not be heedless of this.

As for Ibn Hajar al-Haytami — he had strayed from sound judgment when composing that book, which an insistent request from Sultan Humayun, one of the kings of India at that time, enticed him into writing — as he himself stated in the introduction.

Strange how people went astray in the side alleys of trivialities — they described with virtue certain people who have no place there whatsoever.

What he cited from al-Suyuti's *Tadrib al-Rawi* — that "not sound" does not necessarily imply weakness — makes one contemptuous of the mind of whoever cited it here. It tells us that the man has not understood the matter and has not grasped the issue.

Ibn Hajar al-Haytami deserves to have his words disregarded in every false argument he puts forward in that collapsing book — for in it he was very far removed from reason, transmitted reports, and careful investigation. And our companion imitates him in his catastrophes and disasters.

We do not need to repeat the nonsense of Qasim about that tyrant being a scribe of the revelation and a scribe of the Messenger — for that is a fabrication upon which the evidence, the proofs, and the arguments have wiped out, reducing it to ashes scattered by the wind.

The Claim That Mu'awiya Was the Most Noble of the Companions

Al-Ta'i says [p. 16]: "In that case, what Ishaq ibn Rahawayh mentioned — assuming its soundness — does not diminish Mu'awiya's virtues, for several reasons, among them that he is the most noble of the Companions by lineage both in pre-Islamic times and in Islam, being from the greatest of Quraysh and from the family closest to the Prophet..."

I say to Qasim: Abu Lahab likewise — and Umayya ibn Khalaf and their like. Leave off this empty talk. Mu'awiya's lineage is well known. His father was one of the symbols of disbelief who bore enmity toward the Prophet, may Allah's blessings and peace be upon him and his household, from the very beginning of his mission. His mother was the liver-eater who chewed the liver of the master of the martyrs, Hamza. May they receive from Allah what they deserve.

Muslim narrated in *al-Sahih* (2504) from 'A'idh ibn 'Amr: Abu Sufyan came upon Salman, Suhayb, and Bilal among a group, and they said: "By Allah, the swords of Allah have not taken from the neck of the enemy of Allah what they deserve!" Abu Bakr said: "Do you say this about the elder of Quraysh and their master?" He went to the Prophet, may Allah's blessings and peace be upon him and his household, and informed him. The Prophet said: "O Abu Bakr, perhaps you angered them — if you have angered them, you have angered your Lord." Abu Bakr went to them and said: "O my brothers, did I anger you?" They said: "No — may Allah forgive you, O our brother."[45] Let al-Ta'i take heed of this.

Furthermore, his claim that "Mu'awiya is the most noble of the Companions by lineage" is a misguided, rejected, and false statement. Whoever says it deserves punishment from Allah, Exalted be He, for it — since those from Banu Hashim and others who existed were of nobler lineage than this tyrant. This is a settled matter about which there is no disagreement in the community. In *Sahih Muslim* (2276), from Wathila ibn al-Asqa': the Messenger of Allah, may Allah's blessings and peace be upon him and his household, said: "Allah chose Kinana from the children of Isma'il, and chose Quraysh from Kinana, and chose Banu Hashim from Quraysh, and chose me from Banu Hashim."

---

[45] The claim of some that this statement was made while Abu Sufyan was still a disbeliever is rejected and unsupported, whoever may have said it. This is further confirmed by the fact that Abu Bakr, may Allah be pleased with him, would not defend someone who remained upon disbelief and had not yet outwardly professed Islam.

The Hadith "O Allah, Make Him a Guide, Rightly Guided"

Al-Ta'i then began on page 17 of his book to enumerate the virtues of Mu'awiya as he claims, saying: "And here are the transmitted reports clarifying his virtues: 1. Al-Tirmidhi narrated — and said it is a sound hadith — that the Messenger of Allah, may Allah's blessings and peace be upon him and his household, prayed for Mu'awiya saying: 'O Allah, make him a guide, rightly guided.'"

I say: this hadith is definitively fabricated. Abu Hatim al-Razi said in *'Ilal al-Hadith* (2/362-363): that 'Abd al-Rahman ibn Abi 'Umayra did not hear this hadith from the Prophet, may Allah's blessings and peace be upon him and his household.

Hafiz Ibn Hajar said in *al-Tahdhib* (6/220), transmitting from Hafiz Ibn 'Abd al-Barr regarding this hadith and its narrator: "His companionship is not established as sound and his hadith's chain does not hold."

Hafiz Ibn al-Jawzi included it in *al-'Ilal al-Mutanahiya fi al-Ahadith al-Wahiya* (1/276) and said after it: "Al-Daraqutni said: Isma'il ibn Muhammad is a weak liar." And in its chain is Sa'id ibn 'Abd al-'Aziz, who had suffered mental confusion as stated in *al-Tahdhib* (4/54).

Such are the fabricated and invented virtues.

Delusions Refuted by the Authenticated Sunnah

Al-Ta'i then said after this: "Reflect on this hadith, O Muslim who loves the Companions of the Messenger of Allah — it is a supplication from the truthful and believed one whose supplication for his community is never rejected..."

I say: Muslim narrated in *al-Sahih* (2890) and others that the Messenger of Allah, may Allah's blessings and peace be upon him and his household, said: "I asked my Lord for three things — He granted me two and withheld one. I asked Him not to destroy my community by famine — He granted it. I asked Him not to destroy my community by drowning — He granted it. I asked Him not to make their fighting among themselves — He withheld it."

This hadith demolishes the embellishments and fabrications of Qasim — may Allah guide him.

Al-Ta'i then said, trying to convince himself with the fabrication and lie he tells himself: "So He made Mu'awiya a guide, rightly guided in himself."

I say: glory be to Allah — does one who kills the righteous among the Companions such as Hujr ibn 'Adi, drinks wine, openly practices usury, commands them to consume one another's wealth unjustly and kill one another, and curses Sayyiduna 'Ali, may Allah be pleased with him — does such a person become a guide, rightly guided?

O man — use your reason, by Allah, and think about what you are babbling. May Allah grant you well-being.

Leave writing aside — you have no part in it, even if you blackened your face with ink.

Mu'awiya's Ambition for the Caliphate

Al-Ta'i says [p. 17]: "2. Ibn Abi Shayba transmitted with his chain from Mu'awiya who said: 'I have always aspired to the caliphate since the Messenger of Allah said: if you rule, then do good.'"

I say: al-Dhahabi said in *Siyar A'lam al-Nubala'* (3/131) after citing it with Ibn Abi Shayba's chain: "Ibn Mujahir is weak, and the report is mursal."

Even assuming this were authentic, it contains no virtue, as anyone who has purged his mind of partisanship and committed himself to fairness and the truth would realize. All of that is from al-Haytami's myths in that book of his!

The Hadith: "If You Rule, Then Be Just"

Al-Ta'i then said there: "3. Abu Ya'la transmitted from Mu'awiya who said: the Messenger of Allah, may Allah's blessings and peace be upon him and his household, looked at me and said: 'O Mu'awiya, if you are entrusted with a matter, fear Allah and be just.' He said: I never ceased to believe that I would be tried with a position of authority because of the Messenger's words — until I assumed leadership."

I say: what al-Haytami said when he cited this hadith in *Tathir al-Jinan* was: "Abu Ya'la transmitted it with a chain in which there is Suwayd, and there is something problematic in him that does not affect it" — and al-Ta'i deleted this phrase so that it would not spoil his use of these objectionable reports.

The hadith was narrated by Abu Ya'la (13/370) and Ahmad (4/101) — and there is no virtue or merit in it even if it were sound. Rather, if it were sound, it would indicate that he knew he would not be just and so was advised to be just. Moreover this hadith is among the weak narrations. It is sufficient that its narrator is Mu'awiya himself. And in addition to that, in its chain is Suwayd — whose condition Ibn 'Adi summarized from the statements of the imams by saying: "He is closer to being weak."[46]

Furthermore among its narrators is one who is Umayyad — whose testimony is not accepted in such matters. He is 'Amr ibn Yahya ibn Sa'id ibn 'Amr ibn al-'As, from his grandfather Sa'id ibn 'Amr ibn al-'As. These people's reports are not accepted in such matters. 'Amr ibn Yahya has a biographical entry in *al-Kamil fi al-Du'afa'* (5/122) by Ibn 'Adi — al-Bukhari narrated from him but Muslim avoided him.

Al-Dhahabi listed this hadith among hadiths about which he said: "There are transmitted things in the virtues of Mu'awiya — weak things that are tolerable" — and he counted this among them. Even though it contains no praise or virtue or merit —

---

46 See al-Mizzi, *Tahdhib al-Kamal*, 12:254.

only a trial. And Allah, Exalted be He, said: {"And We will surely test you with evil and with good as trial."} [al-Anbiya': 35]

Al-Ta'i then says — he who blindly transmits the words of al-Haytami: "4. The Imam transmitted with a sound chain, but it contains irsal. And Abu Ya'la connected it with a sound chain and its wording from Mu'awiya is: the Prophet, may Allah's blessings and peace be upon him and his household, said to his Companions: 'Perform ablution.' When they had performed ablution, he looked at me and said: 'O Mu'awiya, if you are entrusted with a matter, fear Allah and be just.'"

I say: Glory be to Allah! So Abu Ya'la's chain of transmission has become authentic, after it had previously been described as 'its chain contains Suwayd, about whom there is some criticism, though not harmful,' meaning, according to his claim, that it was sound but not fully authentic. Then it later changed and became authentic!

And this is exactly how muddled reasoning should be!

Furthermore, the editor of Abu Ya'la's *Musnad* (13/370) commented on it: "Its chain is weak."

And Ahmad's chain with all of that is mursal — and the mursal, even if its chain is sound, is among the categories of weak hadith — as al-Ta'i, who boasts about mentioning issues from books of hadith methodology while using them out of context, should well know.

Al-Dhahabi counted this hadith, as we noted, among the weak ones.[47]

The Hadith: "O Allah, Teach Him the Book and Protect Him from Evil Reckoning"

Al-Ta'i then said there: "5. Al-Bazzar, Ahmad, and al-Tabarani transmitted that the Messenger of Allah, may Allah's blessings and peace be upon him and his household, prayed for Mu'awiya

---

[47] Al-Dhahabi, *Siyar A'lam al-Nubala'*, 3:131.

and said: 'O Allah, teach him the Book and reckoning, empower him in the lands, and protect him from evil reckoning.'"

I say: this too is a worthless fabrication. In its chain is Mu'awiya ibn Salih — and Hafiz Ibn Hajar mentioned in *al-Tahdhib* (10/189) the statements of those who criticized him, saying: "Yahya ibn Sa'id al-Qattan used to find him unacceptable. In a narration from Ibn Ma'in: 'He is not satisfactory.' Abu Ishaq al-Fazzari said: 'He is not fit to be narrated from.' Ibn Abi Khayththama said: 'He transmits very strange things from the people of Syria.'" — And this hadith is undoubtedly among them, given that it contradicts reality.

In its chain is also al-Harith ibn Ziyad — a Syrian whose narration is not accepted for a weak and indeed fabricated hadith that supports his own leanings. No one narrated from him except Yunus ibn Sayf al-Kila'i — and he is unknown. The Hafiz said in his biographical entry in *al-Tahdhib* (2/123): "Al-Dhahabi said in *al-Mizan*: unknown. His condition is that he does not use this word except when Abu Hatim al-Razi said it."

The Hafiz then said: "Yes — Abu 'Umar ibn 'Abd al-Barr said about him: unknown, and his hadith is objectionable."

Ibn Abi Hatim said in *al-Jarh wa'l-Ta'dil* (3/75), transmitting from his father: "Unknown."

Hafiz Ibn al-Jawzi included it in *al-'Ilal al-Mutanahiya fi al-Ahadith al-Wahiya* (1/272). Al-Dhahabi judged the text of this hadith from some of its chains in *al-Mizan* (1/388) as: "Objectionable in the extreme" — and in the chain there is an unknown person and a man who is not recognized.

In another chain mentioned by al-Dhahabi in *al-Mizan* (3/47): through the chain of Ishaq ibn Ka'b — 'Uthman ibn 'Abd al-Rahman, from 'Ata', from Ibn 'Abbas. And 'Uthman ibn 'Abd al-Rahman is al-Waqqasi, as al-Dhahabi stated there in the biographical entry of al-Jumahi — and he is abandoned, as al-Bukhari stated in his *Tarikh* (6/238). And Ibn Ma'in called him a liar as stated in *al-Mizan* (3/43).

Through such objectionable and fabricated reports, narrated by unknown narrators, are the virtues of Mu'awiya completed — for those who have turned a blind eye to the truth and adorned themselves with shameful fanaticism for tyrants.

Al-Ta'i then said: "These reports are explicit in giving him glad tidings of the caliphate." And I say: what evil glad tidings of a trial in which he failed. Rather the sum of his affairs is that he is the leader of the transgressing faction that calls to the Fire.

The Claim That 'Umar ibn al-Khattab Praised Mu'awiya

Al-Ta'i says [p. 18]: "The Commander of the Believers, Sayyiduna 'Umar, may Allah be pleased with him, praised him and commended him and appointed him over Damascus and Syria for the duration of his caliphate. And likewise Sayyiduna 'Uthman, may Allah be pleased with him. And this is a great merit in itself... And if you reflect on Sayyiduna 'Umar's dismissal of Sa'd ibn Abi Waqqas — who is superior to Mu'awiya by many degrees — while retaining Mu'awiya in his position without dismissal, you will know that this indicates a great elevation of Mu'awiya..."

I say: where did Sayyiduna 'Umar and Sayyiduna 'Uthman praise him? As for the appointment over Syria — Sayyiduna 'Uthman appointed al-Walid ibn 'Uqba over Kufa and dismissed Sayyiduna Sa'd ibn Abi Waqqas from it — even though Sayyiduna Sa'd is among the ten given glad tidings of Paradise and among the foremost early Companions, while al-Walid is explicitly declared a depraved sinner in the Quran and was a chronic drunkard. Sayyiduna 'Uthman brought him and flogged him.[48] What great merit for Mu'awiya can be found in anything like this?

The Messenger of Allah, may Allah's blessings and peace be upon him and his household, appointed people who then lied and betrayed, and scribes of revelation who then proved to be

---

[48] Muslim, *Sahih*, no. 1707.

among the most corrupt of people. And he appointed al-Walid ibn 'Uqba to collect the charity taxes of Banu al-Mustaliq — and the Quran descended declaring him a depraved liar.

Through such nonsense does al-Ta'i establish the merits of Mu'awiya — to the point that if they were to discover that he sat for one moment in a town where the Messenger of Allah, may Allah's blessings and peace be upon him and his household, also sat, they would make it a virtue. And this governorship in which Mu'awiya served — the Companions and others testified during the era of Sayyiduna 'Uthman that his conduct and character in it were bad.

'Uthman and 'Ubada ibn al-Samit's Criticism of Mu'awiya

'Ubada ibn al-Samit states that Mu'awiya commands them to do what they consider objectionable — and 'Uthman ibn 'Affan acknowledges this without responding.

Al-Hakim's *Mustadrak* (3/357) narrates from 'Ubayd ibn Rifa'a:

"'Ubada ibn al-Samit stood in the middle of the courtyard of the Commander of the Believers 'Uthman ibn 'Affan, may Allah be pleased with him, and said: 'I heard the Messenger of Allah, may Allah's blessings and peace be upon him and his household — Muhammad, the father of al-Qasim — say: There will rule over your affairs after me men who will familiarize you with what you consider objectionable, and consider objectionable what you know to be right. There is no obedience to one who disobeys Allah.' ... By the One in Whose hand is my soul, Mu'awiya is among those.' And 'Uthman did not reply to him with a single word."

Al-Bukhari narrated in *al-Sahih* (4108) from Ibn 'Umar: "I entered upon Hafsa... I said: 'What has befallen the people you see, and nothing has been assigned to me in this matter.' She said: 'Go — they are waiting for you, and I fear that your absence from them will cause a division.' She did not leave him until he went. When the people dispersed, Mu'awiya gave a speech and said: 'Whoever wishes to speak about this matter, let him raise his head — for we are more entitled to it than he and his father.'[49] Habib ibn Maslama said: 'Why did you not respond to him?' 'Abd Allah said: 'I was on the verge of saying: more entitled to this matter than you is one who fought you and your father for the sake of Islam. But I feared that a word might divide the gathering and cause bloodshed.'"[50]

Al-Dhahabi said:[51] "From Isma'il ibn Umayya: 'Umar singled out Mu'awiya for Syria and allocated to him eighty dinars a month. But the established view is that it was 'Uthman who singled Mu'awiya out for Syria."

Al-Dhahabi's words "the established view" indicate that it was Sayyiduna 'Uthman who singled him out for Syria. The Umayyans had gained dominance over him until he dismissed Sayyiduna Sa'd ibn Abi Waqqas from Kufa and placed al-Walid ibn 'Uqba the depraved sinner over it — the one who led the Fajr prayer one day as four rak'as and in one narration two rak'as, then said: "If you wish, I can add more" — which indicates his contempt for the religion and the prayer — until the people rose against him and complained of him to Sayyiduna 'Uthman, who flogged him for drinking wine — as in *Sahih Muslim* (1707).

Sayyiduna 'Umar, may Allah be pleased with him, said about Mu'awiya: "He is the Khusrau of the Arabs."[52] And this is a statement of censure — for 'Umar ibn al-Khattab likened him to a well-known tyrant who was not a Muslim.

---

[49] Thus Mu'awiya quite openly and brazenly considered his depraved, drunken son more entitled to authority than Sayyiduna 'Umar ibn al-Khattab, may Allah be pleased with him.

[50] Reflect on how the Companions feared objecting to Mu'awiya lest their blood be shed. Let those who fanatically defend this tyrant in falsehood take heed.

[51] Al-Dhahabi, *Siyar A'lam al-Nubala'*, 3:133.

[52] See al-Dhahabi, *Siyar A'lam al-Nubala'*, 3:134; Ibn 'Abd al-Barr, *al-Isti'ab*, 3:1417; Ibn Hajar, *al-Isaba fi Tamyiz al-Sahaba*, 6:153, Dar al-Jil edition; and al-Nawawi, *Tahdhib al-Asma' wa'l-Lughat*, p. 407.

A Serious Error by al-Ta'i

As for his words in the previous text — "and if you reflect on Sayyiduna 'Umar's dismissal of Sa'd ibn Abi Waqqas...and retaining Mu'awiya..." — I say: al-Haytami and his imitator erred and did not understand the issue and did not read the sentence properly. The sentence in the books of historians is as in *Siyar A'lam al-Nubala'* (3/135): "Al-Zuhri said: 'Uthman removed 'Umayr ibn Sa'd and consolidated Syria under Mu'awiya."

They read "Umayr" as "Umar" — and so assumed it was Sayyiduna 'Umar, may Allah be pleased with him, who did that.

In any case, this dismissal and appointment advances nothing and contains no virtue or merit whatsoever — except in the mind of one who invents and fabricates virtues. For Sayyiduna 'Uthman dismissed 'Amr ibn al-'As from the revenues of Egypt and installed 'Abd Allah ibn Sa'd[53] — and it was he who stirred up the people of Egypt against Sayyiduna 'Uthman. With this the merits of the man collapse and fall, one by one.

A Weak Story Used to Praise Mu'awiya

Al-Ta'i says [p. 18]: "7. Ibn Sa'd transmitted that Mu'awiya entered upon 'Umar, may Allah be pleased with them both, wearing a green garment. The Companions gazed at him — with admiration for or from him —[54] and when 'Umar saw them gazing at him, he struck him with his staff. Mu'awiya said: 'Allah! Allah! O Commander of the Believers — why, why?' 'Umar did not speak to him until he returned to his seat. The Companions then said to 'Umar: 'Why did you strike the young man? There is none like him among your people.' — meaning

---

[53] See Ibn al-Jawzi, *al-Muntazam*, 4:362.

[54] These words placed between the two dashes are an addition inserted by al-Haytami. They are not found in the original narration. Rather, they are al-Haytami's own interpretive gloss, by which he reads the report in light of his prior favorable view of Mu'awiya.

his governors[55] — though it is also possible they meant Quraysh, and in either case the comparability is relative. 'Umar said: 'I saw nothing but good from him, but I saw him' — and gestured upward with his hand — 'and I thought I should bring him down.' Meaning: I saw in him something indicating arrogance."

I say: first — I have not found this story in Ibn Sa'd, so let al-Ta'i produce its reference for us. Ibn Kathir mentioned it in *al-Bidaya* (8/125) without attributing it to a book, and likewise al-Dhahabi in *al-Siyar* (3/135). The story, as appears from its truncated chain, is from the narration of the Umayyads — and so cannot be trusted. And in it there is a gap — for the grandfather of 'Amr ibn Yahya ibn Sa'id did not meet 'Umar ibn al-Khattab. This is among the stories and lies fabricated by the Umayyads for Mu'awiya.

Second: in the story, Sayyiduna 'Umar, may Allah be pleased with him, was disciplining him with the staff and recognizing his arrogance, pride, and conceit. And he said on another occasion: "He is the Khusrau of the Arabs"[56] — for Mu'awiya was arrogant toward the caliph and the Companions, since the blood of Abu Sufyan and the family of Harb ran in his veins.

Third: arrogance is blameworthy, and no one with arrogance in his heart will enter Paradise.

Fourth: is it conceivable that Quraysh had no one better than him left — when Quraysh contained Sayyiduna 'Ali, who was superior to him in lineage as the cousin of the Prophet, may Allah's blessings and peace be upon him and his household?

What they have cited here is among his faults — not among what is praiseworthy. And whoever reflects on "there is none like him among your people" will find not a "dazzling merit" but a plain lie.

---

[55] These words placed between the two dashes are also an addition inserted by al-Haytami to complete the meaning he wished to draw from the report.

[56] See al-Nawawi, *Tahdhib al-Asma' wa'l-Lughat*, 2:407; al-Dhahabi, *Siyar A'lam al-Nubala'*, 3:134; Ibn Hajar, *al-Isaba fi Tamyiz al-Sahaba*; Ibn 'Abd al-Barr, *al-Isti'ab*; and others.

Al-Haytami's words are therefore invalid here — as is everything he says in that regard.

The Story That Sayyiduna 'Ali Praised Mu'awiya

Al-Ta'i says [p. 18]: "Sayyiduna 'Ali, may Allah be pleased with him, praised him, saying: 'My slain and the slain of Mu'awiya are in Paradise.' Al-Tabarani transmitted it with a chain whose narrators are considered reliable, with some disagreement regarding some of them."

I say: where is the merit in it? And the statement is among the fabrications and lies.

Let us identify these "reliable" narrators. Al-Tabarani transmitted it in *al-Mu'jam al-Kabir* (19/307), saying: "Al-Husayn ibn Ishaq al-Tustari told us — al-Husayn ibn Abi al-Sari al-'Asqalani told us — Zayd ibn Abi al-Zarqa' told us — from Ja'far ibn Burqan — from Yazid, who said: 'Ali said: 'My slain and the slain of Mu'awiya are in Paradise.'"

Al-Husayn ibn Abi al-Sari al-'Asqalani: a liar. His brother Muhammad ibn Abi al-Sari said: "Do not write from my brother for he is a liar." Abu 'Aruba said: "A liar." Abu Dawud said: "Weak." Ibn Hibban said: "He errs and transmits strange things."[57]

This alone is sufficient to invalidate this report. And we add:

Zayd ibn Abi al-Zarqa': truthful, but Ibn Hibban said he transmitted strange things.[58]

Yazid ibn al-Asamm: Hafiz al-Mizzi said in *Tahdhib al-Kamal* (32/84): "His narration from 'Ali ibn Abi Talib is through a weak chain."

---

[57] See al-Mizzi, *Tahdhib al-Kamal*, 6:469.

[58] Ibn Hibban mentioned him in *al-Thiqat*. See al-Mizzi, *Tahdhib al-Kamal*, 10:73.

It is thus established that this report is among the fabrications and invented narrations.

What has come from Sayyiduna 'Ali contradicts this. Ibn Abi Shayba narrated (5/457) with his chain from 'Abd al-Rahman ibn Jundub: "From 'Ali, who was asked about his slain and the slain of Mu'awiya. He said: 'Mu'awiya and I will come and dispute before the Lord of the Throne — whoever succeeds, his companions succeed.'"

Furthermore, how can the slain of Mu'awiya be in Paradise when the Prophet, may Allah's blessings and peace be upon him and his household, said about Mu'awiya's companions — who call to the Fire — in the authenticated hadith established in *Sahih al-Bukhari* (447): "Ammar will be killed by the transgressing faction — he calls them to Paradise and they call him to the Fire"?

Everything that al-Haytami and al-Ta'i built upon and cited in discussion of that report is refuted and thrown back in their faces. And among it is his statement that "Mu'awiya is a mujtahid who fulfilled the conditions of ijtihad" — and this, by Allah, is among the things that would make even a bereaved mother laugh.

Building Glory on Invented Stories

Al-Ta'i then builds and elaborates upon this fabricated report attributed to Sayyiduna 'Ali, saying: "Therefore Mu'awiya and his followers are rewarded — even though the truth was with Sayyiduna 'Ali and his followers. And reflect on Sayyiduna 'Ali's judgment that the slain of Mu'awiya are in Paradise — you will find that truth was the guide of both."

We say to him: we have reflected well upon it and found it to be a lie not established from Sayyiduna 'Ali — and found you to be trying to comb thorns.

Repeating the Claim That Ibn 'Abbas Praised Mu'awiya

Al-Ta'i says [p. 19]: "And Ibn 'Abbas, may Allah be pleased with them both, commended him when he reported that Mu'awiya had prayed witr with one rak'a, saying — as al-Bukhari narrated in his *Sahih* — 'He is a jurist (faqih)'... And the word 'jurist' is the highest expression of validation and the noblest expression of honor."

I say: Qasim al-Ta'i has repeated this phrase many times. But there is nothing behind it — for a jurist may well be depraved. And the Imam al-Tahawi the Hanafi — who is one of Qasim's own imams — narrated it with the wording "donkey" and not "jurist."

In *Sharh Ma'ani al-Athar* (1/289) by the Imam al-Tahawi the Hanafi, al-Tahawi narrated with a sound chain from Ibn 'Abbas — when told that Mu'awiya had prayed witr with one rak'a — that he said: "From where do you think this donkey got that?"

At the very least it must be said here that the report about Ibn 'Abbas is contradicted — between "jurist" and "donkey" — and thus both cancel each other out, and al-Ta'i is left empty-handed.

Furthermore, Ibn 'Abbas cursed Mu'awiya. In *Musnad Ahmad* (1/217) with a sound chain, Ibn 'Abbas cursed Mu'awiya — but the narrators transmitted this narration in veiled form, using "so-and-so" to conceal Mu'awiya's name out of deference to him.

Ibn 'Abbas said: "May Allah curse so-and-so — they deliberately targeted the greatest days of the Hajj and obliterated its adornment. And the adornment of the Hajj is the talbiya."

That the intended subject of the curse is Mu'awiya is clarified by what Ibn Khuzayma transmitted in his *Sahih* (4/260) from Sa'id ibn Jubayr, who said: "I was with Ibn 'Abbas at 'Arafa and he said to me: 'O Sa'id, why do I not hear the people reciting the talbiya?' I said: 'They fear Mu'awiya.'"[59]

Ibn 'Abbas then came out of his tent and said: "Labbayk, O Allah, labbayk — for they have abandoned the Sunnah out of their hatred for 'Ali."[60]

The Claim That "Jurist" Is the Highest Validation

His statement that "the word jurist is the highest expression of validation and the noblest expression of honor" is invalid on two grounds.

First: Mu'awiya was not a jurist. Ibn 'Abbas criticized him and cursed him as we have clarified — he did not praise him.

Second: there are among the leading imams of jurisprudence and the leading reciters those who were weakened and whose narrations were not accepted. The Imam Abu Hanifa, may Allah have mercy on him — the imam of al-Ta'i, except in matters of Nasb and defending the enemies of the Prophet's household — is among them. And although we disagree with the hadith masters of criticism and accreditation in their weakening of the trustworthy Imam Abu Hanifa, may Allah have mercy on him, and say he is above being merely trustworthy — it is nonetheless necessary to inform al-Ta'i that despite his greatness in jurisprudence, the hadith masters — such as al-Bukhari and others — weakened him.

The Imam Abu Hanifa, may Allah have mercy on him, is among the greatest of the righteous and the foremost of the people of excellence — yet al-Albani the self-contradicting one, and many hadith masters, paid no attention to his righteousness or his

---

[59] This establishes that Mu'awiya used to command what was wrong and forbid what was right, while the Muslims, including the Companions, had no effective power against him at that time.

[60] It is sound. Narrated by al-Hakim in *al-Mustadrak*, 1:464-465, who authenticated it; al-Nasa'i in *al-Sunan al-Kubra*, 2:419, and in *al-Sunan al-Sughra*, 5:253; and al-Diya' in *al-Mukhtara*, 10:378. Al-Albani also authenticated it in *Sahih Sunan al-Nasa'i*, 2:631, no. 2812.

excellence, but rather criticized him and enumerated the statements of those who weakened him — as in his commentary on the *Sunan* of Ibn Abi 'Asim (p. 76) where he said: "Its chain is weak — its narrators are the narrators of al-Bukhari except for Abu Hanifa, for despite his greatness in jurisprudence, the imams weakened him for his poor memory..."

And among the jurists who were criticized and weakened is Ibn Muljam al-Muradi — may he receive from Allah what he deserves. Al-Dhahabi said in *Tarikh al-Islam* (3/653) in his biographical entry: "'Abd al-Rahman ibn Muljam al-Muradi, the killer of 'Ali, may Allah be pleased with him — a Kharijite fabricator... He was among those who read the Quran and jurisprudence... He read the Quran under Mu'adh ibn Jabal, and was among the devout worshippers... And it is said that 'Umar wrote to 'Amr ibn al-'As: bring the house of 'Abd al-Rahman ibn Muljam near the mosque so that he may teach the people the Quran and jurisprudence... I say: then the decree overtook him and he did what he did." End of al-Dhahabi's words.

Hafiz Ibn Hajar said in *al-Isaba* (3/99): "'Abd al-Rahman ibn Muljam... lived into the pre-Islamic era... and he is the most wretched person of this community, by the established text from the Prophet, may Allah's blessings and peace be upon him and his household, for killing 'Ali ibn Abi Talib."

I say to Qasim al-Ta'i: congratulations on this jurist.

There are many other major jurists who were criticized and impugned — and their jurisprudence was not considered among the highest forms of validation and trustworthiness. We will not lengthen this by enumerating their names.

From all of this the collapse and invalidity of al-Ta'i's words becomes apparent — where he said [p. 19]: "The conclusion is that the great scholar of the community, Sayyiduna Ibn 'Abbas — who is among the greatest scholars of the Prophet's household, may Allah be pleased with them, the translator of the Quran, the cousin of the Messenger of Allah, may Allah's blessings and peace be upon him and his household, and the cousin of 'Ali, may Allah be pleased with him, who stood in support of him during his lifetime — commended Mu'awiya with the highest of expressions."

I say: al-Ta'i appears to be daydreaming.

First: you, O Qasim, do not know the right of the Prophet's household and their true rank — even if you claim this with resounding phrases that have no real effect. And if you do not know it, I will — Allah willing — make it known to you before I refute the nonsense you babble in these sentences that carry erroneous thinking.

How do you know the rank and station of the Prophet's household, love them, and honor them — while you commend their enemies and opponents and those who cursed them, headed by their foremost enemy Mu'awiya — and defend them with this frenzied defense built on superstitions, fabrications, lies, and reprehensible and contemptible inventions?

How do you defend Mu'awiya who cursed Sayyiduna 'Ali — while the Messenger, may Allah's peace and blessings be upon him, informed us that whoever curses him has cursed the Messenger of Allah, and that whoever hates him is a hypocrite, and that those who killed 'Ammar are the faction calling to the Fire with Mu'awiya as their leader — like Pharaoh of whom Allah said: {"He will precede his people on the Day of Resurrection and lead them into the Fire — and wretched is the watering place they arrive at."} [Hud: 98]?

Do you think that love for the Messenger and his household is a song you recite in a gathering or a phrase said in a lesson — with no other consequence in belief, action, or word?

Would that we saw you defending Sayyiduna 'Ali and Sayyiduna 'Umar against the attacks of Ibn Taymiyya upon them — especially his attacks on Sayyiduna 'Ali, may Allah be pleased with him. May Allah have mercy on the one who said:

It troubled me about 'Amir that 'Amir comes showing love and sincere counsel each morning, and spends his evenings as a close friend to my enemies. Would that this love and counsel had never been — would that he had been the adversary and the enemy instead.

I return to your words, O al-Ta'i. As for Ibn 'Abbas — he cursed Mu'awiya for abandoning the talbiya out of hatred and scheming against the Sunnah, because Sayyiduna 'Ali was committed to it. And he did not say "he is a jurist" as they claim and as came in al-Bukhari's narration. Rather he said "donkey" — as in al-Tahawi's narration — and this is what is correct in our view, as we have already presented.

And the hadith of Muslim on trimming between al-Safa and al-Marwa has also been presented — and Ibn 'Abbas's statement to Mu'awiya that it is proof against you, not in your favor. He did not consider it proof for him — just as al-Ta'i has not taken heed of any of this.

We seek refuge in Allah from stubbornness, arrogance, and taking pride in sin. We seek refuge in Allah from speech without guidance and without restraint or bridle.

The Claim That Mu'awiya Was a Jurist and Absolute Mujtahid

His subsequent claim that Ibn 'Abbas's word about Mu'awiya — "jurist" — even if established (which it is not, given Ibn 'Abbas's contradictory statement) and even if Ibn 'Abbas — who is not infallible — perhaps said it out of precautionary concealment, or the listener distorted it from him — is "sufficient for accreditation and explicit proof that he is an absolute mujtahid, as transmitted from the legal theorists, hadith masters, and jurists of Ahl al-Sunna" — I say: Mu'awiya was not a jurist, let alone an absolute mujtahid. Rather he followed his own desires. Nothing demonstrates this more clearly than the documented and authenticated matters recorded in the treatise *Statements of the Messenger Concerning Mu'awiya* — that he dealt in usury, drank wine and traded in it, commanded people to consume one another's wealth unjustly as in *Sahih Muslim*, commanded them to abandon the talbiya — which is the hallmark of the Hajj — abandoned the takbir and other acts in the prayer, cursed Sayyiduna 'Ali, may Allah be pleased with him, and ordered the people to do so, and killed those who objected — even if they were noble Companions such as Hujr ibn 'Adi. Are these among the signs of absolute ijtihad?

And is ijtihad permissible where an explicit text exists? The Prophet, may Allah's blessings and peace be upon him and his household, said: "Ammar will be killed by the transgressing faction — they call him to Paradise and they call him to the Fire."

Al-Ta'i then cited on pages 20 and 21 the discussion of Mu'awiya's ijtihad and his flimsy jurisprudence — repeating what has already been critiqued and refuted above. He titled it "The Sixth Pearl: Mu'awiya the Jurist Mujtahid."

I say to him: O Qasim, trying to outwit the Shi'a by turning truth into falsehood and falsehood into truth will not benefit you. Justice demands acknowledging the truth regardless of who states it — even if it were Iblis, about whom the Messenger, may Allah's blessings and peace be upon him and his household, said: "He told you the truth, and he is a liar." Excessive fanaticism and arguing for falsehood bring a man down and render him unreliable.

He then cited on those pages what has already been refuted and demolished — including the fabricated report attributed to Sayyiduna 'Ali containing "my slain and Mu'awiya's slain are in Paradise" — which is a fabricated lie as established above. And what was attributed to Ibn 'Abbas in al-Bukhari saying "he is a jurist" — which is not established from him, and reality contradicts it.

The words of al-Haytami in these matters are thrown aside in every rough and smooth terrain — with no attention paid to them. Especially his words on ijtihad and matters related to it. His books *al-Sawa'iq al-Muhriqa* and *al-Tathir* are among the storehouses of weak, fabricated, and objectionable hadiths — and even if something sound were found in them, its meaning is not what al-Haytami claims through his elaborate, ornate, and useless composition.

The Claim That Ahl al-Sunna Agreed Mu'awiya Was a Rewarded Mujtahid

Among the greatest of fabrications is al-Ta'i's statement: "Ahl al-Sunna wa'l-Jama'a agreed that Mu'awiya is a mujtahid who erred in his ijtihad against Sayyiduna 'Ali and is rewarded for it."

This is among the lies and fabrications — in addition to being the fanaticism that has blinded and deafened its holder from the truth. For Sayyiduna 'Ali and those with him of the noble Companions who call to Paradise — such as Sayyiduna 'Ammar — and Ibn 'Abbas who cursed him and called him a donkey, and the imams of Ahl al-Sunna such as 'Abd al-Razzaq who said: "Do not defile our gathering by mentioning Ibn Abi Sufyan,"[61] and Jarir al-Dabbi the reliable Imam who used to curse Mu'awiya openly,[62] and al-Nasa'i, al-Hakim, al-Taftazani, and great numbers of the leading scholars of Ahl al-Sunna — they all contradict al-Ta'i's fabricated claim.

Or are these not from Ahl al-Sunna?

Where is the consensus, O supposed master of discernment?

Does one who commits such outrages and exercises ijtihad according to his desires in contradiction of explicit texts deserve reward and praise?

Does the perpetrator of sins and such abominations receive reward for them?

And after all of this you claim there is agreement on it.

There are still leading figures of Ahl al-Sunna — those whose minds fanaticism has not clouded and whom blind imitation has not imprisoned — who say what we say: such as the scholar Sayyid Abu Bakr ibn Shihab, Sayyid Muhammad ibn 'Aqil, the

---

[61] See al-Dhahabi, *Siyar A'lam al-Nubala'*, 9:570, in the biographical entry of Imam and hadith master 'Abd al-Razzaq.

[62] Ibn Hajar, *Tahdhib al-Tahdhib*, 2:66: "Al-Khalili said in *al-Irshad*: 'Reliable, agreed upon.' Qutayba said: 'Jarir, the foremost hadith master, narrated to us, but I heard him openly cursing Mu'awiya.'"

Ghumari scholars, the scholar al-Kawthari, Shaykh al-Habashi al-Harari, the scholar Mahmud Sa'id Mamduh, and many, many others from Ahl al-Sunna wa'l-Jama'a.

Do not live in fantasies and illusions.

What he cited here from al-Khattab al-Baghdadi advances nothing. Al-Khattab al-Baghdadi is mistaken in this matter — just as he was mistaken in his *Tarikh* in attacking the reliable Imam Abu Hanifa, may Allah have mercy on him — until the scholars refuted him, among them the Imam and hadith master al-Kawthari, may Allah have mercy on him, in *Ta'nib al-Khatib*, and before him others who refuted him in *al-Sahm al-Musib fi Kabd al-Khatib*.

Furthermore, the statement of al-Khattab and others is not among the legal proofs that you would use to intimidate us. We have presented to you the decisive arguments — all that remains is for you to submit to the truth.

Al-Ta'i then mentioned on page 21 that among those who narrated from Mu'awiya and from whom he narrated were a group of Companions and Successors — and he described Marwan ibn al-Hakam among them as one of the greatest of the Successors.

I say: a man's narrating from the noble and their narrating from him does not validate him. Many of the criticized and impugned narrators — those labeled by the hadith masters as Rafidis, innovators, and so forth — narrated from noble masters and trustworthy masters narrated from them.

I advise you to read the book of the scholar Sayyid Muhammad ibn 'Aqil — *al-'Atb al-Jamil 'ala Ahl al-Jarh wa'l-Ta'dil* — to understand some of this.

The Glorification of Marwan ibn al-Hakam

His statement that "among the greatest of the Successors is Marwan ibn al-Hakam" is something that causes one's composure to dissolve in astonishment. For Marwan ibn al-

Hakam is the accursed son of the accursed[63] — the lizard son of the lizard — on the tongue of the master of all creation, may Allah's blessings and peace be upon him and his household.

Hafiz Ibn Hajar said in *al-Fath* (13/11): "There have come hadiths about the cursing of al-Hakam — the father of Marwan — and what he begat. Al-Tabarani and others transmitted them — most have something problematic in them but some are good."

The Hafiz al-Haythami[64] said in *Majma' al-Zawa'id* (5/241): "From al-Sha'bi, who said: I heard 'Abd Allah ibn al-Zubayr — leaning against the Ka'ba — saying: 'By the Lord of this Ka'ba, the Messenger of Allah, may Allah's blessings and peace be upon him and his household, cursed so-and-so and what came from his loins.' Ahmad and al-Bazzar transmitted it — except that al-Bazzar's wording is: 'Allah cursed al-Hakam and what he begat on the tongue of His Prophet, may Allah's blessings and peace be upon him and his household.' Al-Tabarani likewise with a similar wording, and has a narration like Ahmad's. And the narrators of Ahmad are the narrators of the Sahih."

Al-Tirmidhi narrated in *al-Sunan* (5/444/3350) from al-Qasim ibn al-Fadl al-Huddani, from the trustworthy Yusuf ibn Sa'd:[65] "A man stood before al-Hasan ibn 'Ali after he had pledged allegiance to Mu'awiya and said: 'You have blackened the faces of the believers' — or 'O you who blackened the faces of the believers.' Al-Hasan said: 'Do not reproach me — may Allah have mercy on you. The Prophet, may Allah's blessings and peace be upon him and his household, was shown the Umayyads

---

[63] See al-Bazzar, *al-Musnad*, 6:159; al-Diya' al-Maqdisi, *al-Mukhtara*, 9:310; al-Haythami, *Majma' al-Zawa'id*, 5:241; and others.

[64] This refers to Nur al-Din al-Haythami, with thā' muthallathah, author of *Majma' al-Zawa'id*, not Ibn Hajar al-Haytami, with tā' muthannāh, author of *Tathir al-Lisan wa'l-Janan fi'l-Difa' 'an Ibn Abi Sufyan*.

[65] Al-Tirmidhi's statement after the report that Yusuf ibn Sa'd is unknown is incorrect. Yusuf ibn Sa'd is known, and is among the narrators of al-Tirmidhi and Abu Dawud. Twelve men narrated from him, as stated in his biographical entry in al-Mizzi, *Tahdhib al-Kamal*, 32:427. Ibn Ma'in said: "Reliable and well-known." Ibn Hibban mentioned him in *al-Thiqat*, 5:550. Ibn Hajar said in *al-Taqrib*: "Reliable." Al-Dhahabi also said in *al-Kashif*: "Reliable."

upon his pulpit, and it distressed him. Then {"Indeed We have given you al-Kawthar"} was revealed — O Muhammad: meaning a river in Paradise. And {"Indeed We revealed it on the Night of Power — and what will make you know what the Night of Power is? The Night of Power is better than a thousand months"} was revealed — which the Umayyads will rule after you, O Muhammad.' Al-Qasim said: 'We counted it and it was exactly a thousand months — not one day more or less.'"

Al-Qurtubi said in his *Tafsir* (10/283): "And in a third narration: he saw the Umayyads in his dream jumping upon his pulpit like monkeys — and it distressed him. It was said: this is merely the world given to them — and he was relieved. He had no pulpit in Mecca, but it is possible to dream in Mecca of the pulpit in Madinah. This third interpretation was also stated by Sahl ibn Sa'd, may Allah be pleased with him: 'This dream is that the Messenger of Allah, may Allah's blessings and peace be upon him and his household, would see the Umayyads jumping upon his pulpit like monkeys — and it grieved him. And he never fully laughed from that day until he died, may Allah's blessings and peace be upon him and his household. Then this verse was revealed, informing that their rule and ascent would be made by Allah a trial and test for the people.'" Let al-Ta'i take heed — may Allah guide him.

CHAPTER 5: MISUSED PROOFS AND THE CLAIM OF IJTIHAD

The Verse {That is a community that has passed away}

Al-Ta'i then said [p. 22]: "The Seventh Pearl: Mu'awiya at the Battle of Siffin. O Muslims, know that what took place among the Companions of the Messenger of Allah, may Allah's blessings and peace be upon him and his household, of wars and other matters — the words of Allah, Exalted be He, apply to it: {'That is a community that has passed away — for it is what they earned, and for you is what you earned, and you will not be asked about what they used to do.'}. And all were mujtahids — either correct for two rewards or erring for one — and we are not obligated to investigate their wars or know who was in error and who was correct..." and the rest of his ranting that contradicts its beginning with its end.

This statement contains a chain of errors, contradictions, confusions, and false rejected claims. We mention some of them:

First: His statement "we are not obligated to investigate their wars and know who was in error and who was correct" contradicts himself — for he said the opposite in several passages in the same book. Among them: his words just one page before [p. 21]: "I say: Ahl al-Sunna wa'l-Jama'a agreed that Mu'awiya is a mujtahid who erred..." — this is a stated agreement from Ahl al-Sunna on the opposite of what he claims in his first statement. So note how he twists, stumbles, plays games, and contradicts himself.

And his words also, one page after [p. 23]: "The verifying scholar al-Alusi said in his responses: 'Ali, may Allah honor his face, was in all of that upon the truth without deviating from it by a hair's breadth, and those who fought him in both battles were erring and transgressing — though not disbelievers.'"

And his words [p. 7]: "If you say: what do you say about the errors that issued from them — such as some of them fighting Sayyiduna 'Ali — given that Ahl al-Sunna agreed that he was correct and the other was in error — I say: the occurrence of some errors does not negate their uprightness..."

Reflect on the extent of this contradiction and confusion. Note how he claims that Allah did not oblige us to investigate it — then claims elsewhere that Ahl al-Sunna agreed on the opposite of that.

Such is how every falsifier who stubbornly insists on defending tyrants and transgressors that call to the Fire contradicts himself.

Second: His claim that Allah did not oblige us to know the correct from the erring is refuted by the explicit words of Allah, Exalted be He: {"Fight the one that transgresses until it returns to the command of Allah."} How can we know the transgressing faction to fight it, and the rightful faction to support it, if we do not investigate who was correct and who was in error?

The correct party is the one upon the truth — whom Allah, Exalted be He, commanded us to support and stand with, even if only with words and in our hearts. The transgressor is the erring one whom we must fight even if only with words — and not support or stand beside or defend.

And the erring party has different categories — among them one who calls to the Fire, like Mu'awiya, about whom and whose faction the Messenger of Allah, may Allah's blessings and peace be upon him and his household, said: "They call to the Fire."

Third: The legal texts — such as the words of Allah, Exalted be He: {"Those are the party of Satan..."} and His words: {"Say: If your fathers, your sons, your brothers, your wives, your clan, wealth you have acquired, trade you fear will decline, and dwellings you are pleased with are more beloved to you than Allah and His Messenger and striving in His cause — then wait until Allah brings His command. And Allah does not guide the depraved people."} [al-Tawba: 24] — are clear that a person must investigate to know who was correct and who was in error. The objectives of the Shari'a are built upon this meaning — yet Qasim al-Ta'i wishes to oppose the objectives and Shari'a foundations without realizing it, since his fanaticism for the tyrant has blinded him from many realities.

Fourth: The noble verse {"That is a community that has passed away..."} which he cited contains nothing indicating what he claims. For this verse does not prevent or restrict a Muslim from mentioning those who passed away before us — whether the righteous or the wicked among them. It only clarifies that we are not responsible for their actions. The Noble Quran commanded us to travel through the earth and reflect on the conditions of previous nations. And it is filled with mentions of groups of Companions — such as those who were entrenched in hypocrisy among the Bedouins and the people of Madinah, and the disbelievers of Mecca such as Abu Lahab, and previous nations such as 'Ad, Thamud, Pharaoh, and the Children of Israel — and the community has mentioned them night and day from the time of the Prophet, may Allah's blessings and peace be upon him and his household, to this day while reciting the Noble Quran.

This noble verse only establishes that we are not held accountable for the deeds of those who came before us when we have not followed them — for every person is accountable for himself.

It is thus clear that the verse is not evidence for what al-Ta'i and those like him say — those who defend tyrants.

Fifth: His phrase "we are not obligated to investigate" contains a grammatical error. The correct form is "we are not obligated to investigate" — for "kallafa" is a verb that takes its object directly without a preposition. Allah, Exalted be He, said: {"Allah does not burden a soul beyond what it can bear."} [al-Baqara: 286]

Repeated Preaching and Exhortation

Al-Ta'i says [p. 22]: "As for one who uses the Battle of Siffin as a pretext to curse Sayyiduna Mu'awiya... and whose argument is clarifying the truth and exposing what is right — such a person is a liar and a troublemaker who does not want to clarify the truth and expose what is right, but rather wants to cast doubt on the first generation of the Companions of the Messenger of Allah and overturn the truth that calls for leaving what occurred between them..."

I say: first — it has become clear who the liar and fabricator is, and who wants to overturn scholarly realities.

Second: this is empty, ornate speech built on a fabricated emotion motivated by malice and cunning that will harm its holder on the Day of Resurrection and benefit him nothing.

Third: in that case, the scholars should have erased from the hadith collections and from *Sahih al-Bukhari* and *Sahih Muslim* hadiths such as "Ammar will be killed by the transgressing faction — he calls them to Paradise and they call him to the Fire," and the Prophet's statement to Sayyiduna 'Ali: "None loves you except a believer, and none hates you except a hypocrite," and the sound and explicit texts showing that Mu'awiya used to curse and order the cursing of Sayyiduna 'Ali — some of which are in *Sahih Muslim* and others. And likewise it would have been obligatory for Ahl al-Sunna to erase hadiths such as "Among my Companions are twelve hypocrites..." and the Hawd hadith established in the two Sahihs showing that a group of Companions are driven away from the Hawd and the Prophet says "Away, away."

And according to this twisted understanding, they should have deleted from the Quran the words of Allah about al-Walid ibn 'Uqba: {"If a depraved person brings you news, verify it."} And His words: {"And among those around you of the Bedouins there are hypocrites, and among the people of Madinah there are those entrenched in hypocrisy — you do not know them, but We know them. We will punish them twice, then they will be returned to a great punishment."} [al-Tawba: 101] And likewise His words: {"But when they see merchandise or entertainment they break away toward it and leave you standing."} [al-Jumu'a: 11] — because these cast doubt on the first generation.

This is cold fabrication and madness itself. And madness comes in many forms.

These texts in the Quran and the Sunnah did not come for us to stand before them as spectators — they came so that we love and hate for the sake of Allah, Exalted be He, and so that we know who follows the Messenger, may Allah's blessings and peace be upon him and his household, from those who turn back on their heels — as He, Glorious be He, said: {"...except that We might distinguish those who follow the Messenger from those who turn back on their heels. And indeed it is difficult except for those whom Allah has guided."} [al-Baqara: 143] {"And whoever turns back on his heels will not harm Allah at all."} And He said: {"You will not find a people who believe in Allah and the Last Day making friends with those who oppose Allah and His Messenger — even if they were their fathers, their sons, their brothers, or their clan. Those — He has written faith upon their hearts and supported them with a spirit from Him, and He will admit them into gardens beneath which rivers flow, abiding therein. Allah is pleased with them and they are pleased with Him. Those are the party of Allah."}

From all of this the invalidity of al-Ta'i's subsequent words becomes clear [p. 22]: "Rather he wants division and a fleeting worldly gain and empty fame. What Ibn Hajar stated in *Tathir* applies to him: the imams explicitly stated that it is obligatory to refrain from what caused strife between the Companions, may Allah be pleased with them, and it is not permissible for anyone to mention anything of what occurred between them using it as proof against some of them..."

I say: what demolishes this statement is Ibn Hajar al-Haytami's own words in *Fath al-Jawwad bi-Sharh al-Irshad* (2/295): "Al-Shafi'i, may Allah be pleased with him, said: I derived the rulings concerning transgressors from 'Ali's fighting of

Mu'awiya." Al-Shafi'i derived the ruling on transgressors from Mu'awiya's condition — and this renders al-Ta'i's words "it is not permissible for anyone to mention anything of what occurred between them using it as proof against some" scattered to the winds.

And we say: among those who did not refrain from this but rather explicitly stated what took place between them and took a position on the transgressors — from the imams of the hadith masters — are Jarir al-Dabbi, 'Abd al-Razzaq, al-Nasa'i, al-Hakim, and the teachers of al-Bukhari such as al-Nahdi and al-Fadl ibn Dukayn,[66] following in that the Book of Allah, Exalted be He, the sound Sunnah of the greatest Beloved, and the statements of the noble Companions — such as Sayyiduna 'Umar who called Mu'awiya "the Khusrau of the Arabs" and struck him with the staff. And likewise Sayyiduna 'Ali, Ibn 'Abbas, and all others criticized him.

And upon that the historians proceeded — mentioning in detail what occurred between the Companions: among them Ibn Jarir al-Tabari, Ibn 'Abd al-Barr, Ibn al-Athir in *al-Kamil*, al-Dhahabi in his books, Ibn Kathir in his history, Hafiz Ibn Hajar, al-Taftazani in *al-Maqasid*, al-Qurtubi, and others — to our own day.

His subsequent words — transmitting from al-Haytami: "And this" — meaning delving into what caused strife between them — "can only be from an ignorant person who transmits the sound and the weak, the good and the bad without discrimination; or a feigning ignorant one whose insight Allah has blinded — wanting to diminish the Companions of the Messenger of Allah, without whom neither Book nor Sunnah would have reached us."

I say: all I can say in such a situation is: first — the pot calling the kettle black. Second — we do not know how someone like Hariz ibn 'Uthman and Azhar ibn 'Abd Allah can abuse Sayyiduna 'Ali, may Allah be pleased with him, and the hadith

---

[66] See al-Dhahabi, *Siyar A'lam al-Nubala'*, 10:432.

masters of Ahl al-Sunna validate and praise them. Al-Dhahabi said in *al-Mizan* (10553): "(d t q) Abu Labid al-Jahdami Lamaza — Jarir ibn Hazim narrated from him. He is trustworthy — except that he used to curse 'Ali."

And there is Ibn Taymiyya al-Harrani — of whom Hafiz Ibn Hajar said in *Lisan al-Mizan* (6/319-320): "How many an exaggeration in undermining the speech of the Rafidi led him at times to diminishing 'Ali, may Allah be pleased with him." And his book *Minhaj al-Sunnah* is full of that.

Where is the justice? And this is what you close your eyes to and deliberately ignore.

In any case, the one transmitting the good and the bad, the sound and the weak indiscriminately, is al-Haytami and his imitator al-Ta'i and those like them — those who have not known, examined, or understood the true state of affairs.

The Invalidity of the Rewarded-Mujtahid Claim

His words [p. 22] about Mu'awiya and his followers: "They are mujtahids who are rewarded — their intention was to seek the pleasure of Allah and to establish His boundaries and support His law."

I say: this ijtihad — which involved rebellion against the rightly-guided Imam, killing the believers headed by Sayyiduna 'Ammar, calling to the Fire by the authentic text from our master the Messenger of Allah, may Allah's blessings and peace be upon him and his household, drinking wine, installing the depraved drunkard Yazid over the necks of the people and making him Commander of the Believers — has already collapsed entirely.

Based on these corrupt and rejected notions, among those counted as rewarded mujtahids would be the killer of Sayyiduna 'Umar, the killers of Sayyiduna 'Uthman, and the killer of

Sayyiduna 'Ali, may Allah be pleased with him — Ibn Muljam[67] — whom the hypocrite 'Imran ibn Hittan — who is among the narrators of al-Bukhari — praised with the verse:

What a blow from a pious man — he intended by it nothing but to attain the pleasure of the Lord of the Throne.

From this you will understand the extent of the nonsense of al-Haytami and al-Ta'i.

And Hafiz Ibn Hajar said in *Talkhis al-Habir* (4/45): "His words — meaning al-Rafi'i's — the Kharijites are a sect of innovators who rose against 'Ali believing that he knew the killers of 'Uthman and was capable of dealing with them yet did not retaliate because he approved of their killing and was complicit with them. And they believe that whoever commits a major sin has disbelieved and deserves to abide in the Fire. And for this reason they criticize the imams and do not join them in Friday prayers and congregations — may Allah protect us from their evil...

As for what he mentioned of the Kharijites' belief — the first part is not accurate, for the mentioned belief is the belief of Mu'awiya and the people of Syria."

The Verse {And if two factions of the believers fight...}

Al-Ta'i says [p. 23] about those who fought Sayyiduna 'Ali: "As for their being believers and not disbelievers — the words of Allah, Exalted be He: {'And if two factions of the believers fight, then make settlement between them. But if one of them transgresses against the other, then fight against the one that transgresses until it returns to the command of Allah. And if it returns, then make settlement between them in justice and act justly. Indeed, Allah loves those who act justly.'} [al-Hujurat: 9]

---

[67] Ibn Hajar said in *Talkhis al-Habir*, 4:45: "Al-Shafi'i said: Ibn Muljam al-Muradi killed 'Ali as one acting upon interpretation." That is, he was supposedly a mujtahid acting upon interpretation, according to Ibn Muljam's own claim.

— Allah named both factions as believers and commanded reconciliation between them."

His use of this verse as proof for their not being disbelievers is invalid.

Was this verse revealed about Mu'awiya and his faction for it to be used as proof in their case?

And is every transgressor necessarily a believer or a disbeliever?

And if a faction transgressed while having apostatized or disbelieved — as happened with Sayyiduna Abu Bakr al-Siddiq, may Allah be pleased with him, in the wars against the apostates — must they be fought? And does the verse {"Fight the one that transgresses"} apply to them?

As for Mu'awiya — his condition indicates great danger. For the Prophet, may Allah's blessings and peace be upon him and his household, clarified that he is from a faction that calls to the Fire — as in al-Bukhari. And that one who hates Sayyiduna 'Ali, may Allah be pleased with him, is a hypocrite — as in *Sahih Muslim* — and the hypocrite is in the lowest depth of the Fire. And that he used to curse Sayyiduna 'Ali — while the Prophet, may Allah's blessings and peace be upon him and his household, says: "Whoever curses 'Ali has cursed me." And you know the ruling on one who curses the Prophet, may Allah's blessings and peace be upon him and his household.[68] And that he killed noble Companions such as Sayyiduna 'Ammar in battle and Sayyiduna Hujr ibn 'Adi in cold blood when he objected to their cursing of

---

[68] Umm Salama, Mother of the Believers, may Allah be pleased with her, said: "Is the Messenger of Allah, may Allah bless him and his household and grant them peace, being cursed among you?" I said: "Allah forbid," or "Glory be to Allah," or a similar phrase. She said: "I heard the Messenger of Allah, may Allah bless him and his household and grant them peace, say: 'Whoever curses 'Ali has cursed me.'" Narrated by Ahmad, *al-Musnad*, 6:323; and al-Nasa'i, *al-Sunan al-Kubra*, 5:133. It has numerous routes gathered by al-Haythami in *Majma' al-Zawa'id*, 9:130. It is also transmitted with other wordings by Ibn Abi Shayba, *al-Musannaf*, 12:76-77; al-Tabarani, *al-Mu'jam al-Kabir*, 23:322; Abu Ya'la, *al-Musnad*, 12:444; and others. Shu'ayb al-Arna'ut authenticated it in his commentary on the *Musnad*, 44:329, as did al-Albani in *al-Silsila al-Sahiha*, no. 3332.

Sayyiduna 'Ali, and 'Abd al-Rahman ibn 'Udayd al-Balawi,[69] and he rebelled against the Imam of his time — while the Messenger of Allah, may Allah's blessings and peace be upon him and his household, said: "When allegiance is pledged to two caliphs, kill the second of them" — in Muslim (1853).

Then how much more so when there is added to that the statement of the Prophet, may Allah's blessings and peace be upon him and his household: "There will emerge upon you from this mountain pass a man who will die the day he dies upon a religion other than mine... and Mu'awiya emerged."[70] And what Ahmad narrated in his *Musnad* (5/347) with a chain meeting Muslim's criteria — that he used to drink wine. Allah, Exalted be He, says in His mighty Book: {"Indeed, intoxicants, gambling, stone altars, and divining arrows are but defilement from the work of Satan — so avoid it."} [al-Ma'ida: 90] And the Messenger, may Allah's blessings and peace be upon him and his household, said: "No one commits fornication while he is a believer at the time of committing it, and no one drinks wine while he is a believer at the time of drinking it." Narrated by al-Bukhari (2475).

After all of this they say they were believers and use this noble verse as proof of his faith — as if it were revealed specifically about him.

Hafiz Ibn Jarir al-Tabari said in his *Tafsir* (26/128): "It was revealed about two factions from the Aws and the Khazraj who fought each other over something they were disputing... from Anas, who said: The Prophet, may Allah's blessings and peace

---

[69] Abu 'Abd al-Rahman al-Sulami, who is not the famous Sufi imam of the same name, will shortly be cited as saying: "I never saw the Companions of Muhammad, may Allah bless him and his household and grant them peace, killed in any battle as they were killed that day." Ibn 'Abd al-Barr mentions this in *al-Isti'ab*, 3:1139. This shows that the Companions who called to Paradise were martyred while fighting against Mu'awiya.

[70] Al-Baladhuri narrated it in his *Tarikh* with a sound chain, as stated by the hadith master Sayyid Ahmad ibn al-Siddiq al-Ghumari in *Ju'nat al-'Attar*, 2:154. See also al-Haythami, *Majma' al-Zawa'id*, 5:243, where he mentions al-Tabarani's narration in which the name of the person who appeared is left unnamed.

be upon him and his household, was told: would you not go to 'Abd Allah ibn Ubayy? He went to him riding a donkey... When the Messenger of Allah, may Allah's blessings and peace be upon him and his household, came to him, he said — to the Prophet: 'Keep away from me — by Allah, the stench of your donkey has harmed me.' A man from the Ansar said: 'By Allah, the stench of the Messenger of Allah's donkey is more pleasant than you.' A man from 'Abd Allah ibn Ubayy's people became angry for him. And a man from each side became angry for his companion. There was striking with palm branches, hands, and sandals between them. We were informed that it was revealed about them: {'And if two factions of the believers fight, then make settlement between them.'}"

Al-Tabari also narrated: "Abu Haseen 'Abd Allah ibn Ahmad ibn Yunus told me — 'Abthar told us — Husayn from Abu Malik told us, regarding {'And if two factions of the believers fight, then make settlement between them'}: 'Two men fought and the people of each one became angry for him and gathered until they struck each other with sandals — until there was almost killing among them. And Allah revealed this verse.' He said: it was fighting without weapons."

The Report "They Are Our Brothers Who Transgressed Against Us"

Al-Ta'i says [p. 23]: "And the statement of Imam 'Ali about the people of Siffin — 'They are our brothers who transgressed against us' — is the clearest proof that they were believers and not disbelievers."

I say: our companion has committed a disgraceful act of deception — or he hurls words randomly without knowledge or learning. For Imam 'Ali, may Allah be pleased with him, did not say this about the people of Siffin. He said this about the people of the Camel, O wretched one.

Ibn Abi Shayba narrated (7/535) and al-Bayhaqi in *al-Sunan* (8/173 and 182) from 'Abd Khayr, who said: 'Ali, may Allah be pleased with him, was asked about the people of the Camel and he said: "They are our brothers who transgressed against us — we fought them and they have returned, and we have accepted from them."

The narration, as you can see, is about the people of the Camel — and al-Ta'i attributed it to the people of Siffin through deception, fraud, and lying. Reflect on this scheming with falsehood.

{"And they had already devised their scheme, but their scheme was with Allah."} [Ibrahim: 46]

Furthermore, transgression is not restricted to Muslims or to a believing faction. It can also occur among disbelievers. The Prophet, may Allah's blessings and peace be upon him and his household, said to 'Amir ibn al-Akwa': "Recite your verses" — on the march to Khaybar — and he recited verses including:

The disbelievers have transgressed against us — when they sought to cause strife, we refused.

And the Messenger of Allah, may Allah's blessings and peace be upon him and his household, said to him: "May Allah have mercy on you."[71]

Hafiz Ibn Hajar said in *al-Fath* (7/501): "'Abd al-Razzaq transmitted from him through two chains — one of them: his narration from Ma'mar, from al-Zuhri, from Anas, that the Prophet, may Allah's blessings and peace be upon him and his household, entered Mecca during 'Umrat al-Qada' while 'Abd Allah ibn Rawaha was reciting before him:

Clear the way, O sons of the disbelievers, from his path — for the Most Merciful has revealed it in His revelation. We struck you for its revelation — as we struck you for its sending down.

And it is sound."

And Hafiz Ibn 'Abd al-Barr said in *al-Isti'ab* (3/1139): "'Ammar ibn Yasir on the day of Siffin said to Hashim ibn 'Uqba: 'O Hashim, advance. Paradise is beneath these water vessels.

---

[71] Al-Bukhari mentioned it in *al-Tarikh al-Kabir*, 8:100.

Today I will meet those I love — Muhammad and his party. By Allah, even if they drove us back to the palm groves of Hajar, we would know that we are on the truth and they are on falsehood.' He then said:

We struck you for its sending down — so today we strike you for its interpretation. A striking that removes skulls from their resting place and makes the close friend forget his friend — until the truth returns to its proper course.

He said: I never saw the Companions of Muhammad, may Allah's blessings and peace be upon him and his household, killed in any battle as they were killed that day."[72]

The Peace Settlement of Sayyiduna al-Hasan

Al-Ta'i says [p. 23]: "And if you reflect on Sayyiduna al-Hasan's relinquishment of the caliphate and his peace settlement with Mu'awiya — for the purpose of uniting the community, unifying the ranks, and preventing bloodshed — you will find it a clear proof of the Islam and faith of Mu'awiya and his army."

I say: this is not a legal proof. The summary of the matter is that Sayyiduna al-Hasan saw treachery among the people around him and feared that if the fighting continued, he would destroy the best of the believers who were with him. He also feared that it would open the way for Mu'awiya to kill the household of the Prophet, may Allah's blessings and peace be upon him and his household, and the pure family — wiping them out entirely. He therefore saw fit to hand the matter to Mu'awiya on condition that the caliphate after Mu'awiya would be for Sayyiduna al-Hasan, may Allah be pleased with him. But Mu'awiya did not like this — and so he resorted to treachery and scheming, and sent someone to poison Sayyiduna al-Hasan, the master of the youth of Paradise, who then died — may Allah be pleased with him. For Mu'awiya had planned for his depraved and drunken

---

[72] This shows that Mu'awiya and his faction, who called to the Fire, caused the killing of the virtuous Companions who were in the army of Sayyiduna 'Ali, may Allah be pleased with him, against Mu'awiya, the caller to the Fire.

son to be the caliph — not the master of the youth of Paradise, al-Hasan ibn 'Ali, may Allah be pleased with him, the master of the Prophet's household in his era.

The Prophet, may Allah's blessings and peace be upon him and his household, made peace with the Jews and made covenants and agreements with them — and they broke them, turned against him, transgressed, and conspired against him.

As for the hadith of Sayyiduna al-Hasan's peace settlement — which contains "perhaps Allah will reconcile through him between two factions" — narrated in al-Bukhari (2704): it is not sound in my view; I consider it fabricated to support a political position. Al-Daraqutni included it in *al-Tatabbu'* (222-223) and in *al-'Ilal* (7/161), and Ahmad in *al-'Ilal* (2/444). Muslim avoided it. And the hadith was narrated by Ishaq in his *Musnad* (1/131) as mursal — from al-Hasan al-Basri.

Even if we concede its soundness hypothetically — Sayyiduna al-Hasan's peace settlement with Mu'awiya is not a legal proof indicating Mu'awiya's goodness and virtue. And Mu'awiya was extremely pleased at the killing and death of Sayyiduna al-Hasan, may Allah be pleased with him.

Al-Dhahabi said in *Siyar A'lam al-Nubala'* (3/158): "From Khalid ibn Ma'dan: al-Miqdam ibn Ma'di Karib, 'Amr ibn al-Aswad, and a man from Asad who had companionship came to Mu'awiya. Mu'awiya said to al-Miqdam: 'Al-Hasan has died.' Al-Miqdam said *inna lillah* — invoking Allah's name at the news.[73] Mu'awiya said: 'Do you consider it a calamity?' He said: 'And why not? The Messenger of Allah, may Allah's blessings and peace be upon him and his household, placed him in his lap and said: This one is from me, and al-Husayn is from 'Ali.' He said to the Asadi: 'What do you say?' He said: 'An ember that is extinguished.' Al-Miqdam said:[74] 'I adjure you by Allah — did

---

[73] In the narration of Abu Dawud, no. 4131, the wording is: "al-Miqdam returned it," meaning that al-Miqdam said, "Indeed we belong to Allah, and indeed to Him we return," out of grief.

[74] In the narration of Abu Dawud, no. 4131, the wording is: "As for me, I will not leave today until I anger you and make you hear what you dislike."

you hear the Messenger of Allah, may Allah's blessings and peace be upon him and his household, forbid wearing gold and silk, and using the skins of predatory animals and riding on them?' He said: 'Yes.' He said: 'By Allah, I have seen all of this in your house.' Mu'awiya said: 'I knew I would not escape you.'"[75] Its chain is strong. "And Mu'awiya is among the best of kings in whom justice outweighed injustice,[76] and he is not free of faults — may Allah pardon him." End of al-Dhahabi's words from *al-Siyar*. Reflect on the fanaticism and false defense alongside the acknowledgment of faults.

I say: this hadith is explicit in showing that Mu'awiya violated the commands of the Prophet, may Allah's blessings and peace be upon him and his household, as witnessed by the Companions in his way of life and that of those around him. And that he was extremely pleased at the killing and death of Sayyiduna al-Hasan, the master of the youth of Paradise.

Al-Ta'i then said there [p. 23]: "The conclusion of this Pearl is that refraining from what caused strife between the Companions, may Allah be pleased with them, is the doctrine of the people of truth from Ahl al-Sunna wa'l-Jama'a."

I say: the demolition of this false claim — and its attribution to Ahl al-Sunna wa'l-Jama'a as a doctrine — has already been presented.

Are not Jarir al-Dabbi, 'Abd al-Razzaq, al-Nasa'i, al-Hakim, and other scholars who censured Mu'awiya from Ahl al-Sunna wa'l-Jama'a?

---

[75] Abu Dawud, *Sunan*, no. 4131; al-Tabarani, *al-Mu'jam al-Kabir*, 20:269; and Ahmad ibn Hanbal, *al-Musnad*, 4:132, though Ahmad's narration stops before the part that exposes Mu'awiya's deviation. Baqiyya explicitly states that he heard the report in Ahmad's chain. Al-Albani authenticated the hadith in *Sahih Abi Dawud*, 2:778. Al-Nasa'i also narrated it in abridged form, no. 4255. The commentator on *Siyar A'lam al-Nubala'* also notes that Baqiyya explicitly stated hearing the report in another place.

[76] This is a claim for which there is no evidence. Rather, the evidence points to the opposite [that is, that he was among the worst of kings, and that his injustice far outweighed his justice].

The Testimony and Narrations of Individual Companions

Al-Ta'i then quoted al-Nawawi:[77] "The people of truth and those who count in consensus agreed on accepting the testimonies and narrations of the Companions who lived through the fitna, their complete uprightness, and that they are excused for what issued from them..."

I say: this is a rejected and incorrect idea — regardless of who holds it. It is like the idea that "the early scholars practised tafwid and the later scholars practised ta'wil" — which al-Nawawi, Ibn Hajar, and others also said. Upon investigation, the early scholars did in fact practise ta'wil — and the books of Quranic interpretation are filled with the ta'wilat of the Companions, the Successors, and others from the early generations on the verses of divine attributes and others. The *Tafsir* of Ibn Jarir al-Tabari is among the greatest proofs of this.

Returning to the matter of the Companions: al-Nawawi himself stated the opposite in *Sharh Sahih Muslim* (16/139), where he explicitly mentioned people counted among the Companions who were hypocrites, saying: "The Prophet did not kill the hypocrites because they outwardly professed Islam, and he was commanded to judge by outward appearance while Allah attends to what is inward — and because they were counted among his Companions and waged jihad with him, either out of tribal pride, or in pursuit of worldly gain, or out of solidarity with their clansmen."

This demolishes the words of Qasim al-Ta'i — and Allah is the One we seek for help.

In *Sahih Muslim* (1480), 'Umar ibn al-Khattab rejected the narration of Fatima bint Qays concerning maintenance and lodging, saying: "We will not abandon the Book of Allah and the Sunnah of our Prophet, may Allah's blessings and peace be upon

---

[77] Al-Nawawi, *Sharh Sahih Muslim*, 12:624. However, al-Nawawi later states something in the same work that contradicts this.

him and his household, for the words of a woman — we do not know whether she remembered or forgot."

And the claimed consensus on accepting their narrations is likewise refuted by al-Dhuhali's statement about the noble Companion 'Abd al-Rahman ibn 'Udayd al-Balawi: "It is not permissible to narrate anything from him — he is the head of the fitna."[78]

Hafiz Ibn Hajar said in *Tahdhib al-Tahdhib* (5/72): "Ibn al-Madini said: I asked Jarir: did Mughira dislike narrating from Abu al-Tufayl? He said: Yes." And Abu al-Tufayl is a noble Companion — the last of the Companions to die.

As for testimony — the Companion Abu Bakra's testimony was rejected from the time of 'Umar ibn al-Khattab, may Allah be pleased with him. Al-Dhahabi said in *Siyar A'lam al-Nubala'* (3/6): "The story of 'Umar is well known — his flogging of Abu Bakra, Nafi', and Shibl ibn Ma'bad for their testimony against al-Mughira for fornication. He then asked them to repent — two of them repented, and 'Umar accepted their testimony. But Abu Bakra refused to repent — and whenever someone came to have him as a witness, he would say: 'They have declared me depraved.'"

Al-Bukhari mentioned this in his *Sahih* (*Fath* 5/256) in the Book of Testimonies: "Chapter on the testimony of the one who falsely accused of fornication, the thief, and the fornicator... 'Umar flogged Abu Bakra, Shibl ibn Ma'bad, and Nafi' for accusing al-Mughira... then asked them to repent, and said: Whoever repents, I accept his testimony... And Abu al-Zinad said: the matter among us in Madinah is that when the one who falsely accused repents and seeks forgiveness from his Lord, his testimony is accepted."

Al-Dhahabi said in *Siyar A'lam al-Nubala'* (3/7-8): "'Umar flogged Abu Bakra, Nafi' ibn al-Harith, and Shibl. Two of them repented and 'Umar accepted their testimony. But Abu Bakra

---

[78] See al-Dhahabi, *Tarikh al-Islam*, 3:532.

refused and so 'Umar did not accept his testimony[79] — and he was the best of the three."

This shows that among the Companions there were those whose testimony was rejected by the agreement of the Companions during the era of Sayyiduna 'Umar, may Allah be pleased with him — and this refutes the claim of al-Ta'i that relied on al-Nawawi's statement.

Al-Shafi'i clarified in *al-Umm* (7/26) the rejection of Abu Bakra's testimony, saying: "A trustworthy person from the people of Madinah told me — from Ibn Shihab, from Ibn al-Musayyab: when 'Umar flogged the three, he asked them to repent. Two of them returned and he accepted their testimony. But Abu Bakra refused to return, and so he rejected his testimony."

The Claim That the Transgressing Faction Is Rewarded

Al-Ta'i then said [p. 23], transmitting from Ibn Hajar al-Haytami: "What took place between the Companions, may Allah's pleasure be upon them all, of fighting is confined to this world only — as for the Hereafter, they are all mujtahids who are rewarded."

I say: this is speaking about the unseen and making claims about Allah, Exalted be He, and passing judgment on matters of the Hereafter without proof. Furthermore this contradicts what is established in the Quran and the Sunnah — and what refutes it has already been presented. Among it is the statement of the noble Prophet, may Allah's blessings and peace be upon him and his household, that some of the Companions will be driven away from the Hawd because they changed and altered after him — and that he says of them as they are taken to the left — meaning

---

[79] See al-Shafi'i, *al-Umm*, 6:209; al-Bayhaqi, *al-Sunan al-Kubra*, 10:152; Ibn Hajar, *Tahdhib al-Tahdhib*, 10:418; al-Mizzi, *Tahdhib al-Kamal*, 30:7; and Ibn Hajar, *Talkhis al-Habir*, 4:207.

toward the Fire: "Away, away." And this is among the matters of the Hereafter — not of this world as al-Ta'i claims.

Hafiz Ibn Hajar said in *al-Fath* (11/385): "They are taken to the left — meaning toward the Fire. This was stated explicitly in the hadith of Abu Hurayra in the chapter on the description of the Fire, through the chain of 'Ata' ibn Yasar from him: 'Then a group came — until when I recognized them, a man emerged from between me and them and said: Come. I said: Where? He said: To the Fire.' And in the hadith of Anas the place was clarified... And in the hadith of Abu Hurayra in Muslim: 'Men will certainly be driven away from my Hawd as a stray camel is driven away — I call to them: Come here. A voice will say: Indeed they changed after you...'

Ibn Hajar said: the word 'away, away' means 'far, far away' — the repetition is for emphasis. And in the hadith of Abu Sa'id in the chapter on the description of the Fire: 'It will be said: You do not know what they introduced after you. I will say: Away, away with those who changed after me.' And there is an addition in the narration of 'Ata' ibn Yasar: 'So I see that none of them will escape except like stray camels.'

And Ahmad and al-Tabarani narrated from the hadith of Abu Bakra, raised to the Prophet: 'Men from among those who accompanied me and saw me will certainly come to me at the Hawd' — its chain is sound.

And al-Tabarani narrated from the hadith of Abu al-Darda' similarly, with the addition: 'I said: O Messenger of Allah, pray to Allah that He not make me among them. He said: You are not among them.' Its chain is sound." End of Ibn Hajar's words from *al-Fath* — reflect on it carefully.

Are these Companions who are driven away from the Hawd and taken toward the Fire rewarded and praised — and are these rulings of the Hereafter or of this world as al-Ta'i claims?

Al-Ta'i then cited on page 25 material about Mu'awiya's caliphate and Sayyiduna al-Hasan's relinquishment — repeating previous material whose refutation has already been presented. There is no need for repetition and prolonging the discussion over what holds no benefit. What matters is scholarly speech built upon evidence and following the truth — not transmitting the errors of this person and that without purpose.

CHAPTER 6: MU'AWIYA'S REVILING OF IMAM 'ALI

Al-Ta'i's Denial That Mu'awiya Cursed 'Ali

Al-Ta'i then devoted a special section on page 27 which he titled "The Ninth Pearl: Exonerating Mu'awiya from Cursing Sayyiduna 'Ali and the Prophet's Household." In it he committed a flagrant injustice and an unacceptably rejected arbitrariness and an aggression against knowledge with a fabrication colder than ice: "It is no secret that there is a difference between what historians do in writing history and what hadith masters do in writing hadith. The historians' practice is to transmit without scrutinizing the reports..."

He wishes, through such phrases in which he deliberately blinds himself from the truth, to create in some readers who trust his words — built on ignorance and fabrication — the impression that the hadith masters did not transmit and authenticate the hadiths showing that Mu'awiya used to curse Sayyiduna 'Ali, the cousin of the beloved and chosen one, may Allah's blessings and peace be upon him and his household. Even though that is established in the authenticated collections. For in *Sahih Muslim* (2404) from 'Amir ibn Sa'd ibn Abi Waqqas, from his father:

"Mu'awiya ibn Abi Sufyan commanded Sa'd and said: 'What prevents you from cursing Abu Turab?' He said: 'As for the three things I recall that the Messenger of Allah, may Allah's blessings and peace be upon him and his household, said to him — I will never curse him...'"

And Muslim is not from among the ignorant historians — he is from the precise hadith masters and hafizes.

Ibn Maja narrated (121) with a sound chain[80] from Sa'd ibn Abi Waqqas: "Mu'awiya came on one of his pilgrimage visits. Sa'd visited him, and they mentioned 'Ali. Mu'awiya cursed and reviled him.[81] Sa'd became angry and said: 'You say this about a man of whom I heard the Messenger of Allah, may Allah's blessings and peace be upon him and his household, say: "Whoever I am his master, 'Ali is his master"; and I heard him say: "You are to me as Harun was to Musa, except that there is no prophet after me"; and I heard him say: "I will give the banner today to a man who loves Allah and His Messenger."'"

Is this, O people, the statement of the lying historians as Qasim al-Ta'i claims?

Al-Ta'i's Treatment of Prophetic Reports Against Mu'awiya

He then said there: "This is the way of our scholars[82] from Ahl al-Sunna wa'l-Jama'a — the people of truth. They do not accept any narration that attacks the person of Mu'awiya — even if its chain is sound — because it contradicts Allah's endorsement of them in His Book and His Messenger's endorsement in his purified Sunnah."

I say: this is a manifest deception. Note that he has readiness to declare false the sound hadiths supported by Quranic verses that concern Mu'awiya — as if Mu'awiya were the unambiguous Quranic verses themselves. And we ask Allah, Exalted be He, that he not have readiness to reject the verses that inform of the deviation of a group of Companions from obedience to Allah and His Messenger.

Allah, Exalted be He, said: {"Have you not seen those who make allies of a people with whom Allah has become angry? They are

---

[80] Al-Albani authenticated it in *Sahih Ibn Maja*, 1:26.

[81] That is, he cursed and abused him.

[82] The author's footnote notes that, in Arabic, al-Ta'i wrote the expression for "our scholars" incorrectly.

neither from you nor from them — and they swear to falsehood knowingly."} [al-Mujadala: 14]

We have already refuted this speech and these ideas in what preceded. To summarize: the Noble Quran explicitly stated that groups among those who accompanied the Prophet from the Bedouins and the people of Madinah were entrenched in hypocrisy: {"And among those around you of the Bedouins are hypocrites, and among the people of Madinah there are those entrenched in hypocrisy — you do not know them, but We know them. We will punish them twice, then they will be returned to great punishment."} [al-Tawba: 101] And His words: {"If a depraved person brings you news, verify it"} — and that was al-Walid ibn 'Uqba. And the verses revealed about the hypocrites, the troublemakers, the liars, and those who when they saw trade or entertainment broke away and left the Prophet standing on Friday delivering the sermon from the pulpit. And those who built the Mosque of Harm to cause harm and division among the Muslims. And the hadiths of the two Sahihs about the transgressing faction that calls to the Fire, and those driven away from the Hawd, and the hadith that announces to the one who hates Sayyiduna 'Ali, may Allah be pleased with him, that he is a hypocrite, and the hadith that among his Companions are twelve hypocrites eight of whom will not enter Paradise. And by the import of these verses and authenticated hadiths, the imams and leading scholars of Ahl al-Sunna spoke — such as Jarir al-Dabbi, al-Fadl ibn Dukayn, al-Nahdi, 'Abd al-Razzaq the author of *al-Musannaf*, al-Nasa'i the author of the *Sunan*, al-Hakim the author of *al-Mustadrak*, and many, many others.

All of that demolishes the ideas and words of al-Ta'i and his ilk and renders them fragments — words devoid of soundness and among the empty compositions.

The Claim That Reports of Mu'awiya Cursing 'Ali Are Lies

From all of this the invalidity of al-Ta'i's statement there is also clear: "Know that there is no report mentioned in history saying that Mu'awiya cursed Imam 'Ali and his sons and family from the pulpit and elsewhere — except that it is a fabricated lie. For either in its chain there is a liar or one suspected of lying, or its narrators are unknown, or there is something else — and it is not free of a defect in its narrators that necessitates rejection."

I say: it has become clear that those hadiths are in the two Sahihs or one of them, and in the reliable hadith collections with clean chains — free of liars, fabricators, suspected persons, and unknowns. With that, our companion's words are among the words that have no grammatical basis whatsoever.

The story of Mu'awiya upon al-Miqdam ibn Ma'di Karib's informing him of the death of Sayyiduna al-Hasan, may Allah's peace be upon him — and what that person said in Mu'awiya's presence about the master of the youth of Paradise and one of the two sweet basils of the Prophet of this community — that he was "an ember that Allah extinguished" — is the greatest proof of the corruption of what al-Ta'i and those like him claim and the corruption of his ideas.

The Fabricated Story That Mu'awiya Loved 'Ali

Al-Ta'i then added on page 28, completing his false and rejected ideas — relying on false and fabricated historical narrations. For he permits himself, in constructing the merits and virtues of Mu'awiya, to rely on fabricated and weak historical stories — yet prohibits to others what contradicts his views and rejects it even if its chain is sound and it is established in the two Sahihs. He said:

"What indicates complete love between Sayyiduna 'Ali and Mu'awiya... is that Ibn al-Jawzi transmitted, from Abu Salih, who said: Mu'awiya said to Dirar: 'Describe 'Ali to me'... Mu'awiya's tears flowed... then he said: 'May Allah have mercy on Abu al-Hasan.'"

I say: the astonishing thing is that this man argues with fabrications and invented stories while turning away from the texts of the Quran and the authenticated Sunnah. Beyond this being among the laughable fabrications — for one who loves someone does not curse and revile his beloved, as Mu'awiya was established to have done in the authenticated collections as already presented. Nor does one who loves someone kill those who object to the cursing and reviling of the beloved — as he did with Sayyiduna Hujr ibn 'Adi — this is pure lies.

The chain of this story from Ibn al-Jawzi's *Safwat al-Safwa* (1/316) has already been exposed and its fabricated nature demonstrated at the beginning of this book in the commentary on page 3 of his book. Refer back to it there.

Through such chains and fabrications are Mu'awiya's virtues and his love for Sayyiduna 'Ali, may Allah be pleased with him, completed and transmitted according to Qasim al-Ta'i — who says: "I have only transmitted from the books of history what was authenticated in its chain by the hadith scholars."[83] Which hadith scholar authenticated this?

Al-Ta'i then devoted a section on page 29 in which he wronged the truth — just as he wronged himself — attempting to establish that "transgression" does not mean injustice and sin. For the sake of the tyrant Mu'awiya, he wants to overturn transgression and make it justice and excellence. This is the clear deception, the repugnant fanaticism, the destructive stubbornness, and the manifest misguidance.

The Meaning of Transgression

Al-Ta'i says there [p. 29]: "The Tenth Pearl: Clarifying the Meaning of Transgressors. It may come to a Muslim's mind when he hears that Mu'awiya and his army are transgressors that they are sinners and wrongdoers... And this understanding is an error, because it confuses and fails to distinguish between the linguistic meaning of transgressors and the legal meaning. For the word al-baghi and al-baghiya in the language means the

---

[83] The author's footnote points out that this sentence reflects weakness in al-Ta'i's Arabic expression.

fornicator and the adulteress, or the wicked man and wicked woman, and other meanings."

I say: it is sufficient for the reader to smell the deception, injustice, and stubbornness with falsehood from these words. And it is sufficient to demolish this claim that the author of *al-Qamus* says: "And bagha 'alayhi yabghi baghy-an — he rose above and wronged."

Al-Zabidi said in *Sharh al-Qamus* (10/39): "Al-Azhari said: the meaning of baghy is seeking corruption. So-and-so yabghi 'ala al-nas — when he wrongs them and seeks to harm them... And the Shaykh said: and bagha means he wronged — baghy-an with fath — and it is what appears in the Quran. And al-Lihyani said: bagha 'ala akhihi baghy-an — he envied him. He said: and baghy in origin means envy, then injustice was called baghy because the envier wrongs the envied to the best of his ability."

These are explicit words showing that the meaning of baghy in the language is injustice. And injustice is a type of sin without any doubt — contrary to what our "linguist" companion claims.

Al-Ta'i then said [p. 29]: "In other words, this word in its original linguistic meaning indicates censure — but the legal meaning is not so. For the word al-baghi or al-bughat in legal meaning means rebellion against the just authority."

I say: look, O people, how he deceives openly and claims that baghy in the Quran has nothing to do with injustice and sin. His words are demolished from their foundation and refuted by the Book of Allah, Exalted be He, which says: {"That is how We recompensed them for their baghy."} [al-An'am: 146] — al-Qurtubi and others said: meaning for their injustice. And Allah said: {"And Pharaoh and his soldiers pursued them baghy-an wa 'udwa."} — al-Qurtubi said: meaning transgression, aggression, and injustice.

And all of this injustice, aggression, and transgression — the fanatics want to make it a virtue for Mu'awiya. And thus the Shari'a and linguistic standards are turned upside down.

Attempts to Reinterpret Prophetic Censures of Mu'awiya

Our companion [al-Ta'i] then began the section he devoted to responding to this humble servant's commentary on Mu'awiya in the notes to *Daf' Shubah al-Tashbih* by Imam Ibn al-Jawzi, may Allah have mercy on him, saying [p. 30]:

"Some sound narrations have been transmitted which, upon first reading or hearing, give the impression that they censure Mu'awiya. And some historical reports have been transmitted that convey what is unbecoming of a Muslim — let alone one of the rank of Companion.[84] And if we were to leave the Muslim to understand as he pleases without referring to the learned imams, and without returning to the rules of the Shari'a and the Arabic language,[85] chaos would result and the balance of every Muslim would be disturbed — indeed the words of the truthful and believed one would be fulfilled among us: 'that the later generations of this community will revile the earlier ones.'"

I say: this hadith he cited is a fabricated lie. Al-Dhahabi said in *al-Mizan*: "Al-Barqani said: I asked al-Daraqutni about his hadith from Yahya, from Muhammad ibn 'Ali, from 'Ali: 'When my community does fifteen things...' — he said: it is false." Al-Tirmidhi narrated the hadith through two chains in his *Sunan* (2210 and 2211) — from the hadith of Sayyiduna 'Ali and Abu Hurayra — and each of the two chains contains an unknown narrator. So the hadith is not from the words of the truthful and believed one, may Allah's blessings and peace be upon him and his household, as Qasim al-Ta'i claims — but is from the fabrications of the scheming liars against the truthful and believed one, may Allah's blessings and peace be upon him and his household.

---

[84] Al-Ta'i's wording treats the Companions almost as if they were infallible prophets, even though they are human beings like others: they do good and they may also do wrong. Through his fanaticism, al-Ta'i has effectively raised them to the rank of the prophets, may Allah bless them and grant them peace.

[85] How astonishing, for someone to alter the Arabic and legal meaning of transgression, and then claim that he is returning to Arabic and the Shari'a.

Ibn Hibban narrated this in *al-Majruhin* (2/207) in the biographical entry of Faraj ibn Fadala, saying: "Faraj ibn Fadala al-Shami — his kunya is Abu Fadala, from the people of Homs — narrates from Yahya ibn Sa'id al-Ansari. The Iraqis and the people of his town narrated from him. He was one who reversed chains of transmission and attached weak texts to sound chains. It is not permissible to use him as proof." Ibn Hibban cited this hadith of his among his objectionable narrations.

Upon such falsehoods does Qasim al-Ta'i build his ideas and raise objections against us.

Furthermore, our companion left aside many things I had mentioned there and cited a small portion of it — then pretended he had established its falsity and invalidity. Through this he creates the impression in people that he has refuted me — while I had cited things established in *Sahih Muslim* which he was unable to present or deny, but rather turned a blind eye to them and ignored them.

Al-Ta'i cited on page 30 what I had quoted from *Siyar A'lam al-Nubala'* (5/147) from Ibn Sa'd's *al-Tabaqat*: "The governors from Banu Umayya before 'Umar ibn 'Abd al-'Aziz used to curse a man with whom Allah was pleased..." Al-Ta'i then commented [p. 30-31]: "Let us now examine Lut ibn Yahya — Abu Mikhnaf. The Hafiz al-Dhahabi said in *Mizan al-I'tidal*: 'Lut ibn Yahya — Abu Mikhnaf — is a chronicler who is worthless, not reliable. Abu Hatim and others abandoned him. Ibn Ma'in said: he is not trustworthy. And on another occasion: he is nothing.' The chain thus collapses because of this narrator. This is the state of our writer's preserved material — fabricated reports and weak chains — transmitting nothing but sin in conveying lies and inviting people to harbor ill opinion of this Companion and others."

I say: this is an invalid statement on several grounds.

First: Abu Mikhnaf is trustworthy — like Imam Abu Hanifa, may Allah have mercy on him, whom the hadith critics weakened.[86] In the footnote are the statements of nineteen imams — all of whose statements about him are rejected, refused, and invalid in our view. And you need to be a mujtahid in the evaluation of men before you can determine whether a man is trustworthy or not.

Abu Mikhnaf Lut ibn Yahya was only attacked because he transmitted reports about Mu'awiya and was from the partisans of Sayyiduna 'Ali, may Allah be pleased with him. Ibn 'Adi said in *al-Kamil* (6/93): "He transmitted reports about the early righteous predecessors and it is not unlikely that he would address them critically — he is a fervent Shi'i and a transmitter of their news."

---

[86] They are: Ibn Abi Hatim in *al-Jarh wa'l-Ta'dil* (8:450), where he said: "Abu Hanifa was mentioned in the presence of Ahmad ibn Hanbal, and he said: His opinion is blameworthy, and his body is not to be mentioned... Ibn al-Mubarak abandoned him later on. Ibn al-Mubarak said: Abu Hanifa was poor in hadith... Muhammad ibn Jabir al-Yamami said: Abu Hanifa stole the books of Hammad from me..." I have transmitted these from there briefly and not in order. Criticism of him was also transmitted there from Sufyan al-Thawri and Yahya ibn Sa'id; al-Bukhari in *al-Tarikh* (8:81), who said: "He was a Murji'i. They remained silent about his opinion and his hadith"; Muslim in *al-Kuna wa'l-Asma'*, who said: "Unstable in hadith. He does not have much sound hadith"; al-Nasa'i in *al-Du'afa' wa'l-Matrukin*, p. 57, who said: "He is not strong in hadith, and he makes many mistakes despite narrating little"; Ibn Sa'd in *al-Tabaqat* (6:256), who said: "He was weak in hadith"; al-'Uqayli in *al-Du'afa'* (4:284); Ibn 'Adi in *al-Kamil fi'l-Du'afa'* (7:12), among whose words there are: "because he is not from the people of hadith"; Ibn Hibban in *al-Majruhin* (3:63), where he said: "When his errors outweighed his correct narrations, he deserved to be abandoned as proof in reports. From another angle, it is not permissible to use him as proof because he was a caller to irja', and one who calls to innovations may not be used as proof. Moreover, all our imams collectively, as far as I know, have no disagreement among them that the imams of the Muslims and the people of religious scrupulousness in all lands and regions criticized him and openly impugned him, except one individual after another. We have mentioned what has been narrated concerning this in *al-Tanbih 'ala al-Tamwih*, so there is no need to repeat it"; al-Daraqutni weakened him in his *Sunan* (1:323); al-Hakim in *Ma'rifat 'Ulum al-Hadith*, p. 256; al-Hafiz 'Abd al-Haqq al-Ishbili in *al-Ahkam* (fol. 17b); Ibn al-Jawzi in *al-Du'afa' wa'l-Matrukin* (3:163); and al-Dhahabi in *Diwan al-Du'afa'*, where he transmitted from Ibn Ma'in that he said: "His hadith is not written." These are nineteen men from the imams of this discipline who attacked Imam Abu Hanifa, may Allah have mercy on him. We reject their words altogether and in detail.

This is the reason they attacked him. And one indication of his trustworthiness is that he was not influenced by the political atmosphere of his era and the preferences of the hadith masters influenced by that atmosphere — for he transmitted what contradicted them.

Second: What Abu Mikhnaf said here is correct and beyond reproach. And it is confirmed by what I cited immediately after it — which attests to its soundness. This is what Muslim narrated in *al-Sahih* (2409) from the noble Companion Sahl ibn Sa'd: "A man from the family of Marwan was appointed over Madinah. He summoned Sahl ibn Sa'd and ordered him to curse 'Ali. Sahl refused. The man said: 'If you refuse, then at least say: May Allah curse Abu Turab.' Sahl said: 'No name was dearer to 'Ali than Abu Turab and he used to rejoice when called by it.'"

Muslim narrated in *al-Sahih* (2404) from 'Amir ibn Sa'd ibn Abi Waqqas, from his father: "Mu'awiya ibn Abi Sufyan commanded Sa'd and said: 'What prevents you from cursing Abu Turab?' He said: 'As for the three things I recall that the Messenger of Allah, may Allah's blessings and peace be upon him and his household, said to him — I will never curse him...'"

Ibn Maja narrated (121) with a sound chain[87] from Sa'd ibn Abi Waqqas: "Mu'awiya came on one of his pilgrimage visits. Sa'd visited him, and they mentioned 'Ali. Mu'awiya cursed and reviled him.[88] Sa'd became angry and said: 'You say this about a man of whom I heard the Messenger of Allah, may Allah's blessings and peace be upon him and his household, say: "Whoever I am his master, 'Ali is his master..."'"

All of these sound and established reports confirm the soundness of Abu Mikhnaf Lut ibn Yahya's statement — that the Umayyad governors and their leader Mu'awiya, who established the practice of cursing and abusing Sayyiduna 'Ali for them, were indeed as described. What Qasim al-Ta'i attempted to

---

[87] This was authenticated by al-Albani, the contradictory figure of our age, in *Sahih Ibn Maja*, 1:26.

[88] That is, he cursed and abused him.

argue amounts to nothing and does not advance the question of the established matter in any way — for it is established, indeed mass-transmitted, about Mu'awiya, his governors, and those who came after them.

Al-Ta'i's failure to mention what I cited immediately after the narration of Lut ibn Yahya is a disgraceful act of deception — and misleading the reader from the truth out of fanaticism for the tyrant Mu'awiya.

The Claim That All Faults of Mu'awiya Are Fabricated

O Qasim — after what I have established from the authenticated collections — is it right for you to say about me: "This is the state of our writer's preserved material — fabricated reports and weak chains — transmitting nothing but sin in conveying lies..." and the rest of that reprehensible nonsense?

May Allah grant you well-being and guide you.

Mu'awiya's Killing of Hujr ibn 'Adi

Al-Ta'i then mentioned on page 31 what I had cited about Mu'awiya's killing of the noble Companion Sayyiduna Hujr ibn 'Adi, may Allah be pleased with him. He claimed this was among the fabricated reports — like what preceded it — while then contradicting himself on the following page, acknowledging its establishment against Mu'awiya and claiming he has reward for killing Hujr. He said:

"Then he said: and this is a well-known matter. Ibn Hajar said in *al-Isaba* in his biographical entry: he was killed at Marj 'Adhra' on Mu'awiya's orders. He also transmitted that Mu'awiya killed righteous people, relying on historical reports such as the previously mentioned fabricated report..."

He then contradicted himself on the next page [p. 32]: "Whatever the case, his killing was from a jurist mujtahid who erred in his ijtihad — there is no blame on Sayyiduna Mu'awiya legally, by the consensus of Ahl al-Sunna wa'l-Jama'a. So why does this writer blame him? We ask Allah for propriety in religion and worldly matters. As for the Hafiz's transmission of Hujr's killing — it is sound, and this killing was mentioned previously, so take note."

And here Qasim has reached the degree of madness and stubbornness to the furthest limits of falsehood — for he permitted Mu'awiya, whom he described as the jurist mujtahid — which he is not, as established — to kill the Companions and the innocent. And that he is rewarded for doing so.

And that there is no blame upon the jurist mujtahid if he kills the innocent believers merely because they refused to comply with his command to curse and revile and disavow Sayyiduna 'Ali.

And that we are obligated to show propriety toward the killer of Companions and the righteous. Such is shamelessness in its broadest form.

Al-Ta'i summarized what he wanted to respond and object with on this point [p. 31]: "I respond to all of these matters seeking Allah's help and say: as for the claim that Mu'awiya killed Hujr — there is something to consider here, because most of the reports that transmitted the killing of Hujr came through Abu Mikhnaf Lut ibn Yahya, who is discredited and not accepted as proof."

I say: woe upon this stubborn debater with falsehood, this fanatic defending the enemies of the household of the Messenger of Allah, may Allah's blessings and peace be upon him and his household.

He lied in what he claimed and said. And whoever looks in the hadith and biographical works compiled by the hadith masters — such as al-Hakim's *Mustadrak* (3/468-470) — will find many reports and established sound chains mentioning that Mu'awiya was the one who killed Hujr ibn 'Adi. And in none of them is Abu Mikhnaf the trustworthy mentioned except in one chain.

How then does al-Ta'i say: most of them come from Abu Mikhnaf?

In *Mustadrak al-Hakim* (3/117): "Chapter on the Merits of Hujr ibn 'Adi, may Allah be pleased with him — the monk of the Companions of Muhammad, may Allah's blessings and peace be upon him and his household — and the account of his killing... Abu Bakr Muhammad ibn Balawayh told us — Ibrahim al-Harbi told us — Mus'ab ibn 'Abd Allah al-Zubayri told us: Hujr ibn 'Adi al-Kindi, his kunya is Abu 'Abd al-Rahman — he had visited the Prophet, may Allah's blessings and peace be upon him and his household, witnessed al-Qadisiyya, the Battle of the Camel, and Siffin alongside 'Ali, may Allah be pleased with him — Mu'awiya ibn Abi Sufyan killed him at Marj 'Adhra'. He had two sons — 'Abd Allah and 'Abd al-Rahman — whom Mus'ab ibn al-Zubayr killed in cold blood. Hujr was killed in the year fifty-three." And all the narrators are trustworthy.

Ibn Abi Shayba narrated (6/446): "'Isa ibn Yunus[89] told us — from al-Awza'i — from Hisham ibn Hassan[90] who said: Muhammad — meaning Ibn Sirin — when asked about whether a martyr should be washed, would narrate about Hujr ibn 'Adi when Mu'awiya killed him. He said: 'Hujr said: do not remove my iron chains and do not wash the blood from me — bury me in my bonds and my blood. I will meet Mu'awiya on the path tomorrow.'"

And none of these reports contain a narration from Abu Mikhnaf — and by this what al-Ta'i says collapses.

The Claim That Killing Hujr Was Rewarded Ijtihad

Al-Ta'i then said after that: "Assuming this is conceded — Mu'awiya is a mujtahid who erred, and his killing of Hujr was based on the fact that he was from the army of Imam 'Ali and his followers and those who loved him."

---

[89] Trustworthy and reliable, among the narrators of the Six Collections. His biographical entry is in al-Mizzi, *Tahdhib al-Kamal*, 23:62.

[90] Trustworthy, among the narrators of the Six Collections. His biographical entry is in al-Mizzi, *Tahdhib al-Kamal*, 30:181.

I say: first — how can ijtihad be accepted in the face of an explicit clear text that Mu'awiya knew — namely the Prophet's statement, may Allah's blessings and peace be upon him and his household: "The killer of 'Ammar and his despoiler are in the Fire,"[91] and his statement: "Ammar will be killed by the transgressing faction — he calls them to Paradise and they call him to the Fire"?[92]

Is ijtihad permissible where an explicit text exists?

Perhaps Qasim al-Ta'i has other rules unknown in the books of legal theory and in Islamic law.

What we believe is that Mu'awiya was not a mujtahid — rather ijtihad in his case was forbidden because he was not qualified for it. And despite this his ijtihad was against the explicit texts, alongside rebellion against the rightly-guided Imam — with the statement of the greatest Messenger, may Allah's blessings and peace be upon him and his household: "If allegiance is pledged to two caliphs, kill the second of them" — narrated by Muslim (1853).

Second: When Mu'awiya killed Hujr ibn 'Adi, Hujr was not at that time in the army of Sayyiduna 'Ali, may Allah be pleased with him. Rather, this was approximately twelve years after the caliphate of Sayyiduna 'Ali, may Allah be pleased with him, and his martyrdom.

Al-Ta'i's statement — "his killing of Hujr was based on the fact that he was from the army of Imam 'Ali and his followers and those who loved him" — is invalid on multiple grounds, among them what we mentioned. And among them: that by this logic it would be permissible for Mu'awiya to kill Companions and the excellent ones of the Successors after Sayyiduna 'Ali, simply

---

[91] Narrated by Ahmad, *al-Musnad*, 4:198; Ibn Sa'd, *al-Tabaqat*, 3:186; al-Tabarani, *al-Mu'jam al-Awsat*, 9:103; and al-Hakim, *al-Mustadrak*, 3:386-387, through numerous chains. It is sound, and the contradictory figure of our age authenticated it, as previously mentioned.

[92] Narrated by al-Bukhari, *Sahih*, no. 447, as previously mentioned.

because they had been with him and stood with him supporting the truth — and this invalidity is obvious to any rational person.

The Report "My Slain and Mu'awiya's Slain Are in Paradise"

Al-Ta'i then said [p. 31]: "And Hujr is in Paradise and Mu'awiya bears no sin — by the statement of Imam 'Ali as transmitted by al-Tabarani: 'My slain and Mu'awiya's slain are in Paradise.'"

I say: this statement you attribute to Sayyiduna 'Ali — "my slain and Mu'awiya's slain are in Paradise" — is a fabricated lie, as we demonstrated previously. In its chain is a liar, weak narrators, and a gap.[93]

Ideas built on a crumbling bank.

And from where do you know that Hujr ibn 'Adi, may Allah be pleased with him, is in Paradise — when just three lines later you cast doubt on his companionship? He was an opponent and enemy of "the noble Companion" — in your view — Mu'awiya.

And has any explicit text come stating that he is among those given glad tidings of Paradise?[94]

The Claim That Kinship and Companionship Erase Sins

Al-Ta'i then said [p. 31]: "And even if we concede Mu'awiya's sin — his companionship and family connection to the Messenger of Allah are sufficient to be an expiation, purification, and repentance."

I say: this stubborn deceiver continues his string of errors and sins in defending tyrants. After all this, he acknowledged Mu'awiya's sin through a circuitous route — then claimed that companionship and family connection expiate sins. This is a

---

[93] See the commentary on p. 18 of al-Ta'i's book.

[94] We believe that he is a noble Companion, that he is among the people of Paradise, and that he is a martyr of truth. But what we believe has nothing to do with al-Ta'i and is not evidence for him.

rejected and invalid statement — explicitly contradicted by sound reason and authenticated transmitted texts.

As for family connection — Huyayy ibn Akhtab the Jew was the father-in-law of the Messenger of Allah, may Allah's blessings and peace be upon him and his household, since his daughter Sayyida Safiyya, may Allah be pleased with her, was the Prophet's wife. Yet that benefited him nothing.

And the Coptic Egyptians — the kinsmen of Sayyida Mariya al-Qibtiyya, the Mother of the Believers, may Allah be pleased with her — would that make them uncles of the believers?

No sound text has come establishing that in-laws — even if they committed ruinous and destructive deeds — are thereby purified of sins and transgressions. The Prophet, may Allah's blessings and peace be upon him and his household, said in the authenticated hadith: "O sons of 'Abd Manaf — I cannot avail you anything against Allah. O 'Abbas ibn 'Abd al-Muttalib — I cannot avail you anything against Allah. O Safiyya, aunt of the Messenger of Allah — I cannot avail you anything against Allah. O Fatima, daughter of Muhammad — ask me what you will of my wealth, I cannot avail you anything against Allah." Narrated by al-Bukhari (4771) and Muslim (206) and others.

From these texts it becomes clear that our companion is babbling nonsense.

As for companionship — the disbelievers too are counted among his companions. Allah, Exalted be He, said: {"Your companion has not gone astray nor is he deluded."} [al-Najm: 2] {"And your companion is not mad."} [al-Takwir: 22] {"When he said to his companion: do not grieve."} [al-Tawba: 40] And Allah, Exalted be He, said: {"Say: everyone is waiting — so wait. You will soon know who are the companions of the straight path and who is rightly guided."} [Ta Ha: 135]

Then Allah expressed it with: {"Muhammad is the Messenger of Allah, and those with him..."} — because among his companions are those who are with him and those who are not with him. So take note.

Among his companions are those who apostatized and disbelieved and died upon that — as Hafiz Ibn Hajar mentioned some of them in the introduction to *al-Isaba*.

The Messenger of Allah, may Allah's blessings and peace be upon him and his household, made this clear when he said: "Among my Companions are twelve hypocrites, eight of whom will not enter Paradise..." — narrated by Muslim (2779). And the hadith of the two Sahihs about the Hawd: "Men from among my Companions will come to me at the Hawd and will be driven away from it. I will say: O Lord, my Companions! He will say: You have no knowledge of what they introduced after you — they turned back on their heels and apostatized."[95]

And al-Nawawi[96] said that there was a group of hypocrites counted among the companions of the Prophet, may Allah's blessings and peace be upon him and his household.

The Companionship of Hujr ibn 'Adi

Al-Ta'i then said [p. 31]: "As for the companionship of Hujr — it is disputed. The investigators, such as Imam al-Bukhari, Ibn Abi Hatim, Ibn Sa'd, Ibn Hibban, and Khalifa ibn Khayyat, mentioned him among the Successors — indeed Ibn Sa'd mentioned him in the first generation of the people of Kufa. And a group of scholars held that his companionship is established, as in *al-Isaba* by Hafiz Ibn Hajar, may Allah have mercy on him."

I say: attempts to cast doubt on the companionship of Sayyiduna Hujr ibn 'Adi will benefit Qasim al-Ta'i nothing. Those who mentioned him among the Successors wanted to lighten the burden on Mu'awiya by removing one Companion from the list of those he killed. Otherwise, Mu'awiya's killing of Companions is established, widely known, and famous.

---

[95] Narrated by al-Bukhari, *Sahih*, no. 6585. See also the commentary on p. 3, where the narrations of this hadith are discussed in greater detail.

[96] As previously mentioned, it appears in al-Nawawi, *Sharh Sahih Muslim*, 16:139.

Even assuming hypothetically that Sayyiduna Hujr ibn 'Adi, may Allah be pleased with him, was not a Companion — the cold-blooded killing of a believer because he objected to the cursing and reviling of Sayyiduna 'Ali, may Allah be pleased with him, is one of the major sins that doom their perpetrator to the Fire forever, as stated in the Noble Quran. Allah, Exalted be He, said: {"And whoever kills a believer intentionally — his recompense is Hell, abiding therein. And Allah has become angry with him and has cursed him and has prepared for him a great punishment."} [al-Nisa': 93]

But Qasim al-Ta'i exempts Mu'awiya from this verse — so even if he killed, transgressed, and rebelled against the rightly-guided Imam, he is in al-Ta'i's mistaken view a benefactor who will be rewarded for this beneficence of killing Companions and the righteous. And thus realities and standards are turned upside down.

Furthermore, his claim that "the investigators denied the companionship of Sayyiduna Hujr ibn 'Adi" is not accurate. The source of al-Ta'i's words here is his transmission from Ibn Hajar's *al-Isaba* — for Hafiz Ibn Hajar said there, commenting on Ibn Sa'd: "As for al-Bukhari, Ibn Abi Hatim from his father, Khalifa ibn Khayyat, and Ibn Hibban — they mentioned him among the Successors. And likewise Ibn Sa'd mentioned him in the first generation of the people of Kufa — either because he mistook him for another, or because he was distracted."

Al-Ta'i assumed from this that these scholars explicitly stated he was not a Companion — which is not the case. Moreover he engaged in deception by cutting off from Ibn Hajar's words "or because he was distracted" — so that his purpose would be fulfilled.

Ibn Sa'd mentioned him among the Companions — see *al-Tabaqat* (6/217). Al-Bukhari and Ibn Abi Hatim did not deny his companionship and did not say anything of this kind — as is found by whoever refers to *al-Tarikh* by al-Bukhari (3/72) and *al-Jarh wa'l-Ta'dil* (3/266). Ibn Hibban said in *al-Thiqat* (4/176): "Hujr ibn 'Adi al-Kindi — narrates from 'Ali and

'Ammar — and it has been said that he had companionship." Ibn Hibban did not deny his companionship as al-Ta'i claimed.

And how many errors and mistakes have occurred in such matters — where scholars mentioned a Companion among the Companions and in the same book mentioned him among the Successors. For Hafiz Ibn Hajar said in *Ta'jil al-Manfa'a* (p. 509): "Ibn Hibban said in the Companions: Yassar ibn Sab' Abu al-Ghaddiya al-Juhani — he had companionship. And he said in the third generation, which are the Successors of the Successors: Yassar ibn Sab' Abu al-Ghaddiya al-Muzani — he transmits mursal narrations. I have not seen this from anyone else — rather the words of most of them indicate that he is one person and the difference is whether he is Juhani or Muzani."

Hafiz Ibn Hajar said in *al-Isaba* (1/314): "Ibn Sa'd and Mus'ab al-Zubayri — as al-Hakim transmitted from him — stated that he visited the Prophet, may Allah's blessings and peace be upon him and his household, together with his brother Hani' ibn 'Adi, and that Hujr ibn 'Adi witnessed al-Qadisiyya..."

So our companion's efforts are scattered to the winds.

Know that those people — headed by some hadith masters and hafizes from the early generations — when they saw a criminal, blood-shedding killer Companion, and likewise a wronged Companion killed by Mu'awiya, attempted to deny his companionship or cast doubt on it — lest it reflect on Mu'awiya with grave harm and shatter their rule contrary to the Quran and the Sunnah about the infallibility of the Companions — especially Mu'awiya's infallibility.

Al-Dhahabi said in *Siyar A'lam al-Nubala'* (3/463): "Hujr ibn 'Adi... Abu 'Abd al-Rahman — the martyr — he had companionship and had visited the Prophet." Reflect on this.

His subsequent words [p. 32]: "If the disagreement over his companionship is established, scholarly integrity requires expressing it in a way that acknowledges the disagreement — not asserting his companionship definitively."

I say: you do not understand scholarly integrity enough to say what you say — because fanaticism has blinded you from grasping the truth. Otherwise, the leading verifying hafizes — such as al-Dhahabi and Ibn Hajar and others — definitively established his companionship and had no hesitation about it. Do you say they did not maintain scholarly integrity?

Among that is the statement of Ibn Kathir in *al-Bidaya wa'l-Nihaya* (8/50): "Ibn 'Asakir said: he visited the Prophet, may Allah's blessings and peace be upon him and his household, and heard 'Ali and 'Ammar... And Ibn Sa'd mentioned him in the fourth generation of the Companions and recorded his visit."[97]

So our companion's efforts are scattered to the winds.

Minimizing the Crime of Killing a Muslim

Al-Ta'i says [p. 32]: "Whatever the case, his killing was from a jurist mujtahid who erred in his ijtihad — there is no blame on Sayyiduna Mu'awiya legally, by the consensus of Ahl al-Sunna wa'l-Jama'a."

The refutation of this delirium and this fabricated consensus has already been presented. Otherwise, if there were a consensus, the greatest Messenger, may Allah's blessings and peace be upon him and his household, would not have censured him in the hadiths that came in his censure — nor would Sayyiduna 'Ali, may Allah be pleased with him, nor the hadith imams such as Jarir al-Dabbi, al-Nahdi, 'Abd al-Razzaq, al-Nasa'i, al-Hakim, and others from the scholars who used to censure Mu'awiya and criticize him for his ugly deeds.

His statement "there is no blame upon Mu'awiya" reminded me of the statement of al-'Ijli about 'Umar ibn Sa'd ibn Abi Waqqas:

---

[97] Ibn Kathir then mentioned from Abu Ahmad al-'Askari that most hadith scholars do not authenticate his companionship. This is a clear and rejected error upon which the verifying scholars did not rely. Where are these hadith masters who did not authenticate his companionship? This is false speech to which no attention should be paid. Who are these "most hadith scholars"?

"He is a trustworthy Successor — and he is the one who killed al-Husayn."[98]

Ibn Ma'in said: "How can the one who killed al-Husayn be trustworthy?"[99]

I say: how can the killer of Sayyiduna al-Husayn — the Muslim, the noble Companion, the master of the youth of Paradise, one of the two sweet basils of the Prophet of this community, and the grandson of the Messenger of Allah, may Allah's blessings and peace be upon him and his household — be trustworthy? This is nothing but turning the scales of Islam upside down.

Note how the killer of Imam al-Husayn, the Grandson, may Allah's peace be upon him — who is from the Prophet's household — is considered trustworthy. And one who diminishes and criticizes Mu'awiya is considered a vile Rafidi whose narrations are rejected. So you may understand what deviation is and how the cunning past politics played its role.

Al-Ta'i then said [p. 32]: "As for the Hafiz's transmission of Hujr's killing — it is sound, and this killing was mentioned previously, so take note."

I say: all praise is due to Allah that he acknowledged this after his stubbornness.

We have noted that you contradicted yourself — saying here that the killing is sound and Ibn Hajar said it, while on the previous page saying there is something to consider about it because most of the reports came from the narration of Abu Mikhnaf. Such is the confusion and stumbling.

Avoiding Applying the Verse on Killing

Al-Ta'i then said [p. 32]: "As for his using the verse as proof against Mu'awiya's killing of Hujr ibn 'Adi — this is far-fetched and outside the interpretation of Ahl al-Sunna wa'l-Jama'a. And this is the very essence of Mu'tazilism, since the Mu'tazila say

---

98 See Ibn Hajar, *Tahdhib al-Tahdhib*, 7:396, Dar al-Fikr edition.
99 See Ibn Hajar, *Tahdhib al-Tahdhib*, 7:396.

that the perpetrator of a major sin abides forever in the Fire — and Ahl al-Sunna do not say that."

I say: this is the height of shamelessness. Allah, Exalted be He, says: {"And whoever kills a believer intentionally — his recompense is Hell, abiding therein. And Allah has become angry with him and has cursed him and has prepared for him a great punishment."} [al-Nisa': 93] And the Prophet, may Allah's blessings and peace be upon him and his household, said: "The believer remains in spaciousness regarding his religion as long as he does not shed forbidden blood." Narrated by al-Bukhari (6862).

From 'Ubada ibn al-Samit: the Messenger of Allah, may Allah's blessings and peace be upon him and his household, said: "Whoever kills a believer and is pleased with his killing — Allah will not accept from him either a voluntary or obligatory deed." Narrated by Abu Dawud (4270) with a sound chain.

From Sa'id ibn Jubayr: the people of Kufa disagreed about the killing of a believer — so I traveled to Ibn 'Abbas about it. He said: "It was revealed among the last to be revealed and nothing has abrogated it." Al-Bukhari (4763).

How much more so when to this is added the Prophet's statement, may Allah's blessings and peace be upon him and his household, in the authenticated hadith: "Indeed among my Companions are those who will not see me after I part from them."[100] Narrated by Ahmad (6/290, 307, 317).

And how much more so when to this is also added the statements of the imams, scholars, and hadith masters who censured Mu'awiya and whose names some of we have mentioned.

Al-Ta'i then tries to scandalize, inflate, and impress — presenting to us that what we say is the position of the Mu'tazila.

---

[100] Narrated by Ishaq ibn Rahwayh in his *Musnad*, 1:140; Abu Ya'la, *al-Musnad*, 12:436; and al-Tabarani, *al-Mu'jam al-Kabir*, 23:394. Al-Haythami said in *Majma' al-Zawa'id*, 9:72: "Narrated by al-Bazzar, and its narrators are the narrators of the Sahih."

This made us laugh — and reminded us of the statement of al-Sawi in his commentary on the Tafsir of the two Jalalayns, where he says (3/10): "It is not permissible to follow anything other than the four schools of law — even if it accords with the statement of the Companions, the sound hadith, and the verse. For whoever departs from the four schools is misguided and leads others astray, and this may lead him to disbelief."

Reflect on this, O people.

For this reason our Shaykh, the Imam and hadith master, the Sharif 'Abd Allah ibn al-Siddiq al-Ghumari, said in his book *Khawatir Diniyya* (p. 165): "We wished this statement had come from someone other than Shaykh al-Sawi — whose righteousness and excellence we believe in — and perhaps he wrote it inadvertently, heedless of its gravity. For it is impossible for a sane Muslim — let alone a scholar — to say that taking the apparent meaning of the Quran and the Sunnah is among the foundations of disbelief. We seek refuge in Allah from this statement — which is explicit disbelief in the mind of one who intends its meaning."

Al-Ta'i then set about twisting and turning to reinterpret the verse on killing to prevent its application to Mu'awiya — as if Mu'awiya were exempt from the application of the Shari'a and the Quran. Any verse that praises someone other than Mu'awiya and has no connection to him — he fabricates an application of it for him. And any verse that censures someone who did a deed that Mu'awiya is established to have done — he tries to exclude him from it.

He said [p. 32]: "Ahl al-Sunna hold that the repentance of the killer is accepted unconditionally — by the words of Allah, Exalted be He: {'And indeed I am Forgiving toward one who repents and believes and does righteousness and then continues in guidance.'} And His words: {'Indeed Allah does not forgive that partners be associated with Him, but He forgives what is below that for whom He wills.'}"

I say: the Zaydi, Imami, Mu'tazili, and Ibadi schools also said this — and not Ahl al-Sunna alone. They all agreed that the repentant sinner is like one who has no sin. But Mu'awiya did not repent from his sin for these verses to be brought in his matter and case. For Mu'awiya remained insisting on his tyranny until he exhaled his last breath — and never withdrew from forcing the people to have after him the other tyrant, Yazid the brutal drunkard and depraved one, as Commander of the Believers.

We and the entire community know these verses — and know that Mu'awiya is not included in them because he never repented. Only the fanatics argued against this.

For this reason the fair-minded scholars of Ahl al-Sunna who had no fanaticism and did not fear the force of others and their accusations of Shi'ism and Rafidism criticized and censured Mu'awiya — such as Ibn 'Abbas, Jarir al-Dabbi, 'Abd al-Razzaq, al-Nasa'i, al-Hakim, and others from the pillars of Ahl al-Sunna.

So al-Ta'i's efforts are scattered to the winds.

Hafiz Ibn Hajar said in *al-Fath* (13/70): "Abu Bakr ibn Abi Khayththama transmitted with a sound chain to Juwayra ibn Asma': 'I heard the elders of the people of Madinah saying: when Mu'awiya was on his deathbed, he called Yazid and said: The people of Madinah will give you a day of trouble — if they do, send against them Muslim ibn 'Uqba, for I have found his loyalty. When Yazid took power and 'Abd Allah ibn Hanzala and a group came to him, he honored them and gave them gifts. They returned and incited the people against Yazid, criticizing him and calling them to depose him — and they responded. This reached Yazid, who dispatched Muslim ibn 'Uqba. The people of Madinah met them with large forces — the people of Syria were afraid of them and disliked fighting them. When the fighting broke out, the people of Madinah heard the takbir from within the city — for the Banu Haritha had let in a group of Syrians from the side of the trench. The people of Madinah abandoned the fighting and entered the city out of fear for their families — and the defeat occurred. Those who were killed were killed, and

Muslim took the people's pledges that they were the property of Yazid, to be ruled in their blood, wealth, and families as he wished.' And al-Tabarani transmitted through the chain of Muhammad ibn Sa'id ibn Rummana: 'When Mu'awiya was dying, he said to Yazid: I have smoothed the land for you and subdued the people for you. I only fear the people of the Hijaz — if they cause you trouble, send against them Muslim ibn 'Uqba, for I have tested him and know his loyalty.' He did what he did — al-Hakim let it loose for three days, then called the people to pledge to Yazid and that they were his slaves in obedience to Allah and in disobedience to Him."

Hafiz Ibn Hajar said in *al-Fath* (3/177): "The day of al-Harra saw the killing of countless numbers of Ansar. The noble Madinah was pillaged and the sword was unleashed in it for three days — and that was in the days of Yazid ibn Mu'awiya."

Hafiz Ibn Hajar said in *al-Fath* (4/94), in explaining al-Bukhari's hadith (1877) from Sa'd ibn Abi Waqqas: the Messenger of Allah, may Allah's blessings and peace be upon him and his household, said: "No one schemes against the people of Madinah except that he will dissolve as salt dissolves in water." He said: "It is possible that the meaning is — for whoever intended harm against it in this world — that he will not be left but his power will end soon. As occurred with Muslim ibn 'Uqba and others — for he was seized quickly, and likewise the one who sent him."[101]

Al-Ta'i then said: "And the verse was revealed regarding a disbeliever who killed a believer intentionally and thus deserved to abide forever in the Fire. But Ibn 'Abbas said that the killer of a believer intentionally has no repentance. And Ahl al-Sunna wa'l-Jama'a — the people of truth — answered this by saying: assuming its soundness from Ibn 'Abbas, he only meant emphasis and deterrence and aversion from killing. And the verse does not contain proof for the Mu'tazila and those like

---

[101] Notice here Ibn Hajar's fear of explicitly naming Yazid, who sent Muslim ibn 'Uqba on Mu'awiya's instruction.

them who say that the perpetrator of a major sin abides forever in the Fire."

I say: do you acknowledge, O Qasim, that Mu'awiya will enter the Fire — though not abide forever in it?

As for the statement of Ahl al-Sunna — it is not as you claim, for they have many positions on this matter. Among them: the statement of al-Dhahabi in *Tarikh al-Islam* (3/654) in the biographical entry of Ibn Muljam al-Muradi: "Ibn Muljam, in the view of the Rawafid, is the most wretched of all creation in the Hereafter. And he is in our view — Ahl al-Sunna — one about whom we hope for the Fire, and we permit that Allah may forgive him.[102] Not as the Khawarij and Rawafid say about him. And his ruling is the ruling of the killer of 'Uthman, the killer of al-Zubayr, the killer of Talha, the killer of Sa'id ibn Jubayr, the killer of 'Ammar, the killer of Kharija, and the killer of al-Husayn — all of these we disavow and hate for the sake of Allah." So disavow, O Qasim, Mu'awiya the leader of the transgressing faction that calls to the Fire, and Abu Ghaddiya the one directly responsible for the killing — and they are both Companions. And you must hate them and others among the killers — as is the doctrine of Ahl al-Sunna in al-Dhahabi's view, O fanatical Sunni.

As for the intellectual intimidation you manufacture, O Qasim, to frighten us by labeling our position as Mu'tazilism and the positions of the Mu'tazila — it is an excessive threat we pay no attention to. Welcome the Mu'tazila and whoever agrees with their view. And if taking the apparent meaning of this verse alongside the statements of the Prophet and Ibn 'Abbas about the killer of a believer means holding their position — then excellent is taking it.

---

[102] This statement is rejected, namely that Allah will pardon him after Allah, Exalted be He, threatened the killer of a believer with the Fire and the curse. Ibn Hajar said in *al-Isaba*, 3:99: "'Abd al-Rahman ibn Muljam... lived into the pre-Islamic period... and he is the most wretched of this Ummah by the established text from the Prophet, may Allah bless him and his household and grant them peace, for killing 'Ali ibn Abi Talib."

They interpreted the text of the proof as it came in the rulings of a deceiving scholar — Is the Book of Allah abrogated by the whisperings of their disturbed minds? Or is the hadith of al-Mustafa following their desires in their delusions? The plague of blind imitation is lethal — it strangles the prisoners in their cells. But the majority, who had already recognized the staining of their garments, stayed silent out of cowardice. And some, out of envy from within themselves, remained.

And wretched is the position of Ahl al-Sunna if they say that. And woe upon the cold fabrications and tasteless interpretations that justify to the wicked their ugly deeds and to the killers their evil conduct.

Furthermore, your Hanafi imams are Mu'tazili in belief — for that reason al-Qadir Billah al-'Abbasi lumped them together with the Shi'a and the Mu'tazila. Al-Zamakhshari the Hanafi — great as he is, may Allah have mercy on him — and al-Jassas that Hanafi Imam, may Allah have mercy on him, who denied the vision of Allah in the Hereafter and other things.

It is sufficient now to say to you that Hafiz Ibn al-Jawzi said in *al-Muntazam* (15/125) under the events of the year 408 AH: "From Hibbat Allah ibn al-Hasan al-Tabari: in the year four hundred and eight, al-Qadir Billah, Commander of the Believers, asked the Hanafi Mu'tazili jurists to repent — and they openly returned and disavowed Mu'tazilism..."

You are asleep to the realities — wake up.

Furthermore, the position of Ahl al-Sunna and their doctrine and statement — even if we concede hypothetically that this is their doctrine — is not among the legal proofs of the Shari'a, O supposedly learned one. For it does not count as consensus. Especially since Ibn 'Abbas contradicts them on this — as established in al-Bukhari, which you acknowledged under compulsion and not willingly.

And the Prophet, may Allah's blessings and peace be upon him and his household, did not say "Ahl al-Sunna wa'l-Jama'a will not unite upon misguidance" — rather he said: "My community will not unite upon misguidance."

And 'Abd al-Qadir al-Baghdadi, the Imam of the Ash'aris, says that the positions of the people of deviant desires are considered in the chapters of theological discourse. He stated this explicitly in his book *Usul al-Din* (p. 13): "No consideration is given in such matters to the disagreement of the people of deviant desires from the Rawafid, Qadariyya, Khawarij, Jahmiyya, and Najjariyya — for the people of deviant desires' disagreement is not considered in the rulings of jurisprudence, even though we consider their disagreement in the chapters of theology." The texts on this are very numerous — refer to them in their proper places.

I conclude this point by affirming that in this verse and other Quranic verses there is proof — for the Mu'tazila and others — that the perpetrator of a major sin abides forever in the Fire. It is not a matter determined by your preferences and your temperament. Allah, Exalted be He, said: {"If you avoid the major sins which you are forbidden, We will remove from you your lesser sins."} [al-Nisa': 31] And He said: {"But yes — whoever earns evil and is encompassed by his sin — those are the companions of the Fire; they will abide therein."} [al-Baqara: 81] And His words: {"And whoever disobeys Allah and His Messenger — indeed for him is the Fire of Hell, wherein they will abide forever."} [al-Jinn: 23]

Shaykh al-Kawthari the Hanafi, may Allah have mercy on him, said in the introduction to *Tabyin Kadhib al-Muftari* (p. 18): "The Mu'tazila, contrary to the Hashwiyya, followed a straight course produced by scholarly investigation. The greed of their intellects led them to attempt to comprehend everything — their original opposition was toward intellectual stagnation. Their program was to repel the views seeping into Islam from outside with decisive arguments and rational evidence. And they had honorable positions in defense of the Islamic religion against the materialists, deniers of prophethood, dualists, Christians, Jews, Sabeans, and all kinds of atheists. You see al-Dhahabi expressing mercy for al-Jahiz in *Siyar al-Nubala'* when he mentions his book on prophethood. And we have not seen anything approaching the book *Tathbit Dala'il al-Nubuwwa* by the Judge 'Abd al-Jabbar in strength of argumentation and excellence of composition in repelling the doubts of the doubters. And it is not good to turn entirely away from their books — for how much benefit is in them that still shines in its original garb, not worn by the passage of time." So take heed, perhaps you will understand these hints.

The summary of the matter is that the words of Allah, Exalted be He — {"And whoever kills a believer intentionally — his recompense is Hell, abiding therein, and Allah has become angry with him and has cursed him and has prepared for him a great punishment."} [al-Nisa': 93] — includes Mu'awiya and others.

And the Messenger, may Allah's blessings and peace be upon him and his household, Sayyiduna 'Ali, may Allah be pleased with him, and all the believers who fought the transgressors — the threat of this verse does not include them, because Allah commanded them to fight the transgressors.

So everything Qasim al-Ta'i wanted to reach by twisting the neck of this verse toward what he wanted has been scattered to the winds. And all praise is due to Allah, Lord of all worlds.

Al-Hasan al-Basri's Statement About the Four Qualities

Al-Ta'i says [p. 33]: "The writer also quoted from al-Hasan al-Basri, may Allah have mercy on him: 'Four qualities were in Mu'awiya — had only one of them been in him it would have been ruinous...' I say: this narration was quoted by al-Tabari in his history, and in its chain is Abu Mikhnaf Lut ibn Yahya — who is discredited according to the imams of hadith criticism and accreditation, as we mentioned."

I say: it has been established above that in our view Abu Mikhnaf is trustworthy and reliable — and that they weakened him only because he was a Shi'i from Kufa. And this is not a discrediting factor — rather it is something praiseworthy, given the statement of the Prophet, may Allah's blessings and peace be upon him and his household, to Sayyiduna 'Ali, may Allah be pleased with him: "None loves you except a believer, and none hates you except a hypocrite." And it has been established that they attacked Imam Abu Hanifa, may Allah have mercy on him, and that their criticism of him is worthless — we pay no attention to it and disregard it. He is trustworthy in hadith and in other matters — despite the objections of the criticizing and accrediting hadith masters.

Likewise they attacked Sayyiduna Ja'far al-Sadiq, may Allah's peace and pleasure be upon him, and al-Bukhari did not include him in his *Sahih* — and this is not something to pay attention to.

Indeed, they attacked al-Bukhari himself and abandoned him and placed him among the abandoned narrators — as in Ibn Abi Hatim's *al-Jarh wa'l-Ta'dil* (7/191) in the biographical entry for al-Bukhari.

What al-Hasan al-Basri said is the correct position beyond any doubt — and reality bears witness to it. Al-Ta'i did not mention al-Hasan al-Basri's actual words, lest the reader be horrified at what Mu'awiya did.

Al-Hasan al-Basri said: "Four qualities were in Mu'awiya — had only one of them been in him it would have been ruinous. First: his imposing himself upon this community through fools until he stripped them of their affairs without their consultation, while among them remained surviving Companions and people of virtue. Second: his designating after him his son — a drunkard and wine-drinker who wears silk and beats drums. Third: his claiming Ziyad as his son — while the Messenger of Allah, may Allah's blessings and peace be upon him and his household, said: 'The child belongs to the marriage bed, and to the fornicator belongs deprivation.' Fourth: his killing of Hujr — woe upon him for Hujr, twice over."

The leading hadith masters recorded this story and approved it without criticizing it — Hafiz Ibn Jarir al-Tabari in his *Tarikh* (3/232), Ibn al-Athir in *al-Kamil* (3/337), Hafiz Ibn al-Jawzi in *al-Muntazam* (5/243), and Hafiz al-Suyuti in *al-Nujum al-Zahira* (1/141).

Everything mentioned here in al-Hasan al-Basri's words is correct.

As for his imposing himself upon this community by the sword — nothing demonstrates this more clearly than his rebellion against Sayyiduna 'Ali, the fourth of the rightly-guided caliphs, and the Prophet's statement about Mu'awiya and his faction: "Ammar will be killed by the transgressing faction — he calls them to Paradise and they call him to the Fire." This alone is sufficient to establish that he is ruined by his deed.

As for his designating after him his son Yazid the drunkard and wine-drinker — this is something agreed upon and no rational person disputes it. Al-Dhahabi said in *al-Siyar* (4/37) about Yazid: "He was a Nasibi, harsh, coarse, crude — he consumed intoxicants and committed objectionable acts." Hafiz Ibn Hajar said in *Lisan al-Mizan* (4/293, Indian edition), transmitting from al-Dhahabi: "His uprightness is impugned and he is not worthy of narration from him. Ahmad ibn Hanbal said: it is not appropriate to narrate from him."

This is the depraved one whom Mu'awiya made Commander of the Believers.

Ibn Kathir said in his *Tarikh* (8/224): "As for what is transmitted about him of poetry... this verse that he allegedly cited — if Yazid ibn Mu'awiya said it, then may Allah's curse be upon him and the curse of all who curse... And what was said about him and what befell him — he was not given respite after the massacre of al-Harra and the killing of al-Husayn except for a short while before Allah destroyed him — as He destroys tyrants before and after him. Indeed He is knowing and capable. {'And thus is the seizing of your Lord...'}"

Ibn Kathir said in his *Tarikh* (8/223): "This hadith and its like were used as proof by those who permitted cursing Yazid ibn Mu'awiya — and it is a reported position from Ahmad ibn Hanbal, chosen by al-Khallal, Abu Bakr 'Abd al-'Aziz, Judge Abu Ya'la, and his son Judge Abu al-Husayn. And Abu al-Faraj ibn al-Jawzi defended that in a separate monograph and permitted his cursing."

As for his claiming Ziyad ibn Abih as his son — this is something no rational person denies. Al-Dhahabi stated it explicitly in *Tarikh al-Islam* (4/12, under events of year 44 AH) and declared it definitively.

Hafiz Ibn Hajar said in *al-Fath* (3/545): "His phrase 'Ziyad ibn Abi Sufyan' — this is how it appears in *al-Muwatta'*, as Malik's teacher narrated it during the Umayyad era.[103] But after them he was called nothing but Ziyad ibn Abih. Before Mu'awiya's claiming him, he was called Ziyad ibn 'Ubayd — as his mother Sumayya, a freed slave of al-Harith ibn Kalada al-Thaqafi, was married to the said 'Ubayd and bore Ziyad on his marital bed, and he was attributed to him. Then during Mu'awiya's caliphate, a group testified to Abu Sufyan's acknowledgment that Ziyad was his son — and Mu'awiya claimed him on that basis."

The whole matter revolves around fornication as is known — otherwise why would he be called Ziyad ibn Abih? And the claiming is contrary to the Shari'a — as per the hadith that al-Hasan al-Basri, may Allah have mercy on him, cited.

As for his killing of Hujr ibn 'Adi — the monk and devout worshipper of the Companions of the Messenger of Allah, may Allah's blessings and peace be upon him and his household, as al-Hakim described him in *al-Mustadrak* — this is established beyond any doubt. We have already addressed it at length and do not wish to extend further. With that, the words of this al-Ta'i are scattered to the winds.

---

[103] Notice that Banu Umayya used to punish whoever referred to him as "Ziyad ibn Abih," and the presence of someone like 'Umar ibn 'Abd al-'Aziz among them did not affect them.

An Example of Extreme Brazenness

The astonishing thing after all of this is that al-Ta'i concluded his words on page 33 by saying about us: "So there is no place for this writer to diminish through his fabricated reports the rank of Mu'awiya. And if he had a particle of shame before the Messenger of Allah he would not have written what he wrote and would not have said what he said."

I say: the pot calling the kettle black. And after this clarification that we have presented, people now know that this al-Ta'i — if he had a particle of shame, let alone religion and character — would not have written what he wrote and would not have said anything in defense of a tyrant who bore enmity toward the household of the beloved and chosen one, may Allah's blessings and peace be upon him and his household, and cursed the Commander of the Believers 'Ali, may Allah's peace and pleasure be upon him. But it is shamelessness, lack of shame, and pretense of zeal for the religion — and this corrupt zeal and fanaticism for criminals and Nasibi hypocrites who perish. Woe upon him for what his mouth uttered and woe upon him for what his hands wrote.

We turn his expression back upon him and say: "But when passion overcomes and malice takes hold in the innermost heart — the sun of truth is obscured and one no longer sees by the light of correctness. Rather, darknesses cover him — one upon another. We ask Allah for safety and protection in word and deed."

CHAPTER 7: FINAL REPORTS AND REFUTATIONS

The Prophet's Curse Upon Mu'awiya

Al-Ta'i then cited on page 34 the hadith of Muslim in *al-Sahih* about the Prophet's curse upon Mu'awiya — "O Allah, do not fill his stomach" — and transmitted words of al-Haytami in which he twists and fabricates excuses to turn this hadith from censure into praise.

Mu'awiya deserves the Prophet, may Allah's blessings and peace be upon him and his household, to curse him — given what has been presented of his injustice and transgression, and that he is a caller to the Fire along with those with him. The supplication against him is not purification and mercy — it is anger and retribution from Allah, Exalted be He. Do not be heedless and do not deceive.

And it is sufficient that one of the imams and pillars of Ahl al-Sunna wa'l-Jama'a — Imam al-Nasa'i — considered this to be a fault against Mu'awiya. But the Nasibis turn truth into falsehood and falsehood into truth — may they receive from Allah, Exalted be He, what they deserve.

As for the chapter heading in *Sahih Muslim* — it is not the work of Muslim but of al-Nawawi, as those who are experts in this craft know. So there is no proof in that.

The Hadith "When You See Mu'awiya Upon My Pulpit, Kill Him"

Al-Ta'i then said [p. 35]: "Some lying, ignorant people of strife, stubbornness, slander, and corruption claim that the Messenger of Allah, may Allah's blessings and peace be upon him and his household, said: 'When you see Mu'awiya upon my pulpit, kill him.' And that al-Dhahabi authenticated this hadith. The answer is that al-Dhahabi did not authenticate it — rather he mentioned in his history that this report is a lying fabrication with no basis."

I say: I did not cite this hadith — and he wishes to respond to someone else with these words, so that is his business with that person.

However, this hadith was authenticated by our brother the critic and historian, the excellent Hasan Farhan al-Maliki, in his fine book *Ma'a al-Shaykh 'Abd Allah al-Sa'd fi al-Suhba wa'l-Sahaba* (pp. 185-191), where he said — may Allah preserve him and guide his steps — at the beginning of his discussion: "This hadith is thought by most students of knowledge to be a fabricated hadith with no known chain — even though it will become clear that it is stronger than all the weak hadiths they authenticate in the merits of the man. It is a hadith that at minimum can be described as sound. Otherwise we would be contradicting ourselves and violating the rules of the hadith scholars — indeed it is sound by the totality of its following chains... It is narrated from Abu Sa'id al-Khudri, Sahl ibn Hanif, Ibn Mas'ud, Jabir ibn 'Abd Allah, a group of the people of Badr, and al-Hasan al-Basri in mursal form."

Among its chains of narration: Ibn 'Asakir transmitted it in his *Tarikh* (59/155-156) through a group of trustworthy narrators — from 'Ali ibn Zayd ibn Jud'an, from Abu Nadra, from Abu Sa'id al-Khudri. And this chain is sound. Ibn Jud'an is from the narrators of Muslim — even if some weakened him.

It is corroborated by the hadith of Abu Sa'id, raised to the Prophet: "If allegiance is pledged to two caliphs, kill the second of them." Narrated by Muslim (1853).

The Hadith "The Worst of Arab Tribes Are Banu Umayya"

Al-Ta'i then said [p. 35]: "It was narrated with a sound chain that the Prophet, may Allah's blessings and peace be upon him and his household, said: 'The worst of Arab tribes are Banu Umayya, Banu Hanifa, and Thaqif.' The one objecting says:

Mu'awiya is from Banu Umayya, therefore he is from the evil ones and has no qualification for leadership or caliphate."

I say: I also never cited this hadith in my books — not in my notes on *Daf' al-Shubah* nor elsewhere. Al-Ta'i, as is apparent, intends someone else in citing this hadith and responding to it with stubbornness and falsehood.

In any case, the hadith was narrated by Abu Ya'la (13/417, no. 7421) and (12/198), and al-Hakim in *al-Mustadrak* (4/481) who said: "Sound upon the criteria of the two Shaykhs, though they did not transmit it" — and al-Dhahabi marked it with the symbol of al-Bukhari and Muslim.

Al-Hakim said, one page later there,[104] about Banu Umayya: "Let the student of knowledge know that this is a chapter in which I did not mention a third of what was transmitted. And the first of the trials in this community was their trial — and I could not in good conscience before Allah leave the book without mentioning them."

Al-Haytami cited the hadith in *al-Majma'* (10/71) and said: "Ahmad and Abu Ya'la transmitted it — with the addition: except that he said 'Banu Umayya and Thaqif and Banu Hanifa.' And likewise al-Tabarani. And their narrators are the narrators of the Sahih — except for 'Abd Allah ibn Mutarrif ibn al-Shikhkhir, who is trustworthy."

What al-Ta'i cited from Ibn Hajar al-Haytami in his twisting and excuse-making is invalid and rejected — advancing nothing and availing nothing.

Sunni Disagreement Regarding Mu'awiya

The most al-Ta'i — the imitator of al-Haytami — wants to reach is his statement there on page 53: "Ahl al-Sunna wa'l-Jama'a distinguish between Mu'awiya and his son Yazid the wrongdoer."

---

[104] Al-Hakim, *al-Mustadrak*, 4:482.

I say: first — all praise is due to Allah that he acknowledged Yazid is a wrongdoer. How then did Mu'awiya appoint over the community a brutal, depraved, drunken wrongdoer?

Second: what he attributed to Ahl al-Sunna is not accurate. Ahl al-Sunna fall into three categories.

The first category: those who hated Mu'awiya and declared it openly with courage — such as Jarir al-Dabbi, whose statement we already presented: "Qutayba said: Jarir the foremost Hafiz narrated to us[105] — but I heard him cursing and abusing Mu'awiya openly." Likewise Imam Abu Ghassan al-Nahdi, Abu Nu'aym al-Fadl ibn Dukayn, 'Ubayd Allah ibn Musa, and a group of al-Bukhari's teachers, 'Abd al-Razzaq, al-Nasa'i, al-Hakim, and groups of people of virtue and knowledge from the imams and hadith masters.

The second category: those who hold what the first category holds but cannot state it openly for fear of being labeled with Shi'ism and Rafidism and falling in the estimation of the common people. A group of contemporaries explicitly told me this — and some of the early scholars said it, such as al-Qurtubi.

Al-Dhahabi transmitted in the biographical entry of al-Awza'i in *Siyar A'lam al-Nubala'* (7/130-131) that al-Awza'i said: "We did not receive the stipend until we testified against 'Ali that he was a hypocrite, disavowed him, and pledged divorce, freeing of slaves, and oaths of allegiance on that. When I came to understand my situation, I asked Makhul, Yahya ibn Abi Kathir, 'Ata' ibn Abi Rabah, and 'Abd Allah ibn 'Ubayd ibn 'Umayr — and each one said: there is nothing binding upon you, for you were coerced. But my eyes were not at ease until I divorced my wives, freed my slaves, gave away my wealth, expiated my oaths — and Sufyan informed me that he used to do likewise."

The third category: Nasibis — of two types. Nasibis by inheritance without intention — such as al-Nawawi.[106] And

---

[105] Al-Dhahabi described him in *Siyar A'lam al-Nubala'*, 9:9.

[106] What you must all know is that al-Nawawi is among those who say that the people of the interval, including the parents of the beloved Chosen One, may

intentional Nasibis — such as al-Jawzajani and Ibn al-'Arabi al-Maliki, the author of *al-Qawasim*. And I am uncertain about al-Haytami — whether he holds Nasb by inheritance, influenced by the atmosphere in which he lived, or whether it is intentional and deliberate. But his composition of that excessive book inclines toward intention and deliberateness.

So Ahl al-Sunna are not in agreement on praising Mu'awiya as you claim. It is neither their agreement nor their consensus — and therefore it cannot be said to be their doctrine and method.

Even in this era — we know from Ahl al-Sunna distinguished scholars and individuals who censured Mu'awiya and departed from him: the scholar Sayyid Abu Bakr ibn Shihab, the scholar Sayyid Muhammad ibn 'Aqil, the scholar Sayyid 'Alawi ibn Tahir al-Haddad, the scholar Sayyid 'Abd al-Rahman ibn 'Ubayd Allah al-Saqqaf and others from the 'Alawi Shafi'i sayyids. And the Ghumari scholars — Sayyid Ahmad, Sayyid 'Abd Allah, Sayyid 'Abd al-'Aziz, Sayyid 'Abd al-Hayy, and Sayyid Ibrahim and others. And the scholar Shaykh al-Kawthari — as I clarified in the introduction to *Saf'at al-Burhan*. And the scholar Shaykh 'Abd Allah al-Habashi al-Harari. And the scholar Shaykh

---

Allah bless him and his household and grant them peace, are in the Fire, and refuge is sought with Allah. This is a false and rejected position. He mentioned this explicitly in *Sharh Sahih Muslim*, 3:79, when commenting on the false hadith, "My father and your father are in the Fire," saying: "It contains the point that whoever dies upon disbelief is in the Fire, and that kinship to those brought near does not benefit him. It also contains the point that whoever dies during the interval upon what the Arabs were upon of idol-worship is from the people of the Fire. This is not punishment before the arrival of the call, for the call of Ibrahim and other prophets, may Allah's prayers and peace be upon them, had reached them." I say: this is rejected by Allah's saying: {That you may warn a people to whom no warner had come before you, that perhaps they may remember} [al-Qasas 28:46], His saying: {Rather, it is the truth from your Lord, that you may warn a people to whom no warner had come before you, that perhaps they may be guided} [al-Sajda 32:3], His saying: {That you may warn a people whose fathers were not warned, so they are heedless} [Yasin 36:6], His saying: {And We do not punish until We send a messenger} [al-Isra' 17:15], His saying: {That is because your Lord would not destroy towns unjustly while their people were heedless} [al-An'am 6:131], and His saying: {Your Lord would not destroy towns until He sent a messenger to their mother-town reciting Our signs to them; and We would not destroy towns except while their people were wrongdoers} [al-Qasas 28:59].

Mahmud Sa'id Mamduh. And the scholar Hasan Farhan al-Maliki — and others, dozens of them from the verifying scholars of Ahl al-Sunna wa'l-Jama'a. So do not persist in your error.

Excusing Mu'awiya for Appointing Yazid

Al-Ta'i then devoted a section on page 36 defending and fabricating excuses — claiming there is no blame or censure upon Mu'awiya for appointing the depraved Yazid after him, saying: "The Twelfth Pearl: Mu'awiya's Appointment of Yazid... Indeed this Pearl is convened to repel blame and censure from Mu'awiya for his appointment of Yazid after him."

This is speech that would make a bereaved mother laugh. He built this hollow argument on two matters.

The first: that Mu'awiya did not know Yazid was depraved because he used to pretend piety before him. This is an invalid claim — for Mu'awiya killed and drank and did what he did, then on his deathbed instructed his depraved son and said: "If the people of the city of the Messenger of Allah do something to you, strike them." Ibn Hajar transmitted this in *al-Fath* (13/70) with a sound chain — as already cited.

Ibn Kathir the Nasibi said in his *Tarikh* (8/222): "Yazid made a grievous and outrageous error in telling Muslim ibn 'Uqba to pillage Madinah for three days — a great and outrageous error — alongside the killing of many Companions and their sons that accompanied it... And Allah punished him contrary to his purpose and prevented him from what he desired — and Allah destroyed him as He destroys tyrants before and after him."

I say: what Yazid did in directing Muslim ibn 'Uqba to pillage the city of the Messenger of Allah and kill the remaining Muhajirun and Ansar and their sons — was Mu'awiya's own command and instruction, which Yazid executed through Muslim ibn 'Uqba as Mu'awiya ordered. So upon Mu'awiya is what he deserves — and this is among some of his deeds.

Ibn Kathir said in his *Tarikh* (8/223): "This hadith and its like were used as proof by those who permitted cursing Yazid ibn

Mu'awiya — and it is a reported position from Ahmad ibn Hanbal, chosen by al-Khallal, Abu Bakr 'Abd al-'Aziz, Judge Abu Ya'la, and his son. And Abu al-Faraj ibn al-Jawzi defended that in a separate monograph and permitted his cursing."

And I say: the one who more deserves that — by an even greater degree — is his father Mu'awiya, who planned this, instructed it, commanded it, and insisted that Muslim ibn 'Uqba was the one who knew how to pillage the city of the Messenger of Allah, may Allah's blessings and peace be upon him and his household, and kill the Companion Muhajirun and Ansar and their sons within it.

Al-Dhahabi transmitted in *Tarikh al-Islam* (4/150, under events of year 51 AH): "From Ayyub, from Nafi', who said: Mu'awiya gave a speech and mentioned Ibn 'Umar and said: 'By Allah, he will pledge allegiance — or I will kill him.'"

The second: a false hadith — expressed by al-Ta'i as: "What the truthful and believed one indicated — that when Allah intends to carry out a matter, He strips those of sound mind of their reason until He executes what He intended." This hadith is fabricated. Al-Qa'da transmitted it (1408), al-Daylami in *Musnad al-Firdaws* (1/250), and al-Khattab in *al-Tarikh* (14/99). Al-Dhahabi mentioned it in *al-Mizan* in the biographical entry of Muhammad ibn Muhammad al-Mu'addib and said: "He brought an objectionable report." Then he said: "The defect is either al-Mu'addib or his teacher." And in the chains of al-Daylami and al-Khattab there is Sa'id ibn Sammak — who is abandoned — and likewise Lahiq ibn al-Husayn — who is a liar and fabricator.[107]

So the ideas of al-Ta'i and those who say what he says — such as al-Haytami and the fanatics for tyrants through falsehood — are built upon a crumbling bank that the thirsty person thinks is something.

---

[107] See Ahmad ibn al-Siddiq al-Ghumari, *Fath al-Wahhab bi-Takhrij Ahadith al-Shihab*, 2:352; and al-Munawi, *Fayd al-Qadir*, 1:267-268.

Al-Ta'i mentioned on page 36 that "Mu'awiya said: 'Had it not been for my love of Yazid, I would have seen my purpose clearly.'" This lie is not sound. Al-Tabarani transmitted it in *al-Kabir* (19/306) — and in it is Muhammad ibn al-Hasan al-Hamdani, who was accused of fabrication and was called a liar.[108] Al-Haytami mentioned it in *al-Majma'* (9/355) and said: "In it is an abandoned narrator." And there is more — but I do not wish to extend. I only want to make clear that al-Ta'i's ideas are built on fabricated and worthless narrations in his defense of this tyrant.

And what al-Ta'i cited on page 36 from al-Haytami is the exact truth — where he said: "His excessive love for Yazid blinded him from the path of guidance and plunged the people after him, alongside that depraved renegade, into ruin." By this, Mu'awiya — by the acknowledgment of al-Ta'i and al-Haytami themselves — was blinded from the path of guidance. And this is because he is a caller to the Fire — as stated in the account of Sayyiduna 'Ammar ibn Yasir, may Allah be pleased with him, in *Sahih al-Bukhari* and others.

What al-Ta'i cited from Ibn Hajar al-'Asqalani on page 37 — transmitted by Ibn 'Asakir through the chain of Ibn Abi Zurfa's nephew, 'Abd Allah ibn Muhammad ibn 'Abd al-Karim: "Mu'awiya's Lord is merciful and Mu'awiya's adversary is a noble adversary — what business do you have between the two?" — this statement is unsound. And even if it were sound, there would be no proof in it for anything — it is merely the guesses and hopes of the Nasibis.

The Fabricated Statement Attributed to al-Hasan al-Basri

Al-Ta'i then concluded the topic of Yazid and his appointment on page 37 by citing: "Hafiz Ibn 'Abd al-Barr said in *al-Isti'ab*: Asad ibn Musa told us — Hilal told us — Qatada told us: I said to al-Hasan: 'O Abu Sa'id — there are people here who testify

---

[108] See *al-Kashf al-Hathith 'amman Rumiya bi-Wad' al-Hadith*, p. 225.

that Mu'awiya is among the people of the Fire.' He said: 'May Allah curse them — and what do they know of who is in the Fire?'"

I say: as for Asad ibn Musa — they validated him but he transmits objectionable narrations. In his biographical entry in *al-Mizan* (1/207), Ibn Yunus in *Tarikh al-Ghuraba'* and Ibn Hazm said he transmitted objectionable hadiths. Ibn Hazm weakened him. Al-Nasa'i said, after validating him: "It would have been better for him not to have compiled."

As for his teacher Abu Hilal — he is al-Rasib, one of the weak narrators. Al-Nasa'i said: "He is not strong." Ibn Sa'd said (7/278): "There is weakness in him." Al-Bukhari included him in *al-Du'afa' al-Saghir* and said: "Yahya ibn Sa'id used to not narrate from him." Abu Zur'a said: "He is unreliable." Ibn Hibban mentioned him in *al-Majruhin* (2/283). Al-Daraqutni said: "Weak." And the discussion about him is extensive — see *Tahdhib al-Kamal* (25/292-296).

So this is not established from al-Hasan al-Basri — as you can see. And its narrator is Umayyad. And even if al-Hasan al-Basri's statement were established — which it is not — it would not save Mu'awiya from his deeds and the disasters he committed.

Al-Ta'i then cited a report that 'Umar ibn 'Abd al-'Aziz flogged someone who cursed Mu'awiya three times. This is a report that is not established — for in it is Muhammad ibn Muslim al-Ta'ifi, whom Ahmad ibn Hanbal weakened across the board, from books and other than books.[109] And whoever validated him — such as Ibn Ma'in — said he errs in memory, though his book is sound. And the chain is severed — for Ibrahim ibn Maysara says: "It reached me from 'Umar ibn 'Abd al-'Aziz..."

This appears to be among the things fabricated by the fanatic Nasibis for tyrants. Especially since all its narrators are from

---

[109] Meaning: Ahmad ibn Hanbal weakened him, whether he read from his book or from memory. In either case, he is weak.

Asad ibn Musa ibn Ibrahim ibn al-Walid ibn 'Abd al-Malik ibn Marwan al-Umawi.

Indeed, what is transmitted about 'Umar ibn 'Abd al-'Aziz is that he flogged with twenty stripes anyone who called Yazid "Commander of the Believers" — as in *Siyar A'lam al-Nubala'* in the biographical entry of Yazid.

Mu'awiya's Demise and the Claim of Conquests as Merits

Ibn Jarir al-Tabari said in his *Tarikh* (3/261) under the events of the year 60 AH: "In this year, Mu'awiya ibn Abi Sufyan perished in Damascus."[110]

Al-Ta'i then concluded his collapsing book on page 38 with a section on Mu'awiya's death — adding to his ranting: "The Thirteenth Pearl: On the Death of Mu'awiya. This noble Companion passed away having lived a life full of Islamic conquests..."

I say: al-Ta'i has reminded us of Hulagu and al-Hajjaj and their conquests. What we said earlier about one who wages war in other than the path of Allah has already been presented — refer back to it. I do not wish to add more.

The Claim That the Prophet's Shirt Intercedes for Mu'awiya

Al-Ta'i then said [p. 38]: "When death approached him, he left instructions to be wrapped in a shirt that the Messenger of Allah had given him as a garment — to be placed next to his body. And he had with him clippings of the Messenger of Allah's fingernails, and he instructed that they be ground up and placed in his eyes and mouth. And he said: 'Do this to me and leave me with the most Merciful of the Merciful.'"

---

[110] Likewise, his death is referred to as his "perishing" in Khalifa ibn Khayyat, *al-Tarikh*, 1:232; Ibn Kathir, *al-Bidaya wa'l-Nihaya*, 8:221; Ibn al-Athir, *al-Kamil*, 3:320; and al-Tabarani, *al-Mu'jam al-Kabir*, 20:367.

I say: this is a fabricated story that is not sound. Al-Tabari transmitted it in his *Tarikh* (3/262) and al-Dhahabi mentioned it in *Siyar A'lam al-Nubala'* (3/160). 'Abd al-A'la ibn Maymun is of unknown status — and his father Maymun ibn Mihran, even though he is from the narrators of the Six Collections, used to attack Sayyiduna 'Ali, may Allah be pleased with him,[111] and so his narration is rejected in such matters relating to the virtues of Mu'awiya. Furthermore there is a gap between Maymun ibn Mihran and Mu'awiya — for Maymun says: "Mu'awiya... and recounts the story."

In Ibn Abi Hatim's *al-Marasil* (206-207): "Abu Talib said: I asked Ahmad ibn Hanbal: Maymun ibn Mihran from Hakim ibn Hizam? He said: No — from where would he have met him? He only narrated from Ibn 'Abbas and Ibn 'Umar."

So this story is not sound. And even if it were sound, there would be no proof in it of Mu'awiya's salvation from what he did — since the Messenger of Allah, may Allah's blessings and peace be upon him and his household, as in al-Bukhari and Muslim,[112] wrapped 'Abd Allah ibn Ubayy ibn Salul — the head of the hypocrites — in his shirt and prayed over him. Yet that did not benefit him — neither the Prophet's shirt, nor his prayer and supplication for him.

Allah, Exalted be He, said: {"It is the same for them whether you ask forgiveness for them or do not ask forgiveness for them — Allah will never forgive them. Indeed Allah does not guide the depraved people."} [al-Munafiqun: 6] And He said: {"And never pray over any one of them who has died or stand at his grave. Indeed they disbelieved in Allah and His Messenger and died while they were defiantly disobedient."} [al-Tawba: 84]

With this the invalidity of what al-Haytami said — as transmitted by al-Ta'i on page 38: "And this is the state of the perfect ones, may Allah be pleased with them all — how

---

[111] As in al-'Ijli, *Ma'rifat al-Thiqat*, 2:307.

[112] See al-Bukhari, *Sahih*, no. 1269; and Muslim, *Sahih*, no. 2400.

fortunate that his body was enabled to touch what the body of the Messenger of Allah touched" — becomes clear.

We say: the people of falsehood, licentiousness, and darkness are not helped by the intercession of the angels or the prophets — as Allah, Exalted be He, said: {"And they do not intercede except for one whom He has approved."} [al-Anbiya': 28]

We ask Allah, Exalted be He, to make us from among His righteous, pious, active, humble servants who love the righteous and excellent Companions of the Messenger of Allah, may Allah's blessings and peace be upon him and his household — the pure ones who stood firm upon what they pledged to Allah and His Messenger.

Here the pen halts in what we wished to comment upon regarding what Qasim al-Ta'i wrote — may Allah guide him and pardon him. And Allah is the Guardian of success.

End of *Zahr al-Rayhan fi al-Radd 'ala Tahqiq al-Bayan*

By Shaykh Hasan al-Saqqaf

Translated by Walid Abdurrahim

APPENDIX: PROPHETIC REPORTS AND SCHOLARLY STATEMENTS CONCERNING MU'AWIYA

Translator's Note

The preceding work, *Sweet Basil Blossoms in Refutation of Tahqiq al-Bayan*, is Shaykh Hasan al-Saqqaf's direct response to Qasim ibn Nu'aym al-Ta'i's defence of Mu'awiya ibn Abi Sufyan. It addresses al-Ta'i's arguments one by one: the claim of consensus, the alleged virtues of Mu'awiya, the misuse of reports concerning the Companions, the question of ijtihad, and the established record concerning Mu'awiya's conduct toward Sayyiduna 'Ali and the Prophet's Household.

The material that follows is appended to the original Arabic work. It consists of two related items: first, a treatise gathering Prophetic reports concerning Mu'awiya ibn Abi Sufyan; and second, statements of a group of scholars on the same subject, gathered by some students of knowledge. Together, they serve as an evidentiary continuation of the preceding refutation.

The first work examined al-Ta'i's arguments directly. The appended material now places before the reader a concentrated body of Prophetic reports, scholarly statements, and hadith-critical discussion relevant to the same subject.

The Translator

THE SAYINGS OF THE GREATEST MESSENGER OUR MASTER MUHAMMAD

May Allah bless him and his household and grant them peace
CONCERNING MU'AWIYA IBN ABI SUFYAN

REPORTS OF CENSURE CONCERNING MU'AWIYA ON THE TONGUE OF THE SACRED LAW

Collected by

Some Students of Knowledge

Translated by

Walid Abdurrahim

Reports of Censure Concerning Mu'awiya on the Tongue of the Sacred Law

Many authentic and sound hadiths have come from the Greatest Messenger, may Allah bless him and his household and grant them peace, censuring Mu'awiya ibn Abi Sufyan. The reality of Mu'awiya confirmed the truthfulness of these noble hadiths, because his actions were contrary to the commands and prohibitions of Allah, Exalted be He.

A number of scholars, either deliberately or out of ignorance, attacked these noble hadiths, including Ibn Taymiyya and his fanatical imitators, by means of interpretation, weakening, and denial. Some people of knowledge then followed them in that, out of imitation and fanaticism, without verification.

Fabricated hadiths were also invented to establish the virtue of Mu'awiya, by the will of Mu'awiya and his faction in his Umayyad state. Ibn Taymiyya and his followers then rushed to patch up their chains, authenticate them, and use them as evidence.[113] This is despite the explicit statements of leading hadith masters, such as al-Nasa'i, Ishaq ibn Rahwayh, al-Hafiz Ibn Hajar, and others from the senior scholars of Ahl al-Sunna wa'l-Jama'a, that nothing is authentic concerning the virtue of Mu'awiya.

Al-Hafiz Ibn Hajar said in *Fath al-Bari* (7:104), reporting from Ishaq ibn Rahwayh, al-Nasa'i, and Isma'il al-Qadi al-Maliki:

Nothing is authentic concerning the virtues of Mu'awiya.

Here, then, is some of what has come in the authentic Prophetic Sunnah concerning the clarification of Mu'awiya's state and the judgment upon him by the explicit text of the infallible Messenger, peace and blessings be upon him.

---

[113] In *Majmu' al-Fatawa*, 35:64, and *al-Fatawa al-Kubra*, 4:259, Ibn Taymiyya cited the hadith: "O Allah, teach him the Book and reckoning, and protect him from punishment." It is a fabricated hadith whose chains contain weak narrators and liars, as will come later.

1. *The Hadith of 'Ammar and the Transgressing Faction*

Al-Bukhari narrated in his *Sahih* (447 and 2812), and Muslim also narrated (2916), with several wordings. This is the wording of al-Bukhari in the first place:

"'Ammar will be killed by the transgressing faction. He will be calling them to Paradise, and they will be calling him to the Fire."[114]

Then our master 'Ammar, may Allah be pleased with him, said:

I seek refuge with Allah from trials.

Our master 'Ammar ibn Yasir was in the army of our master 'Ali ibn Abi Talib, the Imam of the People of the Household, fighting Mu'awiya and his faction.

This is an explicit hadith in which our master Muhammad, may Allah bless him and his household and grant them peace, establishes the following matters.

First, Mu'awiya and his group were the transgressing faction. Allah, Exalted be He, commanded us to fight the transgressing faction in His saying:

{Then fight the one that transgresses until it returns to the command of Allah.}

Yet that faction, and its followers, have not returned to the command of Allah, Exalted be He, until our own day.

Allah, Exalted be He, also says:

---

[114] In another wording of al-Bukhari, it states: "'Ammar calls them to Allah, while they call him to the Fire." This hadith was narrated by Ibn Hibban in his *Sahih*, 15:553; Ibn Abi Shayba, 6:385; Ahmad, 3:90; al-Tabarani, *al-Mu'jam al-Kabir*, 12:395; and others. Ibn Hajar said in *Fath al-Bari*, 1:543: "The hadith, 'The transgressing faction will kill 'Ammar,' was narrated by a group of Companions, including Qatada ibn al-Nu'man, as previously mentioned; Umm Salama in Muslim; Abu Hurayra in al-Tirmidhi; 'Abd Allah ibn 'Amr ibn al-'As in al-Nasa'i; 'Uthman ibn 'Affan; Hudhayfa; Abu Ayyub; Abu Rafi'; Khuzayma ibn Thabit; Mu'awiya; 'Amr ibn al-'As; Abu al-Yusr; and 'Ammar himself. All of them are found in al-Tabarani and elsewhere, and most of their routes are authentic or hasan. It is also narrated from another group whose enumeration would be lengthy."

{Say: My Lord has only forbidden indecencies, what is apparent of them and what is hidden, sin, and transgression without right...} [al-A'raf 7:33]

Second, Mu'awiya and the faction he led were calling to the Fire.

Is it permissible after this to defend a man who, along with his faction, calls to the Fire?

Are we not ashamed before our master, the Messenger of Allah, may Allah bless him and his household and grant them peace, who does not speak from desire, but only from revelation revealed?

Third, our master 'Ali and his faction, among them our master 'Ammar, were calling to Paradise and to Allah, Exalted be He.

How can we then say that Mu'awiya erred and receives one reward for his error, when the Prophet, may Allah bless him and his household and grant them peace, says that he and his faction call to the Fire?

Does one who calls to the Fire receive reward and recompense?

Where, then, are the believers who comply with Allah, Exalted be He, and His Messenger, may Allah bless him and his household and grant them peace?

{It is not for a believing man or a believing woman, when Allah and His Messenger have decided a matter, that they should have any choice in their affair. Whoever disobeys Allah and His Messenger has certainly gone far astray.} [al-Ahzab 33:36]

Al-Hafiz Ibn Hajar said in *Fath al-Bari* (1:543):

In this hadith there is one of the signs of Prophethood, an evident virtue of 'Ali and 'Ammar, and a refutation of the Nasibis who claim that 'Ali was not correct in his wars.

The truth is that the one who made this claim was Ibn Taymiyya al-Harrani, whom some people title "Shaykh al-Islam," even though this title is legally forbidden, especially for this man, who authenticated the hadith of the beardless youth, believed in its apparent meaning, and said that it was a waking vision, not a dream.[115]

Allah is exalted far above that, with immense transcendence.

{Glory be to your Lord, the Lord of might, above what they describe.}

Ibn Taymiyya said concerning our master 'Ali, may Allah be pleased with him, in *Minhaj al-Sunna* (4:500 of the critical edition, and 2:232 of the other edition):

Then it is said to these Rafidis: If the Nasibis said to you, "'Ali deemed the blood of the Muslims lawful and fought them without the command of Allah and His Messenger for the sake of his own leadership. The Prophet, may Allah bless him and grant him peace, said: 'Insulting a Muslim is wickedness, and fighting him is disbelief.' He also said: 'Do not return after me as disbelievers, striking the necks of one another.' Therefore 'Ali is a disbeliever because of that," your argument would not be stronger than theirs, because the hadiths they cite as evidence are authentic.

They would also say: Killing souls is corruption, and whoever kills souls for the sake of obedience to himself desires exaltation in the land and corruption. This is the state of Pharaoh...

Ibn Taymiyya forgot that Mu'awiya was the one who killed souls without right, unjustly and aggressively. He did not apply these principles to him. Rather, he went further and compared our master 'Ali to Pharaoh, while he did not compare Mu'awiya to him.

So reflect on how he supported the statement of the Nasibis that the evidence for our master 'Ali, may Allah be pleased with him, being a disbeliever is stronger and more correct in terms of proof.

---

[115] This is in his book *al-Ta'sis fi'l-Radd 'ala Asas al-Taqdis*, 3:241, manuscript.

The Nasibis who say this are none other than him. He invents statements and attributes them to unknown people, while they are his own statements and his own creed.

The poor man forgot the saying of Allah, Exalted be He, in the Noble Qur'an:

{Then fight the one that transgresses.}

He also forgot the description of that faction in the authentic books by the Prophet, may Allah bless him and his household and grant them peace, as the transgressing faction that calls to the Fire. Yet he narrated from his Nasibi brothers the preference of declaring our master 'Ali a disbeliever, supported them, and stated that their argument is the stronger one.

These Nasibis who aggress against the best of the Companions, may Allah be pleased with them, consider declaring our master 'Ali a disbeliever to be an easy and simple matter. But as for the mere thought of saying the slightest word concerning Mu'awiya, they regard that as manifest misguidance, panic at it, and claim that it demolishes the religion from its foundation.

Ibn Taymiyya also forgot the saying of our master 'Ali, may Allah be pleased with him and make him pleased:

I was commanded to fight the oath-breakers, the unjust, and the renegades.

The Messenger of Allah, may Allah bless him and his household and grant them peace, said:

"Among you is one who will fight over the interpretation of the Qur'an, just as I fought over its revelation."

Abu Bakr said: "Am I he, O Messenger of Allah?"

He said: "No."

'Umar said: "Am I he, O Messenger of Allah?"

He said: "No, but the one who mends the sandal."

He had given 'Ali his sandal to mend.

Ibn Hibban narrated it in his *Sahih* (15:385), and Abu Ya‘la (2:341). They authenticated it. Al-Haytami said in *al-Majma‘* (5:186):

Narrated by Abu Ya‘la, and its narrators are the narrators of the Sahih.

For this reason, the small group of Companions who withdrew from fighting and did not fight alongside our master ‘Ali and his faction, which called to Paradise, regretted it. Here is Ibn ‘Umar saying:

I never found in myself anything concerning the matter of this verse like what I found in myself over not fighting this transgressing faction as Allah, Mighty and Majestic, commanded me.

Al-Hakim narrated it in *al-Mustadrak* (3:115), and it is authentic.

Al-Dhahabi said in *Siyar A‘lam al-Nubala’* (2:177):

There is no doubt that ‘A’isha regretted completely her journey to Basra and her presence on the Day of the Camel...

Ibn Taymiyya said in his *Minhaj al-Sunna* (4:514):

‘Ali was incapable of resisting the apostates, who are also from the disbelievers.

This is a lack of discernment and a failure of the pen, in which expression betrayed him, or his desire cast him down into the pit of fanaticism.

Al-Hafiz Ibn Hajar explicitly stated in *al-Durar al-Kamina* (1:155) that Ibn Taymiyya said that about our master ‘Ali. Al-Hafiz said:

Among them are those who attribute hypocrisy to him because of what he said concerning ‘Ali, as mentioned earlier, and because of his saying that he was forsaken wherever he turned, that he sought the caliphate repeatedly but did not attain it, that he only fought for leadership and not for religion, and his saying that he loved leadership, while ‘Uthman loved wealth. He also said that Abu Bakr accepted Islam as an old man who knew what he was saying, while 'Ali accepted Islam as a child, and the Islam of a child is not valid according to one view...[116]

Also because of his words concerning the story of the proposal to the daughter of Abu Jahl, and he died without forgetting it...

And the story of Abu al-'As ibn al-Rabi' and what is understood from its implication, for he spoke severely regarding that.

So they bound him to hypocrisy because of the saying of the Prophet, may Allah bless him and his household and grant them peace: "None hates you except a hypocrite..."

When he was pressed and forced to answer, he would say: "I did not intend this. I only intended such and such," and then he would mention a far-fetched possibility...

The eyes of the Nasibis and the heedless turn blind to all of this that Ibn Taymiyya says by way of attacking a man like our master 'Ali, one of the masters and greatest men of the Companions. They regard it as something trivial. But touching the side of Mu'awiya, according to their mistaken view, is the demolition of Islam and an attack upon it.

Ibn Hajar said in *Lisan al-Mizan* (6:319-320) concerning Ibn Taymiyya:

How many exaggerations he made in weakening the words of the Rafidi, which sometimes led him to diminish 'Ali, may Allah be pleased with him.

Meanwhile, we find Ibn Taymiyya in his books praising Mu'awiya, magnifying him, commending him, and defending him passionately.

2. Mu'awiya Ordered the Cursing of Sayyiduna 'Ali

It is established in the Sahihs and Sunans that Mu'awiya used to order people to curse our master 'Ali, may Allah be pleased with

---

[116] See Ibn Taymiyya, *Minhaj al-Sunna*, 7:155.

him and make him pleased. This is a grave sin, as is explicitly stated in the Sacred Law.

Muslim narrated in the *Sahih* (2404), from ‘Amir ibn Sa‘d ibn Abi Waqqas, from his father, who said:

Mu‘awiya ibn Abi Sufyan ordered Sa‘d and said: “What prevents you from cursing Abu Turab?”

He said: “As for what I remember of three things that the Messenger of Allah, may Allah bless him and his household and grant them peace, said to him, I will never curse him. For one of them to be mine would be dearer to me than red camels.

I heard the Messenger of Allah, may Allah bless him and his household and grant them peace, say to him when he left him behind in one of his expeditions, and ‘Ali said to him, ‘O Messenger of Allah, have you left me behind with the women and children?’ The Messenger of Allah, may Allah bless him and his household and grant them peace, said to him: ‘Are you not pleased that you are to me in the position of Harun to Musa, except that there is no prophethood after me?’

I also heard him say on the Day of Khaybar: ‘I shall give the banner to a man who loves Allah and His Messenger, and whom Allah and His Messenger love.’ So we looked forward to it. He said: ‘Call ‘Ali for me.’ He was brought while suffering from eye pain, so he spat in his eye and gave the banner to him, and Allah granted victory at his hands.

And when this verse was revealed: {Say: Come, let us call our sons and your sons...}, the Messenger of Allah, may Allah bless him and his household and grant them peace, called ‘Ali, Fatima, Hasan, and Husayn, and said: ‘O Allah, these are my family.’”[117]

So reflect on how Mu‘awiya ordered the Companions to curse our master ‘Ali, may Allah be pleased with him.

---

[117] As noted earlier, this hadith was narrated by Muslim, *Sahih*, no. 2404; al-Tirmidhi, *Sunan*, no. 3724; and others.

Ibn Maja narrated (121), with a sound chain,[118] from Sa'd ibn Abi Waqqas, who said:

Mu'awiya came during one of his pilgrimages, and Sa'd entered upon him. They mentioned 'Ali, so he spoke against him.[119]

Sa'd became angry and said: "You say this about a man concerning whom I heard the Messenger of Allah, may Allah bless him and his household and grant them peace, say: 'Whoever I am his mawla, 'Ali is his mawla.' I also heard him say: 'You are to me in the position of Harun to Musa, except that there is no prophet after me.' And I heard him say: 'Today I shall give the banner to a man who loves Allah and His Messenger.'"

This is an explicit narration that Mu'awiya used to speak against our master 'Ali, meaning that he cursed and abused him.

Mu'awiya ordered his governors to curse and abuse our master 'Ali, and to command the people to do so. Among this is what Muslim narrated in the *Sahih* (2409), from the noble Companion Sahl ibn Sa'd, who said:

A man from the family of Marwan was appointed over Madinah. He said: He summoned Sahl ibn Sa'd and ordered him to curse 'Ali.

Sahl refused.

He said to him: "Since you refuse, then say: May Allah curse Abu Turab."

Sahl said: "There was no name more beloved to 'Ali than Abu Turab, and he would rejoice when he was called by it..."

By this it is established that Mu'awiya used to curse our master 'Ali, may Allah be pleased with him, and order the people to curse him. It is authentically established that the Prophet, may Allah bless him and his household and grant them peace, said:

"Whoever curses 'Ali has cursed me."

---

[118] This was authenticated by the contradictory figure of our age, al-Albani, in *Sahih Ibn Maja*, 1:26.

[119] That is, he cursed and abused him.

Ahmad narrated in *al-Musnad* (6:323), with a sound chain, from Abu 'Abd Allah al-Jadali, who said:

I entered upon Umm Salama, and she said to me: "Is the Messenger of Allah, may Allah bless him and his household and grant them peace, being cursed among you?"

I said: "Allah forbid," or "Glory be to Allah," or a similar phrase.

She said: "I heard the Messenger of Allah, may Allah bless him and his household and grant them peace, say: 'Whoever curses 'Ali has cursed me.'"[120]

Al-Hakim also narrated it (3:121), adding:

"And whoever curses me has cursed Allah."

The cursing of our master 'Ali, may Allah be pleased with him, by Mu'awiya and his faction is well-known, indeed mass-transmitted, and this requires the compilation of a separate work devoted specifically to it.[121]

So the summary of the matter now is this: Mu'awiya cursed our master 'Ali and ordered others to curse him, while the Greatest

---

[120] Shu'ayb al-Arna'ut authenticated it in his commentary on the *Musnad*, 44:329, and al-Albani authenticated it in *al-Silsila al-Sahiha*, no. 3332. Al-Nasa'i also narrated it in *al-Sunan al-Kubra*, 5:133, and it has numerous routes of transmission mentioned by al-Haythami in *Majma' al-Zawa'id*, 9:130. It also has other wordings and numerous routes, including what was narrated by Ibn Abi Shayba, 12:76-77; al-Tabarani, *al-Mu'jam al-Kabir*, 23:322; Abu Ya'la, 12:444; and others.

[121] Among this is what appears in Ahmad, *al-Musnad*, 1:187; Abu Dawud, *Sunan*, nos. 4649 and 4650; and others, with an authentic chain, concerning the objection of the Companion Sa'id ibn Zayd to al-Mughira ibn Shu'ba when Sayyiduna 'Ali ibn Abi Talib, upon him peace and Allah's pleasure, was being cursed in his presence. Sa'id ibn Zayd said: "O Mughira ibn Shu'ba, do you not hear the Companions of the Messenger of Allah, may Allah bless him and his household and grant them peace, being cursed in your presence, yet you neither object nor change it?" The contradictory figure of our age, al-Albani, authenticated it in *Sahih Abi Dawud*, 3:880, no. 3887. Also among this is what Ibn Abi 'Asim narrated in his *al-Sunna*, no. 1350, from 'Abd al-Rahman ibn al-Bilmani, who said: "We were with Mu'awiya when a man stood and cursed 'Ali ibn Abi Talib, may Allah be pleased with him, and cursed and cursed. Sa'id ibn Zayd ibn 'Amr ibn Nufayl then stood and said: 'O Mu'awiya, do I see 'Ali being cursed before you and you do not change it? I heard the Messenger of Allah, may Allah bless him and his household and grant them peace, say: He is to me in the position of Harun to Musa.'"

Prophet, may Allah bless him and his household and grant them peace, said:

"Whoever curses 'Ali has cursed me."

Are you, then, with the Messenger of Allah, may Allah bless him and his household and grant them peace, or with Mu'awiya, who cursed our master 'Ali despite knowing that if he did so, he had in fact cursed our master, the Messenger of Allah, may Allah bless him and his household and grant them peace?

Is it permissible for us to defend someone who curses our master 'Ali, may Allah be pleased with him, and who curses our master, the Messenger of Allah, may Allah bless him and his household and grant them peace?

3. The Prophet's Supplication Against Mu'awiya

The Prophet, may Allah bless him and his household and grant them peace, supplicated against Mu'awiya by saying:

"May Allah never fill his belly."

Allah, Exalted be He, answered the supplication of the Prophet, may Allah bless him and his household and grant them peace, and Mu'awiya was never satiated after that.[122] Al-Dhahabi testified that Mu'awiya was one of those known for excessive eating.[123] For that reason, his belly grew large and his appearance became deformed, and he was unable to deliver the sermon except while seated. He was the first person in Islam to deliver the sermon while seated.[124]

Muslim narrated in the *Sahih* (2604), from our master Ibn 'Abbas, may Allah be pleased with them both, that the Prophet,

---

[122] Al-Dhahabi said in *Siyar A'lam al-Nubala'*, 3:123, that al-Hakim added in his narration of the hadith "May Allah never fill his belly": "He was never satiated after that."

[123] Al-Dhahabi said in *Siyar A'lam al-Nubala'*, 3:124: "Mu'awiya was counted among those known for excessive eating."

[124] Narrated by Ibn Abi Shayba in *al-Musannaf*, 7:247. See also *al-Ahad wa'l-Mathani*, 1:380; *Fath al-Bari*, 2:401; and *Siyar A'lam al-Nubala'*, 13:458. The Sunnah of the Prophet, may Allah bless him and his household and grant them peace, is to deliver the sermon standing, as is known.

may Allah bless him and his household and grant them peace, said to him:

"Go and call Mu'awiya for me."

He said:

So I came and said: "He is eating."

Then he said to me:

"Go and call Mu'awiya for me."

He said:

So I came and said: "He is eating."

Then he said:

"May Allah never fill his belly."

Imam al-Nasa'i, the author of the *Sunan*, was killed because he narrated this hadith in Syria. Al-Dhahabi mentioned in *Tadhkirat al-Huffaz* (2:699), from al-Nasa'i, that he said:

I entered Damascus while many of its people were hostile toward 'Ali, so I compiled the book *al-Khasa'is*, hoping that Allah would guide them.[125]

Al-Dhahabi mentioned in *Siyar A'lam al-Nubala'* (14:132):

Al-Nasa'i left Egypt at the end of his life and went to Damascus. There he was asked about Mu'awiya and what had come concerning his virtues. He said: "Is he not satisfied to come out even, such that he must be preferred?" He said: They kept striking him in his testicles until he was taken out of the mosque... Al-Daraqutni said: He left for Hajj, was put to trial in Damascus, and attained martyrdom.

Al-Dhahabi said in the biographical entry of al-Nasa'i, the author of the *Sunan*, in *Siyar A'lam al-Nubala'* (14:129-130):

---

[125] See al-Mizzi, *Tahdhib al-Kamal*, 1:338; Ibn Hajar, *Tahdhib al-Tahdhib*, 1:33; and *Kashf al-Zunun*, 1:706.

It was said to him, meaning al-Nasa'i: "Will you not produce the virtues of Mu'awiya?" He said: "What should I produce? 'O Allah, do not fill his belly'?" So the questioner fell silent.

Al-Dhahabi said there concerning Mu'awiya:

Mu'awiya was counted among those known for excessive eating.

This is an explicit admission from al-Dhahabi that the supplication of the Prophet, may Allah bless him and his household and grant them peace, was fulfilled against Mu'awiya.

It is also an explicit text showing the frailty and weakness of interpreting the hadith "May Allah never fill his belly" through the hadith: "O Allah, whomever I insulted, abused, or cursed, make it mercy and purification for him," and treating that as a virtue of Mu'awiya.

In any case, interpreting the Prophet's statement, may Allah bless him and his household and grant them peace, concerning Mu'awiya, "May Allah never fill his belly," which is established in *Sahih Muslim* (2604), as a virtue of Mu'awiya on the basis of the hadith "O Allah, whomever I cursed or abused, make it mercy for him..." is a false interpretation for two reasons.

The first is that al-Dhahabi admitted that Mu'awiya was among those known for excessive eating. Thus the supplication of the Prophet, may Allah bless him and his household and grant them peace, was answered against him. For that reason, his belly became large, and he was unable to deliver the sermon except while seated. This means that the supplication of the Prophet, may Allah bless him and his household and grant them peace, struck him.[126] This is clear censure.

---

[126] See *Siyar A'lam al-Nubala'*, 3:156-157; *Fath al-Bari*, 2:401; Ibn Abi Shayba, *al-Musannaf*, 7:247; and *al-Ahad wa'l-Mathani*, 1:380. Al-Khatib also narrated in *Muwaddih Awham al-Jam' wa'l-Tafriq*, 1:348, from Jabir ibn Samura that he said: "I saw the Messenger of Allah delivering the sermon standing, so whoever tells you that he delivered the sermon sitting has lied."

The second is that the hadith is qualified and not unrestricted. Muslim narrated it (2603), from the hadith of Anas ibn Malik, with the wording:

"So whichever person from my Ummah I supplicate against with a supplication for which he is not deserving, make it for him purification and cleansing…"

The presence of the phrase "for which he is not deserving" in one of the narrations of the hadith, together with the possibility that Mu'awiya was deserving of it, makes the hadith unfit to be used as evidence according to what is established in the science of legal theory: when a proof is affected by probability, its use as evidence is invalidated.

4. Mu'awiya's Drinking of Wine

Allah, Exalted be He, says:

{Wine, gambling, idols, and divining arrows are only filth from the work of Satan, so avoid it.}

The Messenger, may Allah bless him and his household and grant them peace, said:

"The fornicator does not commit fornication while he is a believer, and the drinker does not drink wine while he is a believer."

Al-Bukhari narrated it (2475). The hadiths censuring the drinker of wine are many and well-known. Indeed, the prohibition of drinking wine is known necessarily, as both the scholar and the ignorant know.

Ahmad ibn Hanbal narrated in his *Musnad* (5:347), from 'Abd Allah ibn Burayda, who said:

My father and I entered upon Mu'awiya. He seated us on couches. Then food was brought to us, and we ate. Then drink was brought to us, and Mu'awiya drank. Then he handed it to my father, and he said: "I have not drunk it since the Messenger of Allah, may Allah bless him and his household and grant them peace, forbade it."[127]

Al-Hafiz al-Haythami said in *Majma' al-Zawa'id* (5:42):

Its narrators are the narrators of the Sahih.

Mu'awiya did not stop at this. Rather, he had caravans carrying wine for him, and he also traded in it. Al-Dhahabi mentioned the matter of Mu'awiya trading in wine in *Siyar A'lam al-Nubala'* (2:9-10), saying:

Yahya ibn Sulaym, from Ibn Khuthaym, from Isma'il ibn 'Ubayd ibn Rifa'a, from his father:

A caravan passed by 'Ubada ibn al-Samit while he was in Syria, carrying wine.

He said: "What is this? Oil?"

It was said: "No, rather wine being sold for so-and-so."[128]

So he took a blade from the market, stood before it, and did not leave a single container except that he split it open.

Abu Hurayra was then in Syria, so so-and-so sent to Abu Hurayra and said: "Will you not restrain your brother 'Ubada from us? In the mornings he goes to the market and ruins the trade of the protected non-Muslims, and in the evenings he sits in the mosque, having no occupation except insulting our honor and faulting us."

He said: So Abu Hurayra came to him and said: "O 'Ubada, what do you have to do with Mu'awiya? Leave him and what he carries."[129]

He said: "You were not with us when we pledged allegiance to hear and obey, to command what is right, to forbid what is

---

[127] Ibn Abi Shayba also narrated it up to this point, 7:271.

[128] As previously mentioned, Muslim narrated it in the *Sahih*, no. 1582, naming him explicitly, while al-Bukhari, no. 2223, left him ambiguous, as was his habit.

[129] This is an authentic narration in which Ibn Ishaq explicitly stated that he heard the report. Al-Bayhaqi narrated it in *al-Sunan al-Kubra*, 9:97, and al-Dhahabi mentioned it in *Siyar A'lam al-Nubala'*, 1:174.

wrong, and not to fear, concerning Allah, the blame of any blamer."

So Abu Hurayra fell silent, and so-and-so wrote to 'Uthman: "'Ubada has corrupted Syria against me."[130]

'Ubada objected to many unlawful matters committed by Mu'awiya, such as dealing in usury, as is established in *Sahih Muslim* (1587), *Sunan al-Nasa'i* (7:275, no. 4562), and elsewhere.

Mu'awiya was not alone in these matters of wine. Rather, his companions, supporters, and loved ones also traded in wine from the time of our master 'Umar, may Allah be pleased with him. It is established that 'Umar ibn al-Khattab cursed Samura because he was the first to permit the sale of wine, and Samura was from the faction and loved ones of Mu'awiya.

Muslim narrated (1582) in the *Sahih*, from Ibn 'Abbas, who said:

It reached 'Umar that Samura had sold wine, so he said: "May Allah fight Samura! Did he not know that the Messenger of Allah said: 'May Allah curse the Jews. Fats were forbidden to them, so they melted them and sold them.'"

It is also in al-Bukhari (2223), but he omitted the name of Samura and replaced it with "so-and-so," in order to cover up the crime.

Sa'id ibn Mansur narrated in his *Sunan* (819), with a sound chain, from Ibn 'Umar:

'Umar ibn al-Khattab said: "May Allah curse so-and-so, for he was the first to permit the sale of wine. Trade is only lawful in what is lawful to eat and drink."[131]

---

[130] The narration of al-Tayalisi, p. 186, has an authentic chain, and it is through the same chain as al-Bukhari above Abu Dawud al-Tayalisi. Al-Bayhaqi also narrated it in *al-Sunan al-Kubra*, 9:97. Al-Bukhari omitted from it what indicates Wahshi's addiction to wine.

[131] It is authentic. The hadith master Sayyid Ahmad ibn al-Siddiq al-Ghumari al-Hasani said in *al-Mudawi*, 4:251: "The hadith is authentic, and al-Dhahabi seems to have used tadlis in his statement that 'Abd Allah ibn Waqid was alone

Naturally, 'Umar ibn al-Khattab did not say "so-and-so"; rather, he mentioned Samura. But the narrators changed it either out of fear of Mu'awiya and Banu Umayya, or because they wanted to cover up his crimes. Ya'qub ibn Shayba clarified in *Musnad 'Umar ibn al-Khattab* (1:47), from Tawus, that the person meant by this was Samura. He said:

It reached 'Umar, may Allah be pleased with him, that Samura had sold wine.[132]

Likewise, the servant of the family of Abu Sufyan, the beloved of Mu'awiya, Wahshi ibn Harb, did not abandon wine even after his Islam, during the time of Mu'awiya in Syria. Here is the text.

Al-Hafiz Ibn Hajar said in *Tahdhib al-Tahdhib* concerning Wahshi and his stipend (11:99):

He settled in Homs and was addicted to wine. 'Umar assigned him two thousand, then reduced him to three hundred because of wine.

Al-Hafiz Ibn Hajar said in *Fath al-Bari* (7:368):

In the narration of 'Abd al-Rahman ibn Yazid ibn Jabir: "I and 'Ubayd Allah ibn 'Adi went out on the summer expedition

---

in narrating it, because the mentioned 'Abd Allah was not alone in narrating it. In the same *Mustadrak*, after his route, there are two other routes which al-Hakim authenticated and al-Dhahabi approved. But he was first compelled to mention that and claim that 'Abd Allah ibn Waqid was alone in narrating it, because the hadith concerns the censure of Banu Umayya and Mu'awiya, as 'Ubada ibn al-Samit, may Allah be pleased with him, swore. Al-Dhahabi cannot tolerate hearing censure of Banu Umayya and Mu'awiya. He only tolerates that regarding the Household of the Prophet and 'Ali, upon them peace."

[132] It is a hasan hadith. It was narrated by al-Bazzar, 4:109, from Abu 'Ubayda; al-Harith ibn Abi Usama, 2:642; Abu Ya'la, 2:175-176; and Nu'aym ibn Hammad in *al-Fitan*, 1:280 and 282. Al-Haythami said in *Majma' al-Zawa'id*, 5:241: "Narrated by Abu Ya'la and al-Bazzar, and the narrators of Abu Ya'la are the narrators of the Sahih, except that Makhul did not meet Abu 'Ubayda." In al-Rafi'i's *Tarikh Qazwin*, 1:475, it is narrated from Hashim ibn 'Urwa, from his father, from Jabir, from Abu 'Ubayda. Al-Munawi mentioned in *Fayd al-Qadir*, 3:94, no. 2841, that among those who narrated it were al-Ruyani and Ibn 'Asakir. The hadith master Sayyid Ahmad ibn al-Siddiq mentioned in *al-Mudawi* that al-Dulabi narrated it in *al-Kuna*, 1:163, from Abu Dharr.

during the time of Mu'awiya. When we returned, we passed through Homs."

His statement: "Would you like to visit Wahshi?" meaning Ibn Harb al-Habashi, the freedman of Jubayr ibn Mut'im.

His statement: "so we may ask him about killing Hamza." In the narration of al-Kushmihani: "so we may ask him about his killing of Hamza." Ibn Ishaq added: "how he killed him."

His statement: "So we asked about him, and it was said to us..." In the narration of Ibn Ishaq:[133] "A man said to us while we were asking about him: 'Wine has overpowered him. If you find him sober, you will find him eloquent in Arabic and he will tell you whatever you wish. But if you find him otherwise, then leave him.'"

In the narration of al-Tayalisi,[134] there is similar wording, and in it he said: "If you find him drinking, then do not ask him."

This is an explicit text showing that Wahshi, the killer of our master Hamza, may Allah be pleased with him, remained addicted to wine after his Islam.

5. 'Ubada ibn al-Samit's Testimony Concerning Mu'awiya

In *al-Mustadrak* of al-Hakim (3:357), from 'Ubayd ibn Rifa'a:

'Ubada ibn al-Samit stood in the middle of the house of the Commander of the Believers, 'Uthman ibn 'Affan, may Allah be pleased with him, and said: "I heard the Messenger of Allah, may Allah bless him and his household and grant them peace, Muhammad Abu al-Qasim, say:

'After me, men will take charge of your affairs who will make you recognize what you reject, and will reject from you what you recognize. There is no obedience to one who disobeys Allah.'"

---

[133] Al-Tabarani also narrated it in *al-Mu'jam al-Kabir*, 20:252. Hamdi al-Salafi al-Wahhabi said in his note there: "Our shaykh said in *Silsilat al-Ahadith al-Sahiha*, 2:703: This is a chain authentic according to the conditions of Muslim."

[134] Narrated by Ibn Abi Shayba, 6:446, with an authentic chain.

"By the One in Whose hand is my soul, Mu'awiya is one of those people."

And 'Uthman did not respond to him with a single word.[135]

I say: this means that 'Uthman ibn 'Affan confirmed the censure of Mu'awiya.

6. The First to Change the Sunnah

The hadith:

"The first to change my Sunnah will be a man from Banu Umayya"

is authentic, and al-Albani authenticated it in his *Silsila al-Sahiha* (4:329, no. 1749).

Ibn Abi Shayba narrated it (7:260), from Abu Dharr, and from him Ibn 'Adi narrated it in *al-Kamil* (3:164). It is also narrated with another wording:

"The affair of my Ummah will continue to stand upon justice until the first one to breach it is a man from Banu Umayya."[136]

7. The Report That Mu'awiya Dies upon Other than Islam

It is established with a sound chain from al-Baladhuri, who died in 270 AH, in *al-Tarikh al-Kabir*, who said:

Ishaq narrated to me: 'Abd al-Razzaq narrated to us: Ma'mar informed us, from Ibn Tawus, from his father, from 'Abd Allah ibn 'Amr ibn al-'As, who said:

---

[135] Narrated by al-Hakim in *al-Mustadrak*, 3:469. It has also been reported from a group of noble and pure Companions, may Allah be pleased with them, who fought alongside our master 'Ali, upon him peace and Allah's pleasure, such as our master 'Ammar ibn Yasir and our master Zayd ibn Suhan, that they said: "Do not remove my garment from me and do not wash my blood from me, for I will be resurrected on the Day of Resurrection as one disputing." See *al-Talkhis al-Habir*, 2:144. It is also narrated in Ibn Sa'd, *al-Tabaqat*, 3:262 and 6:125; *Tarikh Baghdad*, 8:439; 'Abd al-Razzaq, *al-Musannaf*, 3:542; al-Bukhari, *al-Tarikh*, 3:397; Ibn 'Abd al-Barr, *al-Tamhid*, 24:245-246; al-Bayhaqi, *al-Sunan*, 8:186; and others.

[136] Ibn Sirin said that he was killed by the command of Mu'awiya, as in 'Abd al-Razzaq, *al-Musannaf*, 3:242 and 5:273, and its chain is authentic.

I was sitting with the Prophet, may Allah bless him and his household and grant them peace, and he said: "A man will appear before you from this mountain pass who will die, on the day he dies, upon other than my religion."

He said: "I had left my father putting on his clothes, and I feared that he would appear. Then Mu'awiya appeared."

This is a sound chain.

The hadith master, Sayyid Ahmad ibn al-Siddiq al-Ghumari, said in *Ju'nat al-'Attar* (2:154):

This is a hadith that is authentic according to the conditions of Muslim. It removes every gloom from the believer who is bewildered regarding this tyrant, may Allah disgrace him, and it demolishes everything with which the deceivers seek to obscure his reality.

Among the strangest things you will hear is that many hadith masters transmitted this hadith in their compilations and famous dictionaries, but they say, "Then a man appeared," and they do not explicitly mention the name of the accursed Mu'awiya, concealing him and concealing their deviant doctrines of Nasb and depriving the Household of their rights, even if that requires raising the banner of their enemies.

Praise belongs to Allah, who preserved this Shari'a despite the insinuations of the insinuators and the distortions of the falsifiers.

See *Majma' al-Zawa'id* (5:243), where he mentions this hadith from the narration of al-Tabarani with the wording, "Then a man appeared," leaving it ambiguous in this way.

Supporting this is what al-Bazzar narrated in his *Musnad* (6:46), from the noble Companion al-Miqdad ibn al-Aswad, may Allah be pleased with him, who said:

By Allah, I will not testify for anyone that he is among the people of Paradise until I know what he dies upon, after a hadith I heard from the Messenger of Allah, may Allah bless him and his household and grant them peace. I heard the Messenger of Allah say:

"The heart of the son of Adam changes more intensely than a pot when it boils."

Al-Bazzar said after it:

What is correct according to us is that it is al-Miqdad, and its chain is a sound chain.[137]

The Companions are from the children of Adam, and they are not infallible, unlike the prophets, peace and blessings be upon them, for they are the people of infallibility.

8. The Killing of Hujr ibn 'Adi

Mu'awiya killed the worshipful Companion Hujr ibn 'Adi, may Allah be pleased with him, by execution because he objected to Mu'awiya's cursing of our master 'Ali.

Al-Dhahabi said in *Siyar A'lam al-Nubala'* (3:466), in the biographical entry of Hujr ibn 'Adi:

Ibn 'Awn said, from Muhammad ibn Sirin: When Hujr was brought, he said: "Bury me in my clothes, for I will be resurrected as one disputing."[138]

Ibn 'Awn narrated from Nafi', who said: Ibn 'Umar was in the marketplace when the news of Hujr's death was announced to him. He loosened his garment, stood up, and sobbing overcame him.

---

[137] It is an authentic hadith narrated by Ahmad in *al-Musnad*, 4:372; Ibn Sa'd in *al-Tabaqat*, 3:260; and the contradictory al-Albani authenticated it in *al-Silsila al-Sahiha*, 5:18, no. 2008.

[138] This has also been narrated through Lady 'A'isha, Mother of the Believers, as a marfu' report with the wording: "People will be killed at 'Adhra' for whom Allah and the inhabitants of heaven will become angry." It was narrated by Ya'qub ibn Sufyan and, through him, Ibn 'Asakir in *Tarikh Dimashq*, 12:226. There is a break in the chain, but the story is well known. Al-Albani cited the hadith of 'A'isha in his *al-Da'ifa*, vol. 8, no. 3723, and judged it weak. This is good from someone like him, since he did not judge it fabricated, objectionable, or very weak.

Hisham ibn Hassan al-Bakri narrated from Muhammad, who said: When Hujr was brought to Mu'awiya, he said: "Peace be upon you, O Commander of the Believers."

He said: "Am I the Commander of the Believers? Strike his neck."

So he prayed two rak'as and said to his family: "Do not remove the chains from me, and do not wash the blood from me, for I will meet Mu'awiya on the road."[139]

Al-Hafiz Ibn Hajar said in *al-Isaba* (1:315):

He was killed at Marj 'Adhra' by the command of Mu'awiya.[140] Hujr was the one who had conquered it, so it was decreed that he be killed there.

Al-Hafiz Ibn Hajar said before that:

Hujr ibn 'Adi witnessed al-Qadisiyya. After that he witnessed the Camel and Siffin, and accompanied 'Ali, so he was among his Shi'a.

Al-Bukhari (3:72) and Ibn Abi Hatim (3:266) said:

He was killed during the lifetime of 'A'isha.

Some of those whose hearts Allah has blinded among the fanatics said that there is no harm in his killing of our master Hujr and others from the Companions and Successors among the believers and Muslims, because he was a mujtahid. This is a fallen statement, contrary to the explicit text of the Qur'an and contrary to the saying of the Prophet, may Allah bless him and his household and grant them peace:

---

[139] Mu'awiya rebelled against our master 'Ali and marched to fight him.

[140] Reflect on how the Companions feared objecting to Mu'awiya lest their blood be shed. Let those who fanatically defend this tyrant in falsehood take heed, especially those who say: "Would the noble Companions have remained silent about him if he had been committing wrongs and perpetrating injustice?"

"The killer of 'Ammar and the one who despoils him are in the Fire."[141]

And his saying, as in al-Bukhari (447):

"'Ammar will be killed by the transgressing faction. He will be calling them to Paradise, and they will be calling him to the Fire."

The Wahhabis tried to deny that Hujr was one of the Companions, relying upon the statement of some earlier scholars. This denial is false and has no basis in correctness. Leading hadith scholars and imams from Ahl al-Sunna wa'l-Jama'a explicitly stated that he was among the Companions. Among that is the following.

Al-Hakim said in *al-Mustadrak* (3:469):

Mention of the virtues of Hujr ibn 'Adi, the monk of the Companions of Muhammad, may Allah bless him and his household and grant them peace, and mention of his killing.

Al-Dhahabi said in *Siyar A'lam al-Nubala'* (3:463):

Hujr ibn 'Adi... Abu 'Abd al-Rahman, the martyr. He had companionship and delegation.

Some tried to deny the companionship of Hujr ibn 'Adi in order to lighten the crime upon Mu'awiya. But let us suppose, for argument's sake, that Hujr ibn 'Adi was not a Companion. Was he not a believer and one of the righteous worshippers?

Allah, Exalted be He, says in His Book:

{Whoever kills a believer intentionally, his recompense is Hell, abiding therein, and Allah is angry with him, curses him, and has prepared for him a tremendous punishment.} [al-Nisa' 4:93]

Ibn Kathir said in *al-Bidaya wa'l-Nihaya* (6:226):

---

[141] In the narration of Abu Dawud, no. 4131, the wording is: "al-Miqdam returned it," meaning that al-Miqdam said, "Indeed we belong to Allah, and indeed to Him we return," out of grief.

Ya'qub ibn Sufyan said: Ibn Bukayr narrated to us: Ibn Lahi'a narrated to us: al-Harith narrated to me, from Yazid, from 'Abd Allah ibn Zurayr al-Ghafiqi, who said:

I heard 'Ali ibn Abi Talib say: "O people of Iraq, seven men from among you will be killed at 'Adhra'. Their likeness is like the people of the trench."

So Hujr ibn 'Adi and his companions were killed...

Al-Bayhaqi said: "'Ali would not say the like of this unless he had heard it from the Messenger of Allah, may Allah bless him and his household and grant them peace."

9. *The Killing of 'Abd al-Rahman ibn 'Udays al-Balawi*

Among the noble Companions killed by Mu'awiya was 'Abd al-Rahman ibn 'Udays al-Balawi, who was from the People of the Pledge of Ridwan. Al-Dhahabi said in *Tarikh al-Islam* (3:531):

He had companionship and pledged allegiance beneath the tree. He also narrated... He was among those who rose against 'Uthman and marched to fight him.[142] Then Mu'awiya gained power over him and imprisoned him in Palestine with a group of others. He then escaped from prison, and they caught up with him at Mount Lebanon. He was killed. When they caught up with him, he said to the one who killed him: "Woe to you. Fear Allah regarding my blood, for I am from the Companions of the Tree."

He said: "There are many trees on the mountain," and killed him.

10. *Mu'awiya, Yazid, and the Claim to the Caliphate*

In Sahih al-Bukhari, Mu'awiya says that he and his depraved son Yazid are more entitled to the caliphate than 'Umar ibn al-Khattab and his son 'Abd Allah.

---

[142] In the narration of Abu Dawud, no. 4131, the wording is: "As for me, I will not leave today until I anger you and make you hear what you dislike."

Mu'awiya considered his depraved son Yazid more entitled to the caliphate than 'Umar ibn al-Khattab and his son.

Al-Bukhari narrated in his *Sahih* (4108), from Ibn 'Umar, who said:

I entered upon Hafsa...

I said: "You have seen what has happened among the people, yet no share of the matter has been assigned to me."

She said: "Go, for they are waiting for you, and I fear that your remaining behind will cause division among them."

She did not leave him until he went. When the people dispersed, Mu'awiya delivered a sermon and said: "Whoever wants to speak concerning this matter, let him show us his horn, for we are more entitled to it than he and his father."

Habib ibn Maslama said: "Why did you not answer him?"

'Abd Allah said: "I untied my garment and intended to say, 'The one more entitled to this matter than you is the one who fought you and your father upon Islam.' But I feared that I might say a word that would divide the gathering and cause bloodshed,[143] and that something other than what I intended would be carried from me. So I remembered what Allah has prepared in the Gardens."

Habib said: "You were preserved and protected."

So Mu'awiya explicitly states here that he and his son were better than the second of the Rightly Guided Caliphs and more entitled to the caliphate than him and his son 'Abd Allah ibn 'Umar.

Ibn Taymiyya says in *Minhaj al-Sunna* (7:453):

---

[143] Narrated by Abu Dawud, no. 4131; al-Tabarani in *al-Mu'jam al-Kabir*, 20:269; and Ahmad, 4:132, though Ahmad's narration stops before the point that exposes Mu'awiya's misguidance. Baqiyya explicitly stated that he heard the report in Ahmad's chain. Al-Albani authenticated the hadith in *Sahih Abi Dawud*, 2:778. Al-Nasa'i also narrated it in abridged form, no. 4255. The commentator on *al-Siyar* also mentioned that the narrator Baqiyya explicitly stated hearing the report in another place.

No king ever assumed authority who was better than Mu'awiya. He is the best of the kings of Islam, and his conduct was better than the conduct of all kings after him.

You have already seen, and will see further below, the conduct and actions of Mu'awiya: killing Companions and innocents, drinking wine, cursing our master 'Ali and commanding the people to do so, consuming people's wealth falsely by the testimony of the Companions, forbidding what is right and commanding what is wrong by the testimony of our master 'Ubada and the confirmation of our master 'Uthman, may Allah be pleased with them both. All of this, in the view of Ibn Taymiyya al-Harrani, is justice and praiseworthy conduct.

This is how they turn falsehood and wrongdoing into truth and goodness for which its perpetrator is praised.

11. Mu'awiya's Commands to Consume Wealth Falsely and Kill

Muslim narrated in the *Sahih* (1844), and others also narrated, from 'Abd al-Rahman ibn 'Abd Rabb al-Ka'ba, that he said to 'Abd Allah ibn 'Amr ibn al-'As:

This cousin of yours, Mu'awiya, commands us to consume our wealth among ourselves falsely and to kill ourselves, while Allah, Exalted be He, says: {O you who believe, do not consume your wealth among yourselves falsely, except that it be trade by mutual consent among you. And do not kill yourselves. Indeed, Allah is ever merciful to you.}

He said:

So he remained silent for a while, then said: "Obey him in obedience to Allah, and disobey him in disobedience to Allah."

12. Mu'awiya and the Hadiths Forbidding Usury

Muslim narrated in the *Sahih* (1587), and al-Nasa'i in the *Sunan* (7:275, no. 4562), with the wording here being his, from Muslim ibn Yasar and 'Abd Allah ibn 'Ubayd, who said:

The house brought together 'Ubada ibn al-Samit and Mu'awiya.

'Ubada said: "The Messenger of Allah, may Allah bless him and his household and grant them peace, forbade us from selling gold for gold, silver for silver, wheat for wheat, barley for barley, dates for dates..."

And he commanded us to sell gold for silver, silver for gold, wheat for barley, and barley for wheat, hand to hand, however we wished.

This hadith reached Mu'awiya, so he stood and said: "What is wrong with men who narrate hadiths from the Messenger of Allah, may Allah bless him and his household and grant them peace, when we accompanied him but did not hear them from him?"

That reached 'Ubada ibn al-Samit, so he stood and repeated the hadith and said: "We will certainly narrate what we heard from the Messenger of Allah, may Allah bless him and his household and grant them peace, even if Mu'awiya is displeased."

Al-Albani authenticated it in *Sahih al-Nasa'i* (3:946).

The hadith forbidding the sale of gold for gold except weight for weight was narrated by a group of the Companions, and 'Ubada ibn al-Samit was not alone in narrating it. Even if he had been alone, it would have been enough as evidence that Mu'awiya turned away from the Sacred Law in many matters and dealt in usury. Among the Companions who narrated it were 'Umar ibn al-Khattab (al-Bukhari, 2134), Abu Bakra (al-Bukhari, 2175), Abu Sa'id al-Khudri (al-Bukhari, 2177), and others.

This hadith establishes that Mu'awiya used to deal in usury.

Al-Qurtubi explicitly stated in his *Tafsir* (7:392), from Imam Malik, that Mu'awiya openly engaged in usury. Al-Qurtubi said there:

Ibn Wahb narrated from Malik that he said: "The land in which wrongdoing is committed openly is to be abandoned, and residence is not to be established there." He cited as proof the action of Abu al-Darda' when he left the land of Mu'awiya after

Mu'awiya openly engaged in usury, permitting the sale of a gold vessel for more than its weight. He narrated it in the *Sahih*.

13. Mu'awiya's Wearing of Gold and Silk

Al-Dhahabi admitted that Mu'awiya was not free of blemishes. Here is some of that with sound chains.

Al-Dhahabi said in *Siyar A'lam al-Nubala'* (3:158):

From Khalid ibn Ma'dan, who said:

Al-Miqdam ibn Ma'di Karib, 'Amr ibn al-Aswad, and a man from al-Asad who had companionship came as a delegation to Mu'awiya.

Mu'awiya said to al-Miqdam: "Al-Hasan has died."

So he said, "Indeed we belong to Allah, and indeed to Him we return."[144]

Mu'awiya said: "Do you consider it a calamity?"

He said: "Why should I not? The Messenger of Allah, may Allah bless him and his household and grant them peace, placed him in his lap and said: 'This one is from me, and Husayn is from 'Ali.'"

He said to the Asadi: "What do you say?"

He said: "An ember has been extinguished."

Al-Miqdam said:[145] "I adjure you by Allah. Did you hear the Messenger of Allah, may Allah bless him and his household and grant them peace, forbid wearing gold and silk, and the skins of predatory beasts and riding upon them?"

He said: "Yes."

He said: "By Allah, I have seen all of this in your house."

------

144 This is a claim for which there is no evidence. Rather, the evidence points to the opposite.

145 This establishes that Mu'awiya used to command what was wrong and forbid what was right, while the Muslims, including the Companions, had no effective power against him at that time.

Mu'awiya said: "I knew that I would not escape from you."[146]

Al-Dhahabi commented on this narration:

Its chain is strong, and Mu'awiya is among the best of the kings, whose justice outweighed their injustice.[147] He is not free of blemishes, and Allah pardons him.

This is the end of al-Dhahabi's words from *al-Siyar*. So reflect on the fanaticism and defence of falsehood together with the admission of blemishes.

This hadith is explicit that Mu'awiya opposed the Prophet, may Allah bless him and his household and grant them peace, by the testimony of the Companions and those around him.

The commentator on *Siyar al-Nubala'* mentioned that Baqiyya explicitly stated that he heard the report.

14. Reports of Cursing Mu'awiya and His Allies

Al-Hakim narrated in *al-Mustadrak* (4:13), from Lady 'A'isha, that she said:

May Allah curse 'Amr ibn al-'As.

'Amr was one of Mu'awiya's helpers and partners in his actions.

In *Musnad Ahmad* (1:217), with a sound chain, Ibn 'Abbas curses Mu'awiya, but they narrated this report ambiguously with the wording "so-and-so," concealing Mu'awiya.

Ibn 'Abbas said:

May Allah curse so-and-so. They deliberately went to the greatest days of Hajj and erased its adornment, while the adornment of Hajj is the talbiya.

---

[146] It is authentic. Narrated by al-Hakim in *al-Mustadrak*, 1:464-465, who authenticated it; al-Nasa'i in *al-Sunan al-Kubra*, 2:419, and also in *al-Sunan al-Sughra*, 5:253; and al-Diya' in *al-Mukhtara*, 10:378. Al-Albani also authenticated it in *Sahih Sunan al-Nasa'i*, 2:631, no. 2812.

[147] See al-Tabari, *Tarikh*, 3:240; Ibn Kathir, *al-Bidaya wa'l-Nihaya*, 8:67; and Ibn al-Athir, *al-Kamil fi'l-Tarikh*, 3:343 and 7:275.

Ibn Khuzayma clarified that the one meant by the curse was Mu'awiya, narrating in his *Sahih* (4:260), from Sa'id ibn Jubayr, who said:

We were with Ibn 'Abbas at 'Arafa. He said to me: "O Sa'id, why do I not hear the people reciting the talbiya?"

I said: "They fear Mu'awiya."[148]

He said: So Ibn 'Abbas came out of his tent and said: "Labbayk Allahumma labbayk. They have abandoned the Sunnah out of hatred for 'Ali."[149]

Ibn Kathir mentioned in *al-Bidaya*, from Ja'far ibn Sulayman al-Duba'i, who said:

Mu'awiya kept Samura in office after Ziyad for six months, then dismissed him. Samura said: "May Allah curse Mu'awiya. By Allah, had I obeyed Allah as I obeyed Mu'awiya, He would never have punished me."[150]

Ibn Abi Shayba narrated (2:108), with a sound chain, that our master 'Ali, upon him peace and Allah's pleasure, used to say in his qunut:

O Allah, take Mu'awiya and his followers, 'Amr ibn al-'As and his followers, Abu al-A'war al-Sulami and his followers, and 'Abd Allah ibn Qays and his followers.

Al-Baladhuri narrated it with a sound chain in *Ansab al-Ashraf* (vol. 2, p. 75b), with the wording that our master 'Ali said:

O Allah, curse Mu'awiya ibn Abi Sufyan first, 'Amr ibn al-'As second, Abu al-A'war al-Sulami third, and 'Abd Allah ibn Qays fourth.

---

[148] Ahmad narrated it ambiguously in this form, 4:5. Ibn Hajar said in *Fath al-Bari*, 13:11: "Hadiths have been transmitted concerning the curse of al-Hakam, the father of Marwan, and what he begot. Al-Tabarani and others transmitted them. Most of them have some criticism, but some are good."

[149] Narrated explicitly with the wording "al-Hakam," that is, without ambiguity, by al-Bazzar, 6:159, and al-Diya' in *al-Mukhtara*, 9:310-311.

[150] Ibn Hajar, *Tahdhib al-Tahdhib*, 3:101.

As for what al-Bukhari mentioned (3765), namely the statement of Ibn 'Abbas concerning Mu'awiya that "he is a jurist," this is from the alteration of the narrators. Al-Tahawi contradicted that in *Sharh Ma'ani al-Athar* (1:289), narrating it with the wording:

Mu'awiya stood and prayed one rak'a. Ibn 'Abbas said: "From where do you think the donkey took it?"

Its chain is sound.

The learned scholar, Shaykh al-Kawthari, may Allah have mercy on him, explained that Ibn 'Abbas said that out of dissimulation before Mu'awiya. What is authentic from him through two chains is his statement that he was a "donkey," not a "jurist."

He mentioned, may Allah have mercy on him, in his book *al-Nukat fi'l-Tahadduth 'an Rudud Ibn Abi Shayba 'ala Abi Hanifa*, p. 186 of the al-Maktaba al-Azhariyya edition, in the section on witr with one rak'a, the following text:

If this were authentic from Ibn 'Abbas, it would be interpreted as dissimulation, because he had fought him beneath the banner of 'Ali, may Allah ennoble his face. Therefore, there is no reason why he should not take account of him in his public gatherings, unlike in his private gathering.

It has been reported that Mu'awiya was the first person to deliver the Friday sermon while seated, and the deviants of Banu Umayya followed this vile practice, as stated in Ibn al-Athir's *al-Kamil* (4:555). Likewise, Mu'awiya was the first to abandon the takbir in prayer, as stated in *Fath al-Bari* (2:270).

In *Musnad Ahmad* (4:195), *Sahih Ibn Hibban* (7:216), and elsewhere, the noble Companion Shurahbil ibn Hasana, may Allah be pleased with him, used to say:

I accompanied the Messenger of Allah, may Allah bless him and his household and grant them peace, while 'Amr was more astray than his family's donkey.

15. The Curse Upon al-Hakam and His Offspring

Al-Hafiz al-Haythami said in *Majma' al-Zawa'id* (5:241):

From al-Sha'bi, who said: I heard 'Abd Allah ibn al-Zubayr while he was leaning against the Ka'ba, saying:

"By the Lord of this Ka'ba, the Messenger of Allah, may Allah bless him and his household and grant them peace, cursed so-and-so and those born from his loins."[151]

Ahmad and al-Bazzar narrated it, except that al-Bazzar said: "Allah cursed al-Hakam and what he begot upon the tongue of His Prophet,[152] may Allah bless him and his household and grant them peace." Al-Tabarani narrated something similar, and he has a narration like the narration of Ahmad. The narrators of Ahmad are the narrators of the Sahih.

Al-Munawi said in *Fayd al-Qadir* (6:355):

Al-Qurtubi said: What issued from Banu Umayya and their Hajjajs of shedding blood, destroying wealth, and destroying people in the Hijaz, Iraq, and elsewhere is not hidden.

He said: In summary, Banu Umayya met the counsel of the Chosen One concerning his Household and his Ummah with opposition and disobedience. They shed their blood, enslaved their women, captured their children, destroyed their homes, denied their nobility and virtue, and deemed their progeny, captivity, and abuse lawful. They opposed the Messenger of Allah, may Allah bless him and his household and grant them peace, in his counsel, and met him with the opposite of his intent and desire. What shame will be theirs when they meet him, and what disgrace on the day they are presented before him.

Yet according to them, Mu'awiya, despite committing these calamities, reprehensible matters, and explicit violations

---

[151] This means that he and those like him are reliable according to them, and when they need them in the religion of Allah and in narration, they submit to them fully.

[152] See how they express themselves: at one time they say, "He had a little Shi'ism"; at another, "He was accused of extremism"; then al-Juzajani the Nasibi goes further and says, "abusive, openly declaring the evil of his doctrine." Ibn Hajar refuted the excesses of al-Juzajani, saying in *al-Tahdhib*, 10:143: "Al-Juzajani is well known for Nasb and deviation, so his statement does not impugn him."

against Allah, Exalted be He, and against the Prophet, may Allah bless him and his household and grant them peace, may not be disparaged by anyone, nor may his vices be mentioned, nor may he be hated for the sake of Allah, Exalted be He. Rather, he is to be mentioned with lordship and Allah's pleasure.

Thus wrongdoing becomes truth, and truth becomes wrongdoing.

Whoever spoke about him from among the imams of hadith, the people of knowledge, and the imams, they denounced him with their familiar weapon of terror, accusing him of Shi'ism and Rafidism so that he would be silenced and fall in the eyes of the foolish masses. We have witnessed this, touched it, and seen it with our own eyes.

Thus the authentic Sunnah, following the truth and reality, submitting to the commands of Allah, Exalted be He, and His Messenger, and uncovering the truth, become Rafidism in their eyes, perhaps even disbelief and heresy.

Among the examples of imams and hadith masters whom they accused of Shi'ism and extremism is Khalid ibn Makhlad al-Qatwani. He is among the shaykhs of al-Bukhari and Muslim, and both narrated from him in the *Sahih*. Al-Hafiz mentioned him in *Tahdhib al-Tahdhib*,[153] mentioned those who declared him reliable and praised him with goodness, then said:

Al-Ajurri narrated from Abu Dawud: "Truthful, but he has Shi'i leanings."

Ibn Sa'd said: "He was Shi'i, denounced in hadith because of Shi'ism, excessive in that, and they wrote from him out of necessity."[154]

---

[153] Meaning that he used to curse Mu'awiya, disparage him, and speak against him.

[154] Meaning that they were Nawasib who were partisan to the family of Abu Sufyan Sakhr ibn Harb, and who stood in the ranks of Mu'awiya and his faction, concerning whom the Messenger of Allah, may Allah bless him and his household and grant them peace, said, as in al-Bukhari, no. 447: "'Ammar will be killed by the transgressing faction. He calls them to Paradise, and they call him to the Fire."

Al-'Ijli said: "Reliable, with a little Shi'ism, and he had many hadiths."

Salih ibn Muhammad Jazarah said: "Reliable in hadith, except that he was accused of extremism."[155]

Al-Juzajani said: "Abusive,[156] openly declaring the evil of his doctrine."

This is the end of the quotation with some adaptation.

So look, may Allah have mercy on you, at how they express themselves. At one time they say, "He had a little Shi'ism." At another they say, "He was accused of extremism." Then, at another, al-Juzajani the Nasibi adds, "abusive, openly declaring the evil of his doctrine." Reflect.

Statements of Leading Ahl al-Sunna Imams

The statements of the imams of Ahl al-Sunna who used to censure Mu'awiya and turn away from loving and venerating him are very numerous. Here we mention some of the statements of leading imams of knowledge among Ahl al-Sunna wa'l-Jama'a, such as Imam al-Nasa'i, the author of the *Sunan*; al-Hakim, the author of *al-Mustadrak*; 'Abd al-Razzaq, the author of the famous *Musannaf*; and Imam 'Abd al-Razzaq, the shaykh of a group of imams of hadith, such as Ahmad ibn Hanbal, 'Ali ibn al-Madini, the shaykh of al-Bukhari, Muhammad ibn Yahya al-Dhuhali, Yahya ibn Ma'in, and others. He is the shaykh of all of them.

1. Imam al-Nasa'i, Author of the Sunan, Died 303 AH

Al-Dhahabi said in *Siyar A'lam al-Nubala'* (14:133), in the biographical entry of Imam al-Nasa'i:

He had a little Shi'ism and aversion toward the opponents of Imam 'Ali, such as Mu'awiya and 'Amr.

---

[155] See Ahmad ibn al-Siddiq al-Ghumari, *Fath al-Wahhab bi-Takhrij Ahadith al-Shihab*, 2:352; and al-Munawi, *Fayd al-Qadir*, 1:267-268.

[156] See *al-Kashf al-Hathith 'amman Rumiya bi-Wad' al-Hadith*, p. 225.

Al-Dhahabi mentioned in *Siyar A'lam al-Nubala'* (14:132):

Al-Nasa'i left Egypt at the end of his life and went to Damascus. There he was asked about Mu'awiya and what had come concerning his virtues. He said: "Is he not satisfied to come out even, such that he must be preferred?" He said: They kept striking him in his testicles until he was taken out of the mosque... Al-Daraqutni said: He left for Hajj, was put to trial in Damascus, and attained martyrdom.

Al-Hafiz Ibn Hajar said in *Fath al-Bari* (7:104):

Many hadiths have been transmitted concerning the virtue of Mu'awiya, but none of them is authentic through its chain. Ishaq ibn Rahwayh, al-Nasa'i, and others were decisive upon this.

2. Imam al-Hakim, Author of al-Mustadrak, Died 405 AH

In Siyar A'lam al-Nubala' (17:175) and al-Subki's Tabaqat al-Shafi'iyya al-Kubra (4:163):

When it was said to al-Hakim, "Narrate hadiths concerning the virtues of Mu'awiya so that they will stop bothering you," he said: "It does not come from my heart," meaning Mu'awiya.

3. Imam 'Abd al-Razzaq, Author of al-Musannaf, Died 211 AH

In *Siyar A'lam al-Nubala'* (9:570), 'Abd al-Razzaq said to a man:

Do not soil our gathering by mentioning Ibn Abi Sufyan.

4. Imam and Hadith Master Abu Ghassan al-Nahdi al-Kufi and others

Al-Dhahabi cited in *Siyar A'lam al-Nubala'* (10:432), in the biographical entry of Abu Ghassan al-Nahdi, who is among the narrators of the Six Collections:

Abu Ahmad al-Hakim narrated to us: al-Husayn al-Ghazi narrated to us: I asked al-Bukhari about Abu Ghassan.

He said: "What are you asking about?"

I said: "Shi'ism."

He said: "He follows the doctrine of the people of his town. If you had seen 'Ubayd Allah ibn Musa, Abu Nu'aym, and a group of our Kufi shaykhs, you would not ask us about Abu Ghassan."

I, meaning al-Dhahabi, say: Abu Nu'aym and 'Ubayd Allah used to venerate Abu Bakr and 'Umar. They only spoke against Mu'awiya and those connected to him.

As for 'Ubayd Allah ibn Musa, he would not allow anyone named Mu'awiya to enter his house, nor would he narrate to a group among whom there was someone named Mu'awiya, as stated in his biographical entry in *Siyar A'lam al-Nubala'* (9:556-557).

5. Imam and Hadith Master Jarir al-Dabbi, Died 188 AH

Al-Hafiz Ibn Hajar said in *al-Tahdhib* (2:66):

Al-Khalili said in *al-Irshad*: "Reliable, agreed upon."

Qutayba said: "Jarir, the foremost hadith master, narrated to us, but I heard him openly cursing Mu'awiya."

6. The Scholar Sa'd al-Din al-Taftazani al-Hanafi, Died 793 AH

Ibn Hajar included his biographical entry in *al-Durar* (4:350).

Sa'd al-Din al-Taftazani said in *Sharh al-Maqasid* (5:310):

What occurred between the Companions of wars and disputes, in the manner recorded in the books of history and mentioned on the tongues of reliable transmitters, outwardly indicates that some of them departed from the path of truth and reached the level of oppression and wickedness. The motive for that was rancor, stubbornness, envy, obstinacy, seeking dominion and leadership, and inclining toward pleasures and desires, for not every Companion is infallible, nor is everyone who met the Prophet, may Allah bless him and his household and grant them peace, marked by goodness...

As for what occurred after them of oppression against the Household of the Prophet, may Allah bless him and his household and grant them peace, it is so manifest that there is no room to conceal it, and so atrocious that no sound opinion can be confused about it. Inanimate things and animals almost testify to it, those in the earth and heaven weep over it, and mountains are shaken by it... So may Allah's curse be upon whoever carried it out, was pleased with it, or strove toward it. The punishment of the Hereafter is more severe and more lasting.

Ibn Kathir said in his *Tarikh* (8:224), speaking about Yazid ibn Mu'awiya, whom Mu'awiya appointed as caliph over the Muslims and empowered over their necks:

As for what they report from him of poetry concerning that, and his citation of the poetry of Ibn al-Ziba'ra regarding the Battle of Uhud, in which he says:

> *Would that my elders at Badr had witnessed*
> *the panic of Khazraj from the striking of spears;*

> *when al-Khazraj wailed from the blow of the lances,*
> *and killing was fierce among 'Abd al-Ashhal;*

> *We killed the double of their nobles,*
> *and set right the leaning of Badr, so it became straight...*

If Yazid ibn Mu'awiya said this, then may Allah's curse be upon him and the curse of those who curse... As for what has been mentioned about him, what has been said regarding him, and what he used to engage in of actions, abominations, and statements in the coming year, he was not granted respite after the event of al-Harra and the killing of al-Husayn except for a short time, until Allah, who broke the tyrants before him and after him, broke him. Indeed, He is knowing and powerful.

Ibn Kathir said in his *Tarikh* (8:223), commenting on the hadith:

"Whoever unjustly frightens the people of Madinah, Allah will frighten him, and upon him is the curse of Allah..."

He said:

This hadith and others like it were used as evidence by those who permitted cursing Yazid ibn Mu'awiya. It is a narration from Ahmad ibn Hanbal chosen by al-Khallal, Abu Bakr 'Abd al-'Aziz, al-Qadi Abu Ya'la, and his son al-Qadi Abu al-Husayn. Abu al-Faraj ibn al-Jawzi supported that position in a separate work and permitted cursing him.

Further Facts and Clarifications

Abu Sufyan Sakhr ibn Harb, the Father of Mu'awiya

Muslim narrated in the *Sahih* (2504), from 'A'idh ibn 'Amr:

Abu Sufyan passed by Salman, Suhayb, and Bilal among a group. They said: "By Allah, the swords of Allah have not taken from the neck of the enemy of Allah the portion they should have taken."

Abu Bakr said: "Do you say this to the elder of Quraysh and their master?"

He went to the Prophet, may Allah bless him and his household and grant them peace, and informed him.

He said: "O Abu Bakr, perhaps you angered them. If you angered them, then you have angered your Lord."

So Abu Bakr came to them and said: "O my brothers, did I anger you?"

They said: "No. May Allah forgive you, our brother."

The hadith scholar and Hanafi scholar al-Kawthari said in *Saf'at al-Burhan*:

Among the beliefs of this shameless sect are judgment by passing thought, open declaration of anthropomorphism and place, declaring their opponents disbelievers, and partisanship for the family of Harb.

Response to Some Evidences and Objections:

As for some of what they mention of Mu'awiya's virtues, we have already stated that the hadith masters such as al-Nasa'i, Ishaq ibn Rahwayh, and others said:

Nothing is authentic concerning the virtues of Mu'awiya.

Some people have fabricated virtues for him, saying that he is "the uncle of the believers" and "the scribe of the revelation of the Lord of all worlds." We answer these two doubts as follows.

The Myth of Calling Him "Uncle of the Believers"

Who said that Mu'awiya is the uncle of the believers? Was it the Sacred Law, or the fanatics for him who invent virtues for him built upon the edge of a crumbling bank?

Did the Companions used to call Mu'awiya, "O uncle of the believers"?

If Mu'awiya is the uncle of the believers, would Huyayy ibn Akhtab the Jew, the father of Lady Safiyya, be the grandfather of the believers?[157] And would the Copts of Egypt, the people of Lady Mariya al-Qibtiyya, be the maternal uncles of the believers?

Ibn Kathir said in his *Tafsir* of Surat al-Ahzab, verse 6, namely His saying, Exalted be He:

{The Prophet is closer to the believers than their own selves, and his wives are their mothers}

(3:477, Dar al-Ma'rifa, Beirut, second edition, 1407 AH):

Is it said of Mu'awiya and those like him that they are uncles of the believers? There are two views among the scholars, may Allah be pleased with them. Al-Shafi'i, may Allah be pleased with him, explicitly stated that this is not to be said.

The word "not" has been deleted from some modern editions tampered with by sinful hands, thereby reversing the meaning entirely, so pay attention to this.

---

[157] Meaning: Ahmad ibn Hanbal weakened him, whether he read from his book or from memory. In either case, he is weak.

The Myth of "Scribe of the Revelation of the Lord of All Worlds"

We say: writing revelation does not confer infallibility, even though it has not been established that Mu'awiya was among the scribes of revelation.

What is the proof that if a man writes revelation he becomes infallible, cannot be criticized or held accountable, and cannot become wicked, apostatize, or disbelieve?

What was said regarding the "uncle" may also be said regarding this. Mu'awiya was not a scribe of revelation.

Ibn Abi al-Sarh was a scribe of revelation. Al-Hafiz Ibn Hajar said in *al-Isaba* (4:109):

'Abd Allah ibn Sa'd ibn Abi Sarh used to write for the Prophet, may Allah bless him and his household and grant them peace. Satan caused him to slip, so he joined the disbelievers. The Prophet, may Allah bless him and his household and grant them peace, commanded that he be killed, meaning on the day of the Conquest...

Abu Dawud (4358) and al-Nasa'i (4069) narrated it, and its chain is sound.

Al-Bukhari narrated in the *Sahih* (3617), and Muslim likewise (2781), with this being al-Bukhari's wording, from Anas ibn Malik, may Allah be pleased with him:

A man was a Christian, then he accepted Islam and recited al-Baqara and Al 'Imran. He used to write for the Prophet, may Allah bless him and his household and grant them peace. Then he returned to Christianity and used to say: "Muhammad only knows what I wrote for him." Allah caused him to die, and they buried him. In the morning, the earth had thrown him out.

Ahmad narrated with a sound chain (3:120), and Ibn Hibban narrated in his *Sahih* (3:19), from Anas, who said:

A man used to write for the Prophet, may Allah bless him and grant him peace. Then he apostatized from Islam and joined the polytheists. Then he died. That reached the Prophet, may Allah bless him and his household and grant them peace, and he said: "The earth will not accept him."

The Misuse of the Verse: {That Is a Nation That Has Passed Away}

Some people use as evidence for the impermissibility of discussing the state of Mu'awiya and the judgment of the Messenger concerning him the saying of Allah, Exalted be He:

{That is a nation that has passed away. It shall have what it earned, and you shall have what you earned, and you will not be asked about what they used to do.}

Their use of this noble verse as evidence is corrupt, because the noble verse affirms that we will not be asked about the deeds of those who preceded us, meaning that we will not be punished for an action we did not perform, just as we will not be rewarded for an action we did not perform. That is what the noble verse affirms.

Allah, Exalted be He, did not state in the noble verse that it is forbidden for us to mention those of the past and what they did of good deeds and evil deeds. If that were so, Allah, Exalted be He, would not have related to us the stories of Iblis, Pharaoh, 'Ad, Thamud, the people of our master Nuh, the brothers of our master Yusuf and their shameful conduct toward him, and what the hypocrites did during the days of the Prophet, may Allah bless him and his household and grant them peace, in Madinah, and so on.

{We relate to you the best of stories.}

If their use of the verse as evidence were correct, Allah, Exalted be He, would not have censured Pharaoh or made worship through the Qur'an include censuring him and affirming the verses that censure him, and the verses that censure Abu Lahab and those like them, even though they are a nation that has passed away.

Thus their use of this noble verse as evidence for what they want is invalid.

The Hadith of 'Umayr ibn Sa'id: "Do Not Mention Mu'awiya Except with Good"

Some people cite the hadith of 'Umayr ibn Sa'id, who said:

Do not mention Mu'awiya except with good, for I heard the Messenger of Allah say: "O Allah, guide by him."

Al-Tirmidhi narrated it (3843) and weakened it.

Al-Albani authenticated it and erred, because in its chain is 'Amr ibn Waqid, whom al-Albani himself judged to be abandoned in more than one place, including in his *Silsila al-Da'ifa* (2:341). A group of hadith imams declared him a liar. See *Tahdhib al-Tahdhib* (8:102 and 6:220).

The Hadith: "O Allah, Teach Mu'awiya the Book and Protect Him from Punishment"

The fanatical Nasibis also cited the hadith:

"O Allah, teach Mu'awiya the Book and protect him from punishment."

Ahmad narrated it (4:127), and Ibn 'Adi narrated it in *al-Kamil fi'l-Du'afa'* (6:2402).

I say: this supplication is the supplication of the Prophet, may Allah bless him and grant him peace, for Ibn 'Abbas, may Allah be pleased with them both, whose interpretations and explanations of the Book of Allah fill the books of tafsir. The Nasibis, the supporters of Mu'awiya, reversed it and distorted it in favor of Mu'awiya.

In the chain of the hadith is al-Harith ibn Ziyad, who is unknown, as stated in *Tahdhib al-Tahdhib* (2:123) and *al-Mizan* (1:433). Al-Hafiz transmitted from Ibn 'Abd al-Barr that he said concerning him:

Unknown, and his hadith is rejected.

Conclusion of the Appendix

This is a short, concise note on this issue. We ask Allah, Exalted be He, to make us among those who listen to speech and follow the best of it, to make us among those who love for the sake of Allah and hate for the sake of Allah, Exalted be He, to make us firm upon faith, and to resurrect us with His righteous servants, the pure and purified members of His Household, and His good and pious Companions, beneath the banner of the Master of the Messengers, may Allah bless him and his household and grant them peace.

Praise belongs to Allah, Lord of all worlds.

GLOSSARY OF KEY TERMS

Ahl al-Bayt

The Household of the Prophet, may Allah bless him and his household and grant them peace. In this work, the term refers especially to 'Ali, Fatima, al-Hasan, al-Husayn, and those connected to the Prophetic Household through the recognized Sunni understanding of their rank and sanctity.

Ahl al-Sunna wa'l-Jama'a

The mainstream Sunni community. In this work, the term is used for the broad Sunni scholarly tradition, including its hadith masters, jurists, theologians, exegetes, and historians.

Ashab al-Shajara

The People of the Tree. This refers to those who pledged allegiance to the Prophet, may Allah bless him and his household and grant them peace, beneath the tree at al-Hudaybiyya. This pledge is also known as Bay'at al-Ridwan.

Bay'at al-Ridwan

The Pledge of Ridwan, given by the Companions to the Prophet, may Allah bless him and his household and grant them peace, at al-Hudaybiyya. It is mentioned in the Qur'an in connection with Allah's pleasure with the believers who pledged beneath the tree.

Companion / Sahabi

A person who met the Prophet, may Allah bless him and his household and grant them peace, as a believer and died upon Islam. Scholars differed over certain details of this definition and over how the concept of companionship relates to individual uprightness.

Da'if

Weak. A hadith whose chain or text does not meet the conditions of authenticity or soundness. A weak hadith is not automatically fabricated, but it is not treated like an authentic report.

Fitna

Trial, turmoil, civil strife, or religious and political disorder. In this book, it often refers to the conflicts that occurred among Muslims after the death of the Prophet, may Allah bless him and his household and grant them peace.

Hadith

A report attributed to the Prophet, may Allah bless him and his household and grant them peace, or to the Companions or later authorities, depending on context. Hadiths are assessed through their chains of transmission and their texts.

Hasan

Sound or fair. A hadith category below sahih but still acceptable as evidence according to the hadith scholars, provided its conditions are met.

Hawd

The Prophet's Basin or Pool on the Day of Resurrection. Several hadiths mention people being driven away from the Hawd after the Prophet, may Allah bless him and his household and grant them peace, recognizes them.

Ijtihad

Scholarly exertion to derive or apply a legal ruling where the matter is open to interpretation. In this book, the author contests the claim that Mu'awiya's actions can be excused as rewarded ijtihad.

Jarh wa'l-Ta'dil

The science of narrator criticism and accreditation. It examines the reliability, integrity, precision, and defects of narrators in hadith transmission.

Mawdu'

Fabricated. A report falsely attributed to the Prophet, may Allah bless him and his household and grant them peace, or to another authority.

Mujtahid

A scholar qualified to exercise ijtihad. The author rejects the claim that Mu'awiya's disputed actions can be justified by calling him a mujtahid.

Nasb

Hostility toward, hatred of, or denigration of Sayyiduna 'Ali or the Prophetic Household. In this work, Nasb is treated as a serious deviation that affected political and scholarly attitudes toward Ahl al-Bayt.

Nasibi

A person characterized by Nasb. The term is used polemically in the book for those who display hostility toward 'Ali or defend those who wronged him and the Prophetic Household. wrongdoing.

Rafidi / Rafidism

A polemical label historically used for those accused of rejecting the first three caliphs or holding excessive devotion to 'Ali and the Prophetic Household. In later usage, it is often applied broadly to accuse or silence those who criticize certain Companions or defend Ahl al-Bayt strongly.

Rawafid

Plural of Rafidi. It is a polemical term and should be read in context, especially where the author is discussing how accusations of Rafidism were used to marginalize critics of Mu'awiya or defenders of Ahl al-Bayt.

Sahih

Authentic. A hadith that meets the recognized conditions of authenticity, including a connected chain, reliable narrators, precision, absence of hidden defects, and absence of contradiction with stronger evidence.

Siffin

The battle fought between the army of Sayyiduna ʿAli, may Allah be pleased with him, and the forces of Muʿawiya. It is central to the book's discussion of the transgressing faction and the hadith of ʿAmmar.

Tafsir

Qurʾanic exegesis or commentary. The book cites tafsir works in discussing verses such as the verse of the accursed tree and verses concerning praise, censure, hypocrisy, and transgression.

Tulaqa'

Those released by the Prophet, may Allah bless him and his household and grant them peace, at the Conquest of Mecca. The term is used in the book in relation to Muʿawiya and his family background.

Umayyads / Banu Umayya

The clan and later ruling dynasty associated with Muʿawiya, Yazid, Marwan, and their successors. In this book, the author distinguishes between lineage as such and the political project associated with Umayyad rule.

Al-Fi'a al-Baghiya

The transgressing faction. This refers to the faction mentioned in the hadith of ʿAmmar: "Ammar will be killed by the transgressing faction." The author argues that this identifies Muʿawiya's faction as the one in transgression.

Zindiq / Zandaqa

Heretic or concealed unbelief, depending on context. The term appears in polemical settings and should be read according to the author's usage in the relevant passage.

BIBLIOGRAPHY

Ahmad ibn Hanbal. *al-Musnad.*

Ahmad ibn al-Siddiq al-Ghumari. *al-Jawab al-Mufid li-l-Sa'il al-Mustafid.*

Ahmad ibn al-Siddiq al-Ghumari. *Fath al-Wahhab bi-Takhrij Ahadith al-Shihab.*

Ahmad ibn al-Siddiq al-Ghumari. *Ju'nat al-'Attar.*

Ahmad ibn al-Siddiq al-Ghumari. *al-Mudawi li-'Ilal al-Jami' al-Saghir wa-Sharhay al-Munawi.*

al-Albani, Muhammad Nasir al-Din. *Silsilat al-Ahadith al-Sahiha.*

al-Baladhuri, Ahmad ibn Yahya. *Ansab al-Ashraf.*

al-Baladhuri, Ahmad ibn Yahya. *al-Tarikh al-Kabir.*

al-Bayhaqi, Ahmad ibn al-Husayn. *al-Sunan al-Kubra.*

al-Bazzar, Ahmad ibn 'Amr. *al-Musnad.*

al-Bukhari, Muhammad ibn Isma'il. *al-Jami' al-Sahih.*

al-Dhahabi, Muhammad ibn Ahmad. *Siyar A'lam al-Nubala'.*

al-Dhahabi, Muhammad ibn Ahmad. *Tarikh al-Islam.*

al-Dhahabi, Muhammad ibn Ahmad. *Mizan al-I'tidal fi Naqd al-Rijal.*

Abu Dawud, Sulayman ibn al-Ash'ath. *al-Sunan.*

Abu Ya'la al-Mawsili, Ahmad ibn 'Ali. *al-Musnad.*

al-Hakim al-Naysaburi, Muhammad ibn 'Abd Allah. *al-Mustadrak 'ala al-Sahihayn.*

al-Haythami, 'Ali ibn Abi Bakr. *Majma' al-Zawa'id wa-Manba' al-Fawa'id.*

Ibn 'Abd al-Barr, Yusuf ibn 'Abd Allah. *al-Isti'ab fi Ma'rifat al-Ashab.*

Ibn 'Adi, 'Abd Allah ibn 'Adi al-Jurjani. *al-Kamil fi Du'afa' al-Rijal.*

Ibn al-Athir, 'Izz al-Din. *al-Kamil fi'l-Tarikh.*

Ibn Hajar al-'Asqalani, Ahmad ibn 'Ali. *al-Durar al-Kamina fi A'yan al-Mi'a al-Thamina.*

Ibn Hajar al-'Asqalani, Ahmad ibn 'Ali. *Fath al-Bari bi-Sharh Sahih al-Bukhari.*

Ibn Hajar al-'Asqalani, Ahmad ibn 'Ali. *al-Isaba fi Tamyiz al-Sahaba.*

Ibn Hajar al-'Asqalani, Ahmad ibn 'Ali. *Lisan al-Mizan.*

Ibn Hajar al-'Asqalani, Ahmad ibn 'Ali. *Tahdhib al-Tahdhib.*

Ibn Hajar al-'Asqalani, Ahmad ibn 'Ali. *al-Talkhis al-Habir.*

Ibn Hazm, 'Ali ibn Ahmad. *al-Fasl fi'l-Milal wa'l-Ahwa' wa'l-Nihal.*

Ibn Hibban, Muhammad ibn Hibban. *al-Sahih.*

Ibn al-Jawzi, 'Abd al-Rahman ibn 'Ali. *Manaqib al-Imam Ahmad ibn Hanbal.*

Ibn Kathir, Isma'il ibn 'Umar. *al-Bidaya wa'l-Nihaya.*

Ibn Kathir, Isma'il ibn 'Umar. *Tafsir al-Qur'an al-'Azim.*

Ibn Khuzayma, Muhammad ibn Ishaq. *al-Sahih.*

Ibn Maja, Muhammad ibn Yazid. *al-Sunan.*

Ibn Sa'd, Muhammad ibn Sa'd. *al-Tabaqat al-Kubra.*

Ibn Taymiyya, Ahmad ibn 'Abd al-Halim. *al-Fatawa al-Kubra.*

Ibn Taymiyya, Ahmad ibn 'Abd al-Halim. *Minhaj al-Sunna al-Nabawiyya.*

Ibn Taymiyya, Ahmad ibn 'Abd al-Halim. *al-Ta'sis fi'l-Radd 'ala Asas al-Taqdis.*

al-Kawthari, Muhammad Zahid. *al-Nukat fi'l-Tahadduth 'an Rudud Ibn Abi Shayba 'ala Abi Hanifa.*

Muslim ibn al-Hajjaj. *al-Jami' al-Sahih.*

al-Munawi, 'Abd al-Ra'uf. *Fayd al-Qadir Sharh al-Jami' al-Saghir.*

al-Nasa'i, Ahmad ibn Shu'ayb. *al-Sunan al-Kubra.*

al-Nasa'i, Ahmad ibn Shu'ayb. *al-Sunan al-Sughra.*

al-Nawawi, Yahya ibn Sharaf. *Sharh Sahih Muslim.*

al-Qurtubi, Muhammad ibn Ahmad. *al-Jami' li-Ahkam al-Qur'an.*

al-Suyuti, Jalal al-Din. *al-Durr al-Manthur fi'l-Tafsir bi'l-Ma'thur.*

al-Tabarani, Sulayman ibn Ahmad. *al-Mu'jam al-Kabir.*

al-Tabari, Muhammad ibn Jarir. *Jami' al-Bayan 'an Ta'wil Ay al-Qur'an.*

al-Taftazani, Sa'd al-Din. *Sharh ul-Maqasid.*

al-Tirmidhi, Muhammad ibn 'Isa. *al-Jami' al-Sunan.*

ABOUT THE AUTHOR

Al-Sayyid Hasan ibn Ali ibn Hashim ibn Ahmad ibn Alawi ibn Ahmad ibn Abd al-Rahman al-Saqqaf is a contemporary Muslim scholar from the noble Prophetic household, as indicated by the honorific "al-Sayyid," a title traditionally used for descendants of our master the Messenger of God, peace and blessings be upon him and his family, through Sayyida Fatima al-Zahra and Imam Ali, may God be pleased with them both. His great-great-grandfather, Sayyid Alawi ibn Ahmad al-Saqqaf, who died in 1335 AH, was the Shafi'i mufti and the shaykh of the noble Husayni Ba Alawi sayyids in Mecca.

He is known among serious students of creed and hadith for his critical care, his concern for verifying the scholarly heritage, and his authentication and examination of Prophetic hadiths and reports, including the statements of the Companions and the scholars who came after them in the first three centuries.

He has continuous efforts in defending the transcendence of God Most High and rejecting anthropomorphism and corporealism. Among his most prominent shaykhs and teachers was the great hadith master Sidi Abdullah ibn al-Siddiq al-Ghumari, may God have mercy on him, one of the major hadith scholars of the twentieth century. Shaykh al-Saqqaf follows the Shafi'i school in matters of Islamic jurisprudence.

His scholarly work focuses especially on Islamic creed, hadith criticism, purifying religious understanding from weak evidences, correcting ideas, exposing inherited errors, rejecting extremism and narrow sectarian excess, and opposing interpretations that compromise the transcendence of God Most High.

He is known for scrutinising theological claims in light of the Noble Quran, the sound Sunnah, sound reason, and the verified statements of recognised scholars from within the heritage of Ahl al-Sunna wa'l-Jama'a. One of the distinguishing features of

Sayyid al-Saqqaf's scholarship is his command of hadith science in its broad sense: knowledge of narrators, chains of transmission, subtle defects, and the principles of authentication and weakening. This hadith-based method is evident in his treatment of questions of creed and other Islamic issues.

Where many later discussions rely heavily on scholastic logic or philosophical frameworks, Sayyid al-Saqqaf returns to the sources themselves: the Noble Quran and the hadith reports as assessed according to their own precise internal criteria. He then weighs every claim on that basis.

The method of Sayyid Hasan al-Saqqaf is both critical and reformative. He examines inherited formulations with scholarly scrutiny, always returning to the foundational evidences and calling the reader back to the principles of belief. In his method, every matter of creed must be weighed by evidence, not merely by repetition, attachment to the dominant or widespread view, or adopting positions merely in reaction to other schools.

One of the clearest features of his scholarly project is his ongoing correction of doctrines and reports that lead to corporealism, anthropomorphism, or the attribution of bodily meanings to God Most High. In this regard, his writings continue the method of the imams of transcendence, affirming that God Most High is not a body, is not contained by place or direction, and is not described by limbs, organs, motion, sitting, settling, or any attribute of created beings.

Sayyid Hasan al-Saqqaf has approximately 150 authored works and books. Among the most famous are:

1. *Sahih Sharh al-'Aqida al-Tahawiyya*, a critically verified commentary on the text of al-'Aqida al-Tahawiyya.

2. *'Iqd al-Zabarjad al-Nadid fi Sharh Jawharat al-Tawhid*, a commentary on the poem *Jawharat al-Tawhid* by Shaykh Ibrahim al-Laqqani. In this commentary, he follows the method and approach of the hadith scholars.

3. *Tanaqudat al-Albani al-Wadihat fima Waqaʻa lahu fi Tashih al-Ahadith wa Tadʻifiha min Akhtaʼ wa Ghalatat*, a scholarly documentation of the contradictions found in al-Albani's rulings on hadiths and narrators.

4. *Tanqih al-Fuhum al-ʻAliya bima Thabata wa ma lam Yathbut fi Hadith al-Jariya*, a critical study of what is and is not authentically established in the hadith of the slave girl.

5. *al-Tandid bi-man ʻAddada al-Tawhid*, a work demonstrating the invalidity of dividing divine unity into divinity, lordship, and names and attributes.

6. *al-Tanbih waʼl-Radd ʻala Muʻtaqid Qidam al-ʻAlam waʼl-Hadd*, a work of warning and refutation against the belief in the eternity of the world and limit.

7. His critical edition and substantial scholarly introduction to *al-ʻUluw* by al-Hafiz al-Dhahabi.

8. His critical edition of *Dafʻ Shubah al-Tashbih bi-Akuff al-Tanzih* by the Hanbali hadith master Ibn al-Jawzi.

9. His critical edition and substantial scholarly introduction to *Ijtimaʻ al-Juyush al-Islamiyya* by Ibn Qayyim al-Jawziyya.

10. *Iʻlam al-Thaqalayn bi-Khurafat al-Kursi Mawdiʻ al-Qadamayn*, a book on the issue of the Footstool and the rejection of corporealist interpretations.

In addition to these, he has many other scholarly works and in-depth studies of weak, fabricated, and Israelite-influenced reports that entered discussions of creed.

These works reflect his broader scholarly project: to return Islamic creed to the clarity of the Noble Quran, the sound Sunnah, and the method of the verifying scholars.

In this book, which we publish today, Sayyid Hasan al-Saqqaf presents the creed of Islam in a coherent, evidence-based manner, accompanied by deep reverence for the meanings of faith and divine unity. His aim is to clarify sound creed, purify it, and protect it, so that the reader may approach the foundations of religion with certainty, understanding, and confidence.